An Angel on His Wing

An Angel on His Wing

The Story of Bill Gordon, Alaska's Flying Bishop

Tay Thomas

WIPF & STOCK · Eugene, Oregon

Wipf and Stock Publishers
199 W 8th Ave, Suite 3
Eugene, OR 97401

An Angel on His Wing
The Story of Bill Gordon, Alaska's Flying Bishop
By Thomas, Tay
Copyright©1989 by Thomas, Tay
ISBN 13: 978-1-5326-7915-5
Publication date 4/10/2020
Previously published by Morehouse Publishing Company, 1989

Dedication and Acknowledgments

This book could never have been written without the help of the many friends and family of Bill Gordon. When I wrote my other books, I always struggled over the dedication, but with this one there has been no doubt since the beginning—it is dedicated to all of the following people:

To Billie Williams, the Gordons' and my long-time friend, who traveled all over Alaska and the Lower 48 to tape more than a hundred interviews; to Sheyna Rieger who devoted endless hours to typing and retyping the manuscript; to Bev Dodge who re-checked my Alaskan historical facts; to my husband, Lowell, Chuck Eddy, Tad Bartimus, Cynthia Merman, George Harris (fifth Bishop of Alaska), Andy Fairfield, and Don Hart, who all helped and inspired me in indispensable ways; and to all of the following persons who contributed through interviews:

Charlotte Adams
Bill Anderson
The late John Bentley
Everitt Calhoun
Gordon and Cutty Charlton
Tom and Charlotte Cleveland
Leighton and Elinor Collins
Charlie and Linda Croski
Moses Cruikshank
The late Jean Aubrey Dementi
Rick and Anne Draper
Sally Fairfield
The late John and Betty Flanagan
Richard and Bobbie Freer
Mary Ann Gallagher
Emmet Gribbin
Syd Alexander

Joe Aprill
Isabel Baumgartner
Mark Boesser
Henry Chapman
Dick and Katie Clarke
David Cochran
Don and Jan Craddick
Archie Crowley

Phil and Marilyn Dietz
Norman and Stella Elliott
Scott Fisher
Anna Frank
The late Wesley Frensdorff
Trimble Gilbert
Wes Gregg

Dorothy and Allan Hall
Betty Hart
Arthur Henry
Harold and Mary Fran Hill
Bertha Stalker Jennings
Ethel Joseph
Elaine Johnson
Corrinne Kenway
Keith and Jackie Lawton
Ella Lisbourne
Ed and the late Bertha Meier
Milton Nicholia
Ann Parsons
Titus Peter
John Phillips
Norma Reich
Mildred Sage
Wilson Sam
Mary Richards Sarvello
Bill Shafer
Berkman Silas
Maudry Sommers
Mary Ellen Starr
Doris Stewart
Charlotte Swan
The late Martha Swan
Lola Tilley
Charlie and Annie Titus
Matthew Titus
Murray Trelease
Seymoure and Claudia Tuzroyluk
Glen Wilcox
John Williams
Clover Jean Ward Yarborough
Stan and Charlotte Hadley

Walter and Louise Hannum
Kitty Harwood
Sally Herron
Teddy Hunter
Peter and Elsie John
Bob Jones*
Solomon Killigavuk
Mary Elizabeth Lee
Alaska Linck

Sandy McClain
Evolyn Melville
Maryann Munroe
The late Daniel Norton
Louise Paul
Helen Peters
Elsie and Elman Pitka
Al and Joanne Reiners
David Salmon
Dale and Joyce Sarles
Paul and Robin Sherry
Dick Simmonds
Marion Stevens
Lee Stratman
Joseph Swan
Pauline Swenson
Bessie Titus
Luke Titus
Caggie and Charlie Trapp
Tom Tull
Alice Weber
Joe Williams
Pat Williams
Sandy and Margie Zabriskie

FAMILY MEMBERS:
Shirley Gordon
Anna Gordon
Becky Gordon Chisum
Almeria Gordon
Mary Irwin Gordon
The late Nina Lewis
Laura Gordon Williams

Bill and Bonnie Gordon
Nancy and Sandy Dameron
Jocelyn Gordon
Sharon Mertsching
Grace Gordon Pless
Lynn Lewis Sathe
The late Mina Ballard

*Note: Judy Edwards Jones died in a tragic fall at her home in Laramie, Wyoming, on 13 June 1989 just as this book went to press.

FOREWORD

In the mid 1980's, ten years after moving on from his post as the Episcopal Bishop of Alaska, Bill Gordon—he liked to be called Bill, or just "Bishop" if absolutely necessary—asked my mother Tay Thomas if she would write his biography. She already had published four books and earned a name for herself as an Alaskan author, and she and my father had been friends with Bill Gordon since the early 1960's. Without hesitation she said yes. Years later she commented that perhaps she should have thought twice before taking on the job.

The book took four years of her life. Folders piled higher and higher on her desk, filled with hundreds of pages of anecdotes, names, dates, place descriptions, all from interviews with over one hundred people—family members, friends, priests—who had lived or worked with Bill Gordon. A friend had helped her tape the interviews, but only Tay could do the writing. And then, after finally launching into the first chapters, she received in the mail 20 hour-long tape recordings from Bill which became more piles of pages of anecdotes and recollections of his early life and first years as a priest and then Bishop in Alaska. Tay wrote to a journalist friend, "I look at the two foot high piles of papers all about me, then force myself to begin a chapter outline. It comes to forty pages . . . what have I gotten myself into?"

The biggest challenge Tay faced in the writing of the book was Bill Gordon himself. He was a remarkable and charismatic man of great intelligence, energy and vision; he was used to going full speed ahead and making things happen. In the early 1960's, elected Bishop of Alaska at the age of only 29, he began pushing for the Episcopal church to raise up and train native clergy in place, which necessitated a change in the Church canons. By the early 1970's there were 27 native Alaskan men and women ordained to the priesthood (this also was very early days in the discussion of allowing women to be priests in the Episcopal Church). It was hard for this driving force of a man to sit back and let someone tell the story of his life. He wanted Tay to write the book, but he wanted control over it.

Bill Gordon was extremely stubborn, but so was Tay Thomas. When she finally shared the in-the-galleys manuscript with him in the fall of 1989, their long friendship teetered on the brink. He insisted on making many changes before the book was published, and she refused, maintaining that it was a biography and not an autobiography, this was what she had signed on for and what she was delivering, whether he was completely happy with the final product or not. Some heated letters went back and forth, but at the same time they each strove for honesty and hearing the other party out, and I am sure they each spent much time in prayer on this topic.

To their great credit—and much credit goes also to Bill Gordon's wife Shirley, with her quiet sense of humor, and perspective—their friendship did survive the book and indeed outlasted it. Before Bill Gordon died of cancer in 1994 at the age of 75, he and Tay had parted as warm friends, and he had declared that the book was all right, though inaccurate in places. Shirley Gordon comments today, "His kids and I hoped that Tay would not write the typical saintly missionary story. We got our wish."

It has now been exactly 30 years since the publishing of *An Angel On His Wing*. Thanks to Wipf and Stock Publishers, and to editor Al Ullman, we are able to reprint *An Angel On His Wing* with a couple of corrections that the Bishop so wished for.

First of all, many thanks to the Gordon family for providing the new cover photo of Bill with one of his beloved airplanes. This is so fitting for a biography of a man who learned to fly for the sole purpose of caring for his far-flung flock. Upon his retirement Bill Gordon estimated that he flew nearly 9,000 hours as chief pilot of what he liked to call "Episcopal Airlines of Alaska."

And then there is the story behind the title of the book, or more accurately, two stories. We'll never know how there came to be two stories of an angel flying with Bishop Gordon, but at least now, in this Foreword, you can hear the Bishop's story: he strongly disputed my mother's version of Bishop Bentley, Bishop of the Second Missionary District of Alaska (Bill's predecessor who moved on to become director of Episcopal Overseas Missions), sending a letter of support for Bill Gordon to use an airplane for his regular visitations around the state, closing with the comment, "Keep an angel on your wing." Bishop Gordon insisted there was no such letter of approval from Bishop Bentley, who did not approve of the ministerial use of small planes; instead he said the comment came from legendary Alaska bush pilot Don Sheldon, after the Bishop had had a crash landing in the fog at the Fairbanks airfield that unfortunately involved two other planes (unoccupied, with no injuries in the incident). Don Sheldon happened to stop off at the airport, and surveying the wreckage of the three airplanes, he shook his head and remarked in his laconic way, "Well, the Bishop sure had an angel on his wing this time."

Finally the reprint of the book gives us the opportunity to include the Bishop's suggested last six paragraphs for the book's ending. Thirty years later it seems only fair to give him the final word, and I have a feeling my mother would approve.

Anne Thomas Donaghy
May 2019

Contents

Chapter 1

Heading North

The young man stood at the rail near the bow of the ship; the cold March breeze ruffled his dark brown hair as he looked north across the gray water. Alaska, and a life of mission work, lay beyond the horizon. Bill Gordon had spent his life until now in the southeastern United States, sheltered by secure home and school walls. Yet, with supreme confidence, he knew he was now where he belonged. He was eager—impatient in fact—to find out what lay ahead.

Longshoremen were loading the holds of the *S.S. Yukon* with cargo, hauling heavily laden nets from the dock to the hatches above. Bill watched intently from the upper deck as a jumble of boxes and cases dangled in mid-air. Was his own well-worn trunk there? He hoped so; it contained all his worldly possessions. Bill thought back to the five-day trip from North Carolina; travel was difficult in 1943 wartime. The trip was one of many firsts: his first ride on a Pullman train; the first time he had been west of Birmingham, Alabama. When they stopped in Bluefield, West Virginia, he had twenty minutes in which to say goodbye to the oldest of his six sisters, and during his eleven-hour break in Chicago he had a visit with another one. For the rest of the journey he stared out the window for hours at a time at the grandeur of the western United States. At dinner in the dining car, which was preceded by hours of waiting because the train was jammed with troops, he had his first encounter with a finger bowl.

However, Bill would never forget his departure at the railway station in the little town of Ridgeway, Virginia, twelve miles from his home in Spray. At midafternoon he stood on the crowded platform with his father, mother, an aunt, his youngest sister, and a girlfriend. He had been waiting for this big moment for a week and plans had been carefully laid for the trunk to be sent ahead by truck. But thirty minutes before departure it had still not arrived. Never very patient, Bill paced the platform, stormily complaining of the delay.

"We will pray about it," his father announced quietly, and "Preacher" Will Gordon gathered his family into a circle. "Good grief, Dad, we've got to do something! That trunk has everything I need for Alaska!" Nonetheless young Bill joined the family in the midst of the crowd as his gentle parent asked God to produce the wayward trunk. While their heads were still bowed, Bill heard the sound of the truck's engine just as the train's whistle shrieked in the distance. The driver had gone past the turn off, but remembered and turned back.

Now, pulling his coat collar higher, Bill felt a pang of homesickness. He would miss the strong support of his parents. With the exception of one summer at camp in New Jersey, the farthest north he had ever gone, he had always lived at, or close to, home. Tired, Bill leaned on the railing. The past two days had been a tedious battle of paperwork with the Alaska Travel Control Office. Since U.S. soldiers were fighting in the Aleutian Islands due to the Japanese invasion, wartime restrictions were tight: No one could go to Alaska without a job or a good reason for being there. But his fatigue was due to more than bureaucratic paper work. Bill had met a very pretty young lady behind the desk and had taken her out to dinner and a movie last night. His southern gallantry required that he, not realizing the great distance to some of Seattle's suburbs, accompany her home on the bus. He caught the last ride back at two A.M.

Suddenly, Bill spotted two most attractive young women among the crowd of men preparing to board the ship. His fatigue vanished. Bill could not take his eyes off the slim one on the right; she was beautiful, with long brown wavy hair, sparkling dark eyes, and even features. Her face was animated as she came up the gangplank while talking with an older man in Army uniform.

Too bad! She must be seeing that major off—her father, maybe. Bill watched enviously as the pretty girl hugged and kissed him good-bye on the deck below. Then the major disembarked while the two girls, waving excitedly moved to the rail. Bill headed quickly toward the stairs. In light of approximately 500 men sailing on this ship, as compared to twelve or fifteen women, most over forty years of age, he would have to act fast. Taking the steps two at a time the slim, five-foot, ten-inch athlete unhindered by his heavy overcoat "just happened" to find a place next to her at the rail and quickly struck up a conversation, enough for them to agree to sit together at dinner that night. This meeting would change Bill's life, but the entry in his small black pocket diary notes only: "I met Shirley Lewis at 6:40 p.m. on March 3."

Shirley came from a middle-class family in Longview, a Weyer-haeuser Pulp Mill Company town in southern Washington State. Life at Lower Columbia Junior College, a few blocks from home, had become boring, her tuition funds needed replenishing, and she was ready for something new. A secretarial job with the Army Corps of Engineers in faraway Seward, Alaska, was newer than anything Shirley could imagine. In spite of her striking good looks, she was an unaffected, genuine young woman of twenty, with a sharp mind and strong sense of values.

Shirley was a diary writer and she and her companion, Jean Evans, had purchased a brown and gold leather book to record every detail of their adventure. The first page, headed "Oddities (their signatures)" is followed by the names of four men and their addresses. William Jones Gordon, Jr., with no address, is at the top.

Shirley's companion, Jean, begins the joint diary, describing the long, low, single-stack passenger ship built in the 1920s leaving the dock and heading across Puget Sound. "Then we strolled on the deck long enough for Shirley to meet Bill Gordon, twenty-four, a clergyman going to Alaska to take over the Epis-copal Church in Seward." She adds that he has a cute southern accent, dark curly hair, deepset eyes, and a catching smile.

After dinner that first night, Shirley and Bill strolled on deck. The next afternoon and two strolls later, Shirley confided in her friend, Jean, that she wanted to marry Bill. They had known each other only twenty-four hours, but to Shirley it seemed like a year. "Shirley Gordon does sound pretty," she writes in the book. With only six more days to go, the shipboard romance progressed rapidly. The sky was clear, the air mild, and snow-covered mountains lined the waterway. All perfect excuses for lengthy walks outdoors. The brisk evenings were even more pleasant because they had the decks to themselves—dark decks on a ship sailing under strict blackout rules.

One night Bill and Shirley ensconced themselves in a sheltered nook on the upper level, watching the phosphorous in the water. "It looked just like the stars in the sky—the only difference being that they were all falling stars, and I made a thousand wishes all the same," Shirley wrote. At that moment a young seaman decided to throw out a pot of water, squarely in the faces of the young couple. "We were speechless, then we laughed heartily about it forever after."

That night Shirley made a date to meet Bill to see the sunrise. "I stood on the port side and waited. The sun didn't rise—neither did the little minister. Finally he appeared from the leeward side and explained in words of one syllable or less that "the sun usually rises in the east—at least in this country."

"That's her story," Bill recalls. "I don't think she showed up."

"I was there," Shirley retorts, "on the wrong side of the ship. He was angry—I should have known then what I was getting in for!"

Shirley incurred further ire when she showed up for dinner one night wearing a pair of gray slacks. (The women on board always changed to skirts or dresses.) She announced to her friends at the table that pants were the only practical attire for the ship. The young people teased her and Bill stated that southern women never wore them. Shirley left in a huff, announcing that she was not hungry after all. She continued to wear slacks.

The ship docked at Juneau, Alaska's capitol, late on the third day but no one was allowed ashore because the Captain did not want to lose precious hours trying to round up straying passengers. A dangerous stretch of open water lay ahead, and a destroyer escort was joining him. The Aleutian battlefield was not far beyond their present horizon.

From the deck, Juneau is a quaint sight. The wooden buildings of the town, then home to 5,700 people, cling to the steep green and rocky mountainsides which drop straight to the shore of Gastineau Channel. The houses rise in tiers, perched on cliffs or stilt-like foundations. Rickety wooden stairways connect various levels, as do steep, narrow streets.

The girls had their first encounter with Alaskan prices after fresh supplies were taken on board and breakfast was served following a five A.M. departure. Shirley wrote that fresh milk was available again, if one wanted to pay one dollar a glass. They decided they would buy a cow when they reached Seward, and then board it in the church's back yard.

On Sunday 7 March about 100 passengers gathered in the ship's social hall to hear Bill give his first sermon since his graduation from Virginia Seminary in January. It was very successful, but Shirley was not entirely pleased with the consequences. Afterward, "everyone from the bos'n's third mate to the Ancient Mariner has wanted a conference with him—and he obliges," leaving little time for romance.

Bill recalls that having the service, which he did not volunteer to do, was an agonizing endeavor, but it brought a surprisingly pleasant result. The Chief Purser decided he was entitled to a cabin to himself on the main deck. Bill had enjoyed the company of his two tough construction worker roommates, but one had consumed much of two bottles of whiskey smuggled aboard at Juneau, and he caused considerable trouble in his drunken stupor. To show his remorse, he insisted on passing the hat for Bill after his sermon.

"Now that I had a nice place of my own," Bill remembers, "Shirley could visit me more easily."

Shirley retorts, "I came to visit you on shipboard?"

"Sure you did." The sparring resumes.

"I don't remember that. I remember visiting the assistant purser."

"I remember that, too." Bill can laugh over the rivalry today. "He had a new victrola and a big record collection."

The ship arrived in Valdez on 10 March and the passengers were allowed to go ashore. Alaska is a surprise to most people, but for a southerner like Bill it was amazing. Valdez, surrounded by majestic glacier-laden mountains, received twenty-two feet of snow a year and there were huge drifts everywhere.

Bill and Shirley were glad for a chance to walk and headed directly for the Episcopal Church, built in Gold Rush days. They found the Reverend Mervin Wanner in the small wood structure, having just finished his Ash Wednesday service—to a congregation of six parishioners. Shirley was worried that Bill would be discouraged, but he was undaunted, eagerly looking forward to his work in nearby Seward.

Following the brief stop, the ship knifed its way between massive rock cliffs to enter the calmer waters of Resurrection Bay (so named by Russian sailors on Easter Day of 1791). At dawn the next morning the passengers lined the decks, awed by the sight of a circle of snow-covered mountains ringing one of the finest and busiest ice-free harbors in the northern hemisphere. Seward occupied a fringe of flat land along the western shore.

Docks, storage facilities, and a railroad yard dominated the site because the town served all of Alaska's interior with its vital railroad connection. (No paved roads connected any Alaskan settlements until 1960.) Seward's population was about 900, but Fort Raymond, on the north end of town (a stopover for the military en route to the Aleutian fighting) housed 2,300 soldiers. The war had brought other changes to the strategically important seaport: The Army built gun emplacements on the mountainsides, encircling the town and bay, and barbed wire had been laid along the shoreline and across the heads of mountain canyons.

Seward was founded in 1903 by a group of eastern businessmen who planned to build a railroad to Alaska's interior. Houses of all shapes and sizes sprang up almost overnight. Shops, restaurants, and bars lined the dirt main street. A two-story bank building stood on a slight hill, appropriately marking the section of homes dubbed "Millionaire's Row." The handsome Victorian-style buildings with front porches and scrolled eaves indicated the prosperity enjoyed by those residents who invested in small but wealthy gold mines beyond the fringe of mountains.

The private efforts failed in attempting to build the railroad and the U.S. government bought them out, establishing a construction base on the site of present-day Anchorage in 1915, pushing the vital rail link through to Fairbanks in 1923. In 1943 the coal-burning train ran twice a week between Anchorage and Seward. The 150-mile trip took eight hours.

Bill disembarked on the night of the ship's arrival and was met by Episcopal Chaplain Justin Edwards, stationed at Fort Raymond. The church-owned house where Bill was supposed to live had been rented for many years. Since the occupants were still there, Mr. Edwards had arranged for Bill to stay temporarily with Mrs. Cal Brosius, "a plump sixty-year-old widow and member of the church."

Mrs. Brosius, who lived above a machine shop on the main street, mothered Bill during the three weeks of his stay with her. "She was given to wonderful hospitality," Bill relates, "but she was also given to conversation, and before I had a chance to meet most of my congregation, I'd had some analysis of them and their strengths and foibles."

Seward's St. Peter's Mission is a small wood building with brown painted siding and white trim around arched windows. A circular steeple perches at the rear of the steep roof and a small white cross is mounted on the front peak. At that time, the mission had been without a resident minister for ten years, but Chaplain Edwards helped with services. On Bill's first Sunday, the congregation numbered twenty-five. The small group puzzled him because he had been shown a petition signed by seventy-three people in Seward asking for a resident priest.

At the conclusion of the service, five stalwart ladies, pillars of the Mission, fluttered about Bill, apologizing for the rectory situation. They were startled by the boyish, handsome priest who had almost bounded down the aisle. "My, he's so young!" murmured one, while another added, "So good looking, and a bachelor . . ." with a sigh. She was the unmarried member of the group. "Well, he'll be better than no one," stated their cynical companion.

The following two months were busy ones for Bill. First he gave the small rectory a sparse house cleaning (the living room ceiling remained covered with a heavy layer of soot, where he wrote, "What are you looking up here for?"). He retained the

three boarders, which helped pay some of his expenses. Then
he made some repairs to the church, adding new pews to replace
rickety benches.

Most of Bill's time, however, was spent in other areas. "I'll
admit I didn't do a whole lot in the church there." In late March
the Seward High School English teacher was drafted. Since Bill
had a degree, he was asked to take the man's place for half days
the rest of the year. He also became assistant director of the U.S.O.
The extra pay came in handy since his deacon's salary was only
ninety-five dollars a month.

In the little time he had to himself, Bill continued to pursue
Shirley Lewis. Shirley and Jean had found a ten by twelve room
for rent over a plumbing shop on the main street. The area had
been partially gutted by a fire the previous winter and the charred
remains of buildings, combined with the mud and dirt revealed
as the winter's snow melted, was a bleak setting, but the young
people never noticed. They met at the ice cream parlor nearby
(where shakes were made of canned milk) and Bill invited Shirley
for meals at Mrs. Brosius's home, to the movies, and on long
walks.

By early May, Bill came to the conclusion Shirley had reached
two months earlier—he was in love. Their courtship, however, was by no means smooth and predictable. All month they
squabbled and made up, over and over again. They didn't doubt
their feelings for each other, but both were strong-willed and
independent.

Shirley was caught up in a frenzy of dances and parties in a
town with an Army base (where two battalions from the National
Guard of Longview were stationed) and about twenty single
young women. How long could Bill's quiet evening dates—
dinners with Mrs. Brosius, the movies, and walks—compete with
the glamorous whirl twenty-year-old Shirley was thoroughly
enjoying?

The matter was brought to a head in late May when the bishop
of the Missionary District of Alaska arrived for a visit.

Bill assumed that Bishop John Bentley was coming to check
on his progress at St. Peter's, and in fact, that had been the
bishop's initial plan. But before leaving his headquarters at

Nenana, an Interior town 470 miles north of Seward and a three-day train trip away, he received word that his elderly priest in charge of remote Point Hope was ill with a failing heart and would have to retire. This village post was the focal point of the work of the Episcopal Church along the entire length of the Northwestern Coast. It was also the most rugged and remote mission in the district. In desperation he thought of Bill Gordon, a young deacon just out of seminary and new to Alaska.

John Bentley was aware that Bill came from a remarkable family in North Carolina whose descendants had rendered notable service to both Church and State for generations, and that Bill had been reared with a keen sense of duty and obligation. Bill's clergyman father was considered a saint by the people of rural Spray, an impoverished mill town, home to the Gordon family since 1912. His mother was a woman of equally strong faith and dedication. In addition to bringing up seven children—six girls and Bill—she was active in many facets of Church life; a gifted speaker and teacher, she traveled all over the South to hold seminars and retreats, speak to women's auxiliaries and conduct Bible studies.

Bishop Bentley was honest with Bill. He explained that Point Hope was the most difficult isolated mission they had in Alaska. "Will you go?" he asked bluntly.

"I will go anywhere and do anything my Bishop asks me to do," was Bill's response. This was true; Bill was a dedicated young clergyman. But he "did have some private problems." It was hard to imagine any place more isolated and difficult than Seward. And what about Shirley? He asked Bentley for a day to think about it, and then he told him he would go, that the bishop knew the need far more than he.

They then proceeded to make plans. When Bishop Bentley attended a church service, he noticed a very attractive young woman assisting in arranging the altar, straightening up after people left. Later Bill introduced him to Miss Shirley Lewis, but it never occurred to the Bishop that there was any serious relationship between the two of them; after all, Bill had been in Seward such a short while!

In Bill's letter to his mother after the Bishop left, he reveals more human feelings about his new assignment: "Well, your geography lesson starts again! I am going to Point Hope to replace Archdeacon Frederic Goodman, who is ill and has to come out, and there is no one else to replace him. It is quite isolated, with one boat going there a year—in August. The rest of the time it is icebound. Winters are long and there is total darkness for eight weeks. I know it is going to be lonesome, but I believe I can stand anything for a year. [The Bishop had suggested trying it for that length of time.] Frankly, I am a little afraid of the job, but I am going to do my best. There is no doctor there, or even a nurse. Anyone, when seriously ill, must radio out and have a plane sent in. Planes go there occasionally—that's how I'll get in."

He concludes wistfully, "I wish I could take Shirley Lewis along as my wife, but, of course that seems a little impractical, but not impossible in the future. She has a desire for service just as deep as mine—she is surely a wonderful girl and worth waiting a long time for. She will stay on with her job here with the Engineers until her year is up, but I wouldn't be surprised to see her go to work in one of our missions in Alaska after that. She likes Bishop Bentley very much, and he is crazy about her, but who wouldn't be? He has invited her up to spend her vacation in Nenana. I never thought I'd be so completely helpless around a woman.

"Do ask everyone to remember this new opportunity in prayer for I surely cannot handle that job alone. I must have much power from on high. I definitely seem to be guided to go there; every objection I have thought up has been selfish—Shirley, loneliness, isolation, living conditions, etc. If God wants me there He will provide for every need. I love you all."

At that time, Bill and Shirley had not yet talked of marriage. But, while Bill was making preparations to move, Chaplain Edwards and Mr. Knight, Seward's Methodist minister, began talking to him about marrying Shirley and going north together. Bill couldn't imagine asking a woman, even one as intrepid as Shirley, to endure the inevitable hardships of such a remote village.

The two men took Bill on a two-day fishing trip along the Russian River in the mountains behind Seward and spent much of the time encouraging him to marry. When they returned with a good catch, they came to Bill's house for a fish dinner and invited Shirley. The entire conversation centered on why the two should go to Point Hope together. "It was a little embarrassing, since I had not asked Shirley to marry me. But out of that evening came the thought—why not!"

Shirley recalls her first comment following the proposal: "I can't marry you—I can't even play an organ!" She was ambivalent about marriage, and particularly about going to Point Hope at that stage in her life. She was having too much fun, and besides, she wanted to return to college. But she loved Bill, and he was the kind of man she was looking for. "Bill was, (and is) a southern gentleman. I had no family church background but was baptized on my own at age eleven in the Disciples of Christ Church. I dropped out when I was in high school and they told me that dancing was a sin. I liked Bill's brand of religion. Also, he read poetry to me—one of my loves—but that didn't last very long into the marriage. He didn't drink, and I don't think I ever knew a man who didn't."

Two weeks after he returned to Nenana, Bishop Bentley received a letter from Bill asking if Shirley might go to Point Hope with him. This possibility had not occurred to the Bishop, but he couldn't think of any reason to refuse.

"You tell her to get packed," he said simply.

And with that settled, they proceeded to set a date for the wedding. Bill wired his family the news that he and Shirley would be married on 16 July and then proceed to Point Hope together. Shirley sent a similar telegram to her family: "BILL AND I TO BE MARRIED JULY 16 MUST LEAVE HERE JULY 20 BISHOP BENTLEY APPROVES AND WILL PROBABLY PERFORM CEREMONY PLEASE SEND WEDDING DRESS AND VEIL IMMEDIATELY SEND ANYTHING ELSE TO ME AT POINTHOPE ALASKA BY JULY FIRST YEARLY BOAT LEAVES ABOUT THEN WIRE REPLY. SEND JEANS DRESS—SHIRLEY LEWIS."

To say that the Lewis family was stunned is an understatement; they had not been aware of the seriousness of their daughter's romance, much less her move to Point Hope, in their minds the place closest to the North Pole. Bill's parents felt that Point Hope was a great opportunity for him to provide the missionary service of which his father had long dreamed. "Preacher" Gordon had wanted to go to China before he even entered seminary, but war intervened and he accepted a call from the small church in Spray for one year only. He was to work among impoverished and illiterate families who lived in mountain isolation, their children laboring with them in the local mills. Bill's mother, Anna Clark, was principal of a girl's school in East Carolina when his father invited her to come to Spray to teach school and church school classes. He really wanted to see how she would react to a missionary situation, still thinking of China. She rose to the challenge with equal fervor and they were married in 1913, but the China dream never became a reality; "Preacher Will" and his family remained in Spray for thirty-seven years. When Bill was born, his parents dedicated him to God for missionary work in foreign fields.

Shirley's mother, who was not a churchgoer, questioned whether her daughter knew Bill well enough, and Point Hope seemed truly at the end of the earth. But then Shirley had always been adventuresome and independent, and her mother trusted her judgment. In later years, Mrs. Lewis admitted that she had to battle a lot of "what ifs": What if she has a baby, gets sick, or homesick, or has a crash.

Shirley's father, an Army Major stationed at Excursion Inlet near Juneau, had strong feelings against the church as an institution. Nevertheless, he wrote his daughter assuring her of his support, promising to make every effort to be present at her wedding. He added, "When I was home last month, Mother and I were discussing you and Bill. I would be remiss if I did not quote her as nearly as I can remember her words: 'If Shirley contemplates marriage, there is one thing she must always remember: A minister's wife must subordinate at all times her own life, her home, her family, and her wishes on all things to the Church, the community, and to the demands which others will make on her husband, no matter how unreasonable they may be.'

"In this war-torn world, with all of its baser natures so exposed as they are today, it is indeed comforting to know those who have faith—as you and Bill must have faith—in God, in each other, and in your ability to carry that faith to others.

"Of one thing I am certain, and that is wherever you and Bill may go, you both have the intelligence, the faculty, and the ability to make your immediate environment much finer because of your presence. May God Bless you both."

Bill's mother wrote Shirley: "The girl William loves already has a warm place in my heart. I admire the courage that goes with your love in facing this challenge of the far north, and yet I think it is the most wonderful experience that two people who really care for each other could have—an opportunity to mean everything to each other and with it to serve in a quiet and blessed way.

"I have always loved William with a deep devotion and I rejoice in his happiness. I trust it to you, even as I pray that he may always worthily cherish you—and cherish is such a lovely word."

The six sisters were amused that Bill should marry someone before they even had a chance to say whether they liked her or not. Perhaps it should be no surprise that Bill picked a girl who looked so much like the Gordon daughters that when Shirley later stood in a family picture, friends could not pick her out! Nancy, the oldest, suggests that Shirley is the only person in the world who is sure enough of her own self that she could be Bill's wife and not be intimidated by him.

Even Bill and Shirley's "adopted" mother had to have her say. Mrs. Brosius took Shirley aside one evening after dinner and offered to write her mother, suggesting she feign illness so that she would have to return home, and thus escape the sudden marriage! "You know, my dear," she advised Shirley, "I'd be very wary of marrying any man who leaves his socks all over his room."

Marriage plans moved ahead at a fast pace. First, Shirley's belongings had to be sent to Seattle immediately, in hopes of making that one boat to Point Hope. Bill then took on the responsibility of preparations because Shirley had never been to a wedding! Shirley's mother sent the wedding and bridesmaid dresses, and Bill's mother sent her own ring. Anna Gordon had long ago told Bill that if she approved of the girl Bill married, she would provide the diamond ring that had belonged to her mother. And now she sent it to Shirley, sight unseen.

It was a traditional wedding. Bishop Bentley officiated at the

evening ceremony, assisted by Chaplain Edwards from Fort
Raymond. Shirley's father gave the bride away and Mrs. Brosius
served as mother, beaming from the front pew. The church was
filled with wildflowers: tall vases of magenta Fireweed, blue
Lupine, and graceful ferns. Two arrangements of white daisies
framed the small cross on the altar. Shirley's princess styled dress
was of white chiffon, and she carried a white prayer book with
a shower marker of the same daisies.

Bill had neglected none of the details of a traditional "Lower
48" wedding, while Mrs. Brosius was in charge of the reception,
given in the rectory by the Women's Guild of the Church, where
Bill and Shirley cut a small, two-tiered wedding cake.

Following a short night's stay in the small Seward hotel, Bill
and Shirley, along with Bishop Bentley, took the train north. The
threesome stopped over in Anchorage for two days. At that time
Anchorage was a town of 4,200 people, sitting high on the bluffs
above Cook Inlet. In 1939, the military had arrived to select land
for an airfield, and with the start of World War II an Army base
was built as well. Now it was a bustling town.

Bill and Shirley made the two-hour drive toward the Matanuska
Valley to visit the Eklutna Native School, and talk with two young
Eskimo girls, Madeline and Alice, daughters of Peel Tooyak,
interpreter for the Point Hope Mission. The youngsters told the
Gordons much about life at Point Hope, and described the Mission
house as "very nice."

They arrived in Nenana at three P.M. on 21 July, and the party
transferred to the mission launch to reach the Bishop's lodge—
home and headquarters a mile upriver. The rambling one-story
building stood on the riverbank surrounded by a lawn, spruce
and birch trees, and had a magnificent view of Mt. McKinley
and the snow-covered Alaska Range beyond the swift, silt-laden
Tanana river.

Nenana was one of the Tanana Valley missions begun among
Athabaskan Indian villages in the early 1900s, but it has a unique
history. A genteel missionary woman, Annie Craig Farthing, was
given charge of the Mission and the work of starting a school for
native youngsters. Miss Farthing did just that, at the cost of her
life, and the resulting boarding school had a profound effect on

the native people of the whole valley.

The following day, Bill took his canonical exam, a verbal test given by priests Warren Fenn of Anchorage and Elsom Eldridge of Fairbanks, a requirement for deacons before ordination to the priesthood. Normally there is a year's wait before this final step, but the Bishop needed a priest at Point Hope now.

Bill was ordained by Bishop Bentley on Sunday 25 July in St. Mark's Church, Nenana, nine days after his wedding in Seward. Shirley was confirmed into the Episcopal Church just before the service, the only non-Eskimo person Bill ever presented for confirmation. She had momentarily cast off her usual sweater-skirt, bobby socks, and oxfords outfit for a handsome blue tweed coat, matching beret, and navy pumps with three-inch heels. The Reverend Arnold Krone, priest-in-charge of St. Mark's Mission was presenter for Bill, and Father Fenn gave the sermon. Bill acquired another substitute mother: Miss Bessie Blacknall, a long-time lay worker in the Nenana Mission school, originally from North Carolina.

Miss Blacknall later wrote to Bill's mother: "Isn't it proper for mothers to get tears in their eyes when their children are graduating from high school, and later getting married, and certainly when a son is being ordained? Well, I could not keep the tears back. Both so young, so good looking, so happy. Bill made a splendid choice in a wife we all think. She is pretty, most attractive, and sweet, and I think will be a great help to him all through life."

Bill wrote his parents that the congregation in the mission church that day consisted mainly of local Athabaskan Indians, a few soldiers stationed at a small communications center there, and the mission school staff; very different from his ordination as deacon six months earlier in the stone church in Spray. His father had participated in that ceremony, but only after much wrestling with his conscience. Father and son had parted ways on some theological issues during Bill's freshman year in college. "Preacher Will" held more fundamental beliefs, which to Bill meant retreating into a cocoon. Bill believed in a God "whose service is perfect freedom." Their divergent views became an issue just before Bill's ordination, when his father asked, "Can you sign those vows?''

Bill replied, "Yes—you don't have to believe that every word in the Holy Scripture was written by the finger of God." Bill's theology was closer to that of his mother's. "She had a wider horizon, saw the Big Picture," he says. "She taught it, and my father lived it." Three of Bill's sisters followed their father's views and three followed their mother, but each child was allowed to find God in his or her own way, in his or her own time. However, parental rules required Sunday church attendance and morning family worship services for anyone at home.

Following his ordination, Bill and Shirley went by train to Fairbanks, the terminus of the railroad, and while waiting for an available plane to take them to Point Hope, they shopped for winter clothing. "If only we knew what we would need!" was Bill's frustrated comment in a letter to his family. He also met the bishop's secretary while in Fairbanks and wrote, "She is very attractive, though I guess it is a little late for that observation now! I'm not complaining about my acquisition anyway. She is more wonderful every day. . . .''

Chapter 2

The Land that God Forgot?

On Friday 30 July the weather cleared. After obtaining an available plane, Bill, Shirley, and Bishop Bentley took off for Point Hope at midmorning. The single-engine orange and black Bellanca was piloted by Sig Wien, who later became a much-loved person in the Gordons' lives. One of four Minnesota farm brothers who came north in 1924 to fly the rugged northland and start Wien Airlines in 1930, Sig was a man of few words—known for flying five hours with passengers and never saying anything. He was also called "Sigwien" by the Eskimos who looked forward to his comings, bringing supplies for trading posts, mail, and fresh food gifts. Sig's Arctic Coast routes were the most hazardous in Alaska, with no navigational aids, no large mountains or rivers to follow. Villages along the undented coastline are small and blend in with the surroundings, especially in winter when buried beneath the snow. The weather is treacherous—fog can develop in minutes—and runways at that time were the most primitive in the Territory, the frozen Bering Sea often the only choice.

The five-hour flight from Fairbanks to Kotzebue was over the desolate Alaskan interior, devoid of anything human except a few widely scattered Athabaskan Indian villages. It took them along the Tanana River until it joined the mighty Yukon; then the small plane left the river highways behind, heading northwest over low hills. This was Shirley's first plane flight, other than a quick hop a friend had once given her over Longview; the same was true for Bill.

Looking down on the landscape brought back many memories

for John Bentley, who had come to Alaska in 1921. He had been attending William and Mary College in Virginia, but had to drop out to go to work. He got a job as a carpenter in a shipyard, but he really wanted to go into the mission field. He wrote Peter Trimble Rowe, the first Bishop of Alaska, who turned out to be desperate for help in this far-flung missionary district. In those days one could travel to Interior Alaska only in the summertime, so Bishop Rowe suggested that in the meantime Bentley attend Virginia Seminary that spring. The young man did so, sitting with the senior class, but not permitted to take part. John Bentley was surprised and proud when the Seminary printed his name beneath the eighteen men who graduated, but with a line drawn between them. Later, after becoming a deacon and then a priest "on the job," and eventually elected Alaska's second bishop, Bentley was given an honorary degree at the seminary. That line was then scratched out.

As Bishop Bentley looked down on the two large rivers, he thought of the years he had spent as a jack-of-all-trades in the Indian village of Anvik. And then later, as Archdeacon of the Yukon, of his many winter travels by dog team. His favorite times, though, were spent on the Mission boat. He would leave his Nenana home the first Monday in June and return in mid-August. He traveled the Yukon and its tributaries during those ten weeks, stopping to hold services at the fish camps where most villagers spent summers. Little did Bill know that the next years of his life would be spent similarly—traveling from one remote settlement to another.

While the Bellanca was being refueled in Kotzebue, the largest Eskimo village along the western Arctic Coast with all of 372 residents, the Gordons visited the government hospital, the closest medical facility to Point Hope, 170 miles north. Shirley was wearing her new navy blue shoes, and had no idea what an impact they would have on the local populace. Three months later, when the Superintendent of Reindeer Herds came to Point Hope, he said to her, "Oh, you were the lady who arrived in the Arctic with high heels!" Sig Wien had noticed more than her footwear; upon his return to Fairbanks he told friends he had just flown the most beautiful woman he had ever seen to Point Hope, of all places.

They started off on the last lap, flying over what Shirley called, "very peculiar looking country—no trees, very few hills and lots of small lakes and streams—like something in Walt Disney's 'Fantasia.' " They followed the coastline north, passing over Kivalina, one of Bill's village posts. Sig got the weather report from Point Hope by wire, but his decoder was missing, so they just trusted to luck. About five miles from their destination, the fog ahead was so thick they had to land on the beach near two tents, the site of the old village of Jabbertown.

One of the tents was occupied by a man named Antonio Weber, whose life was to be interwoven with Bill's in incredible ways in the years ahead. He was there with his family hunting sea animals. He had a large skin boat made out of *ugruk* ("seal") skins and Sig hired him—for about five dollars—to take his passengers the rest of the way. Antonio loaded the boat and then he hooked a long seal skin line between the bow and his team of ten dogs. Everyone climbed in, with Antonio in the stern with a paddle while the dogs pulled from the beach, driven by Antonio's thirteen-year-old daughter, Dolly. She ran behind, prodding them by tossing an occasional stone, keeping the traces untangled, and never once stopping for breath. She ran the entire way in soft gravel, and when they arrived at the village an hour later, Dolly didn't even rest, but cavorted along with the other children.

The whole village turned out to greet the new arrivals. They were taken to the school to meet Peel Tooyak, the Mission interpreter. It turned out that Archdeacon Goodman, the ailing priest, had no idea Bill was coming; he had expected to remain there for the rest of the year. Bishop Bentley had written him, but no mail had been delivered since May. He had sent a follow-up telegram from Kotzebue, but Mr. Sams, the Point Hope school teacher and radio operator had not passed along the message yet. Such are communications in the Arctic!

The trio walked the mile from the village to the Mission, following a trail marked with four-foot-high whale bones which guided the people during white-out conditions, and they greeted a totally surprised Mr. Goodman. Bill recalls that the Bishop and the Archdeacon had a lengthy talk while the younger couple waited in another room. It was easy to hear every word spoken because the walls were thin partitions, and the Gordons were stunned to hear the old man propose that he remain in charge of the Mission, while directing Bill's activities there and at outstations. And Shirley would be a marvelous housekeeper for them both! As soon as he could, Bill drew the Bishop aside and told him firmly that when the Bishop's plane left there would either be two or three on board.

The Sunday church service started at eleven A.M. and ended at one-thirty. St. Thomas's Mission Church was a simple green frame structure with two pairs of small square windows on each side and a large rectangular foyer. A slim white wooden cross rose above the roof peak. It was packed with 225 of the 257 villagers. Shirley was particularly taken by the beauty of the old oak pews, the bright candlelight surrounding the ornate brass cross on the altar, and behind it a large, colorful painting of St. Thomas examining the nail prints in the hands of Jesus.

Thirty-one people were presented to Bishop Bentley for confirmation. The bishop preached with Peel Tooyak as interpreter. Peel also read the Bible lessons in Eskimo, and Archdeacon Goodman officiated at his last Communion. Bill wrote his family: "It was a very impressive service. The people really sing, [in Eskimo and English], we have a good choir and Peel plays the small organ. The Archdeacon has trained them well in the service. He is very high church—he has fourteen candles on the altar— and the people here call me Father!"

Bill observed the whole village assembled for worship and thought of the four remarkable clergy who had preceded him. All had spent years working here, beginning with Dr. John Driggs, a medical missionary who arrived in 1890 and stayed for eighteen years. He began his ministry by teaching school and treating what ailments he could. Thirteen years after his arrival, in 1903, Bishop Rowe went to Point Hope on the U.S. Revenue Cutter (the only means of transportation) and ordained John Driggs as a deacon in the Episcopal Church.

In 1908 Dr. Driggs was sent to Seattle for retirement; the isolation, loneliness, and terrible hardships had taken their toll. He returned a year later, to make his home farther north, near

Cape Lisburne. He died there in 1914 and a lonely grave now
marks the site.

Bishop Rowe appointed the Reverend A. R. Hoare to take over
Dr. Driggs's work in 1908. A former engineer in Alaska who was
advanced to the priesthood, Hoare left his wife and children
behind, living alone at Point Hope for twelve years. He built the
Mission house and Browning Hall for recreation in 1912, but his
ambitious plans were cut short when he was shot to death by
a crazed white man, the teacher in the village.

Archdeacon Goodman, an Englishman, arrived in 1925, following a five-year stint by the Reverend W. A. Thomas. He continued
the extensive work of his predecessors—building the Augustus
Hoare Memorial Hospital, and translating into Eskimo the most
frequently used Episcopal Prayer Book services (the first time the
Eskimo language was printed). His plans for further work at the
coastal outstations of Kivalina and Point Lay were thwarted by
lack of funds from the National Church, a perennial problem. By
1943, when his health was deteriorating and he was long past
retirement age, he had to be taken to and from the church by
sled. These were big shoes for twenty-five-year-old Bill Gordon
to try to fill!

On Tuesday morning, when the plane returned for the Bishop
and Archdeacon, a message arrived asking Sig Wien to fly north
325 miles to Barrow instead, to search for the thirteen-year-old
son of the Barrow schoolteacher. He had wandered off from a
reindeer camp in the fog and had been missing three days.

Bill and the Bishop went along on the flight as far as the
Presbyterian village of Wainright, just south of Barrow, where
the two visited the few Episcopal families in their homes and Bill
baptized two babies. "I had to go nearly to the end of the world
to have my first baptism! We spent the night in the school house.
I slept in a sleeping bag for the first time and found it very
comfortable. Supper was caribou—good meat."

Meanwhile, Sig found the boy and guided him back to camp,
then flew the two men south again to Point Lay, a mission
outstation, where Bill baptized twelve more babies. From Point
Lay, they continued to Point Hope, but hit fog and had to turn
back. Bill was deeply disappointed—he missed Shirley—but they

made it in the following morning. In two days, Bill had baptized fourteen babies, visited Eskimo families in their sod igloos, and flown 1500 miles—he was off to a running start!

Nearly a week after the arrival of the Gordons and the bishop, Archdeacon Goodman picked up three small suitcases, put on his black hat and his overcoat, and stepped out of his Arctic home for the last time, a place where he had spent most of his ministry. The whole village gathered in a large semicircle around the plane. Each person shook hands with Father Goodman and they all sang "God Be With You Till We Meet Again," in English and in Eskimo. The Archdeacon pronounced his blessing, then he and Bishop Bentley climbed into the plane and flew off.

Shirley and Bill immediately moved into the mission house, and discovered that Goodman had left behind just about everything he owned, including a thousand books, 900 of which were detective stories. There was even a pot of tea on the stove. Later, he wrote often, asking them to send along various items. He wanted some books and a half-empty can of curry powder for which Americans would have no use. The Gordons dutifully mailed them, only to receive a letter weeks later taking them to task; the package had arrived in bad array, the curry all mixed in with his books. The most bizarre item the Archdeacon left behind was in the bedroom. It looked like a chest with a hinged lid, but it was actually a coffin that Goodman had made for himself, exactly to his dimensions. Inside were careful instructions about how he would be laid out and buried. The Gordons used it for storage, although Shirley had some anxious moments over it.

Both Bill and Shirley were pleased with their first home, which was a California bungalow shipped north piece by piece. The house, painted green with white trim, stood on pilings five feet off the permanently frozen ground. Wood siding covered this open area and the space inside was used as a storeroom. Originally, the house was encircled by a porch, not very useful in its present location! Part of the front porch was closed in forming a vestibule which opened into a little hall, a small living room complete with a coal heating stove, a tiny kitchen, and a dining room which they used for freezer storage because it had no heat.

The second floor contained a bedroom and a storeroom (Bill converted it to an office). Bishop Bentley was shocked to find there was only a single bed and he promised he would order a larger one. The Gordons were not concerned—it was a good way to keep warm! The upstairs had no stove, and frost often formed on their blankets during a cold spell.

Utilities consisted of a generator and storage batteries for a few light bulbs, and an ancient washing machine which gave out within a matter of days. Water came from a shallow well in summer, but during the long winter water for drinking came from ice blocks, brought from a river fifteen miles away while melted snow was used for washing. The drifts around the house were hardpacked and Bill sawed them into blocks. An oft-repeated comment in his letters was, "They never taught us this in seminary!"

The Gordons also inherited numerous buildings at the mission complex: Browning Hall, a sixty-foot-long rectangular building used for all sorts of recreational functions, another large, empty structure built to serve as a hospital, a coal house, a storage shed for gasoline, a workshop, a boat house on the beach, and a greenhouse.

Just beyond the church was a most unusual graveyard, encircled by 812 eight-foot-tall whale ribs. Most of the graves were marked with small wooden crosses, but some, particularly those of great whalers of the past, had a single monstrous whale rib. A small marble monument marked the resting place of the Reverend Hoare.

At this stage in their lives, the young newlyweds would have been happy in a tent at the North Pole. In fact, both say they felt ashamed to have such good quarters in a village of single-room sod houses. With the onset of winter darkness and icy winds, however, their accommodations no longer seemed luxurious. The walls were painted a dismal dark green with black trim, the floors were covered with brown linoleum which could be icy cold, even in midsummer. The wiring was exposed and the twenty-three-year-old generator gave them constant trouble until they were often reduced to the light of one gasoline lamp and, at one point in midwinter, candles. Once the electric washing machine gave out, the washing had to be done by hand, and it took a lot of snow to make enough water. The latter was heated in a five-gallon can on the coal stove, and the laundry hung on galvanized pipes covering the kitchen ceiling. Today Bill recalls one of his most vivid memories of the house: "Walking through that room with wet clothes flapping me in the face." In one letter Shirley mentioned having washed by hand twelve sheets, worn by "angels" in the Christmas pageant and heating the old-fashioned flat iron on their coal stove.

Fortunately Bill and Shirley were young, imbued with the spirit of adventure and of dedication to Bill's work, as well as equipped with a superb sense of humor. Some troubled times lay ahead, but the months of August and September of 1943, before winter set in, were a joyous honeymoon period. Many of the Point Hope people had traveled north to their fish camps on the Kukpuk River, so Bill's work was lighter and both had a chance to become more acquainted with each other and with their surroundings. Bill wrote his parents, "The sun goes down here about 10:30 now, over the water, and the coloring has been magnificent. We have a beautiful setting, with ocean on two sides, a lagoon on the third. The place is completely flat and treeless, with little flowers all over the point. And the point is unmistakably that—a long, narrow sand spit, with a maximum elevation of eight feet, sticking way out into the Chukchi Sea toward Siberia [200 miles away]. The snow-capped hills from Cape Lisburne to Cape Thompson form a half-circle behind us, and the view off our back porch of the sea and its waves is perfect. After supper [the first night in the house] Shirley and I went down to the beach—just fifty yards in back—and went wading in the Arctic Ocean! It was plenty cold but a lot of fun. I don't suppose there are many people living on two beaches who never can go swimming at either."

The point of land is called Tikeraq by the Eskimos, meaning index finger. It is treeless and bushless, but sections of the sand and gravel dunes are covered with green tundra growth. The village houses were situated in four rows, with ditches between them. Wet in summer, luxurious grass grew there and provided the sod for blocks needed to re-cover the homes each year. These ditches were a source for drinking water when the snow was gone—an unsanitary situation. In 1943, with the exception of the rambling old wood-framed schoolhouse, a small trading post, and one home (owned by the village leader, Peter Koonoyak), all the houses were semisubterranean, made of two-foot-thick sod covering a driftwood frame. Called igloos, but not the kind pictured in geography books, they consisted of a single ten foot by ten foot room with a window in the ceiling made of semitranslucent seal intestine. It was flexible and could be hit from the inside to knock off snow. A long, low passage (a *connichuck,* or "vestibule") with a small opening formed the entrance. One had to stoop, or even crawl to enter.

Inside the igloo itself the odor of ancient blubber hung in the air, thick with smoke from the cooking fire of sod soaked in seal oil. A stove made from a gasoline drum or can was used but usually not for heat (kerosene oil lamps gave off some warmth). Coal was too expensive and driftwood was rare. Villagers ranged up and down the beach for up to thirty miles during the summer, collecting whatever they found into piles above the high water mark. When snow came, they took their dog sleds to gather it. On frigid days, the people wore parkas indoors, and ice formed on their water overnight. Sod huts, however, were far warmer than the later frame buildings, and kept the temperature close to freezing in spite of minus ten to minus thirty degree readings outside. Many of the families had six or more children, so body heat helped, especially when they slept wall-to-wall, using caribou skins on the floor.

The westernmost house was a quarter mile from the very tip of the point, where a unique lighthouse stood. A twenty-foot-tall pyramid of white wooden latticework, with a large gas lantern at its apex, was kept lighted from early August until 15 April, when twenty-four-hour daylight returned. Although the lighthouse had been set up by the Coast Guard as a beacon for ships, its other important function was to guide hunters returning across the pack ice.

In late August of 1943 Bill began visitations to the elderly and sick of the village, accompanied by interpreter Peel Tooyak. He also preached his first sermon with Peel interpreting. Patrick Attungana, a village elder then, later to become an Eskimo priest,

comments on this service: "The first time I went to hear about
the new preacher. I enjoy. After sermon hymn Gordon welcomed
Point Hope people. He said, 'I have first sermon in the village,
on Lord's Prayer.' He explain it. I won't forget. I remember
sometimes when I start same sermon in church. Later on he teach
us Psalm Twenty-three. He gave it to congregation. Tried to learn.
I learn good, all right. I have it right here now in my mind."

Some of the villagers held their own service on Sunday afternoons, all in Eskimo, led by Peter Koonoyak in his home. Bill
was invited to attend. Everyone sat in a circle on the floor for
an hour or longer. They read from the Bible, discussed the reading
and sang hymns all in Eskimo—Bill recognized one or two—and
several people said spontaneous prayers. The faith and witness
of this lay group had a profound impact on Bill and his own
ministry in later years.

The village store's thirty-two-foot open launch was going to
make a trip south to Kivalina, one of the Mission's outposts, and
Bill and Shirley hitched a ride, their first on a small boat. It was
quite a trip (eighty miles in thirteen hours), and they arrived at
Kivalina at four A.M. Sunday morning! On the way down some
of the men saw a thousand-pound walrus on the beach, so they
drifted in and killed it and cut it up on the spot. The walrus added
some aroma to the already tightly packed narrow boat.

Kivalina is about halfway to Kotzebue along the smooth, flat
Arctic coastline. In fact, the only landmark between Point Hope
and Kivalina is Cape Thompson, a series of sheer, rocky cliffs
rising several hundred feet straight out of the water. The clefts
are filled with thousands of nesting birds, which flee in clouds
when disturbed by human noise.

Kivalina itself is on a spit of land similar to Point Hope, although
both spit and village are much smaller. Three rows of sod houses
lined the narrow sandy strip between the ocean and a lagoon,
which is fed by two small rivers. The two wood-frame buildings
in the village belonged to the school and the trading post. Bill
and Shirley stayed with the teachers, Dan and Eunice Stalker. Both
Eskimos, educated in Anchorage and Fairbanks, they opened their
arms to the young couple. That same morning, in spite of only
two hours' sleep, Bill held a service in the school (Kivalina had

no church). There was a sizable congregation (about sixty-five people). This was the first time Bill celebrated the Holy Communion with no altar, cross, or candles. After dinner, Bill visited all his people in their igloos. In the evening he had another service and baptized three babies, making twenty for the month of August. The next morning Bill hired the store launch and, with Milton Swan, (the village leader who was to become one of Bill's closest friends over the next thirty years) went five miles up the Kivalina River to the reindeer camp.

Domestic reindeer had been introduced to Alaska in 1892, when Dr. Sheldon Jackson, a Presbyterian missionary, purchased them in Siberia, bringing them back on a U.S. Revenue Cutter. His purpose was to provide Eskimos with a reliable source of food. Over the next ten years, 280 more were imported, and by 1930 the government estimated the herd had increased to over 600,000 animals. Herders were brought from Siberia and Lapland to teach the people how to care for them.

The first site for the project was at Teller, on the Seward Peninsula south of Kotzebue. In 1894 two men were sent from Point Hope to learn about herding and they were given some reindeer to take back to the Point Hope-Kivalina area. At first the herd did well, expanding to about 6,000. By 1940 it had dropped to 2,000, and in 1948 the last 250 animals at Point Hope disappeared when the herders came to the village for Christmas festivities.

The project was unsuccessful for a number of reasons. The coastal Eskimos foraged for food from a home base following a definite cycle of hunting and fishing activities that are foreign to the nomadic routine of close herding. Even the most dedicated men left their herds for spring whaling activities, at a time when the caribou were migrating, so large numbers of reindeer joined their wild cousins.

Three of the Episcopal families in Kivalina had become reindeer herders, living in tents near the reindeer, and Bill and Milton found them about noon. "I had lunch with them by a beautiful clear water stream," Bill wrote, "excellent reindeer meat, then I had a service in one of the tents. It was about ten feet by fifteen feet and full of everything from their stove and cooking utensils

to reindeer skins and dogs. But we got twenty-six people into
it and I preached and celebrated the Holy Communion, using a
food box as an altar. I couldn't straighten up! We sang some
hymns from a few Wayside hymnals [small paperbacks published
by the Episcopal Church] I'd brought. It was a fine service and
a real blessing to me. I was quite touched when, afterwards, one
of the women came up and gave me a nickel for an offering. It
may have been the only cash she had."

Back in Kivalina, Bill appointed Milton and Martha Swan to take
charge in his absence, and he obtained permission for them to
use the school. He left a note for the annual supply boat to leave
an extra ton of coal there. "We need a church building here very
badly, and have the money to build, but can't get the materials
now," he recorded. (There are no trees in Kivalina, so lumber
would have to come in by supply boat the following year.) Bill
adds, "I hope we can get around to it soon—a group of the
California Friends Church [not the American Quakers, but an
independent sect] have started work in Kivalina."

Bill felt very strongly that the Eskimos be allowed to live their
lives as they saw fit. "Seeing the way a few of the narrow sects
have dealt with the Eskimos here in the Arctic has more and more
convinced me of the basic wrongness of these methods. They
have forbidden them to do the native dance—part of their very
life and fiber, and how they can possibly find any ill in this form
of expression I cannot see. The hates and jealousies they breed
in the people against those who disagree with them is downright
sinful. Religious faith cannot be built on law and negativism.
There is none of the love of God to be seen."

Bill often commented on his theological differences with the
Friends. He accepted the Eskimos' traditions: the dancing, the
whaling festivities as part of their church life, and while Bill
himself never smoked cigarettes, he did not ban this pleasure
among his people. Also, he and Shirley played cards and other
games, and loved to dance. Bill's strong reaction to strict negative
theology runs counter to his father's fundamentalism. Yet Bill
states, "My religious experience at home was not negative. My
father was a very positive Christian, with some trend toward
fundamentalism. The slight legalism that might appear was mostly

because of the attitudes of the people in the community who would come down out of the Virginia Mountains, most of them illiterate. So, their understanding of the faith was simplistic, limited by their educational experience."

Bill's faith was influenced by his mother's broader interpretation of the Bible, and also by the priests at the church camps he attended every summer while growing up. He was in constant informal contact with them; they were solid in their faith, and yet there was a freedom about them that appealed to him.

Milton and Martha Swan, the couple Bill left in charge of the mission outpost, were long-time leaders in the village and devout Christians who held Sunday services in their home following the earlier guidance from Archdeacon Goodman. Martha had a few intermittent years of formal schooling, so she had struggled to learn to read the Bible on her own. Then Milton memorized passages that she read to him before bed each night. Milton also taught himself to play the small folding organ in the school.

Returning to Point Hope, the Gordons were just in time for the visit of the annual supply boat, bringing mail and all the supplies for the coming year. It also brought along three young soldiers to be stationed there for weather observation. Four others accompanied them temporarily to help set up a quonset hut for living quarters. Bill persuaded the lieutenant in charge to rent the empty hospital building (never used as such) as well. He felt it was good to have the men nearby—only a few hundred yards from the mission house—and for the well-built, well-maintained structure to be used. His control of the soldiers' housing proved to be good leverage for him those few times when men or situations threatened to get out of control. The Gordons were delighted to be joined by outsiders of their own age. These Army men were to play an important supportive role for Shirley during Bill's frequent absences, and almost daily games—especially cards and Monopoly—helped everyone pass the long winter nights. Dances were fun for all of them, holidays were shared, and imported food delicacies were constantly exchanged.

The supply boat unloaded supplies on the south beach near the village because a north wind had come up. It grew so strong that the boat was forced to sail on to Barrow before leaving coal and

gas for the coming year. Fortunately for the Gordons, down to
their last two bags of coal, the ship was able to stop on its return
voyage.

Archdeacon Goodman had put in some "railroad" tracks and
a pushcart which could easily bring supplies the hundred yards
from the north side of the spit, but his ingenuity was of no use
when the ship used the south beach, so Bill was forced to hire
six dog teams to bring everything up over the tundra—a long
day's hard labor. Each September in the years ahead, Bill's letters
were punctuated with comments about the supply boat using the
south beach once again, as though the captain took perverse
pleasure in watching the missionary do manual labor. Of course,
this particular priest welcomed the exercise—it was the expense
of hiring dog teams that concerned him. The 300 hundred-pound
sacks of coal already cost the mission sixty dollars a ton to ship
from Seattle. Bill had grown up counting his pennies.

For Bill and Shirley, the happiest part of the supply boat arrival
was receiving Bill's well-traveled trunk, suitcases belonging to
them both, several packages, and thirty-two letters, a full afternoon of reading their first news from home. The only regular
mail deliveries were once a month by dog team from Kotzebue
between November and April, and limited to items of small size.
The rest of the year they had one delivery by boat, in late summer.
However, there was an occasional plane to take mail out. This
was a major disappointment to Bill and Shirley, as was the
discovery that the only radio in Point Hope was at the schoolteacher's home, more than a mile away.

With their food supplies stored for the coming year, Shirley's
major challenge was to learn how to cook. Although she and her
sister had grown up in a home where chores were done by
everyone, the two girls fought over who was going to wash and
dry an endless number of dishes, while her mother took care of
all meal preparation.

Now Shirley had to learn with a temperamental coal stove, and
since no grocery store existed down the street, substituting
ingredients was the rule. Also the milk was powdered, butter was
in tins, and eggs were fresh on arrival (they developed a stronger
taste as the months went by and had to be turned every two

weeks). This posed problems for recipes, as well as taste buds. A further challenge was learning how to cook the local produce, such as ptarmigan, reindeer, seal liver, and caribou tongue. Bill's early letters frequently refer to Shirley's new skill. "Shirley is developing into a remarkable cook. We had a mighty good reindeer steak recently and roast reindeer today." Later, when Bill hired village men to help him build an ice house and Shirley had to cook them lunch, Bill boasted that Shirley fed five hungry working men for a week, and she really measured up to the task.

In a letter later that fall, Bill commented that Shirley was studying a cookbook at his instigation. She was looking for a recipe that did not take five eggs. He and Peel Tooyak tried to help by putting dampers in the oven. A few months later Bill had to admit that both he and Shirley were gaining weight from eating so much starchy food.

Bill's job in the kitchen was to make ice cream with a hand-cranked machine and snow. He had such a craving for his favorite dessert that he could not wait for winter and took a wheelbarrow over three quarters of a mile of tundra to the lagoon to fill it with newly formed ice. Then he began to hunt with his .22 rifle, proudly bringing home duck and ptarmigan.

Once Shirley's cooking had progressed, they began inviting Eskimo families for dinner, one every Friday evening. Shirley also started a Girls Friendly Society for the young women her age, having them to the house once a week for Bible study and fellowship. She had begun making friends by visiting every home in the village.

"I am having a marvelous time," she writes. "These people are so genuine and such good friends. The wife of our church usher, Moses Melik, has adopted me! She has three other adopted children and insists they call me Sister. She calls me *Paneen*, which is the Eskimo word for "daughter," as she speaks no English. I visited them in their igloo and had *pineapple* with them, which looked for all the world like canned peaches to me. We sat on the floor at a little table which stood about six inches high. Fanny, my Eskimo mother, said grace."

Bill's everyday chores—it took half of his time just for them to survive—increased with the onset of winter. The biggest job was converting an old storeroom into an ice house. With the five village helpers Shirley had fed, they hauled in great blocks of sod to make walls four to six feet thick for insulation. Then they began hauling ice from the Kukpuk River, their winter drinking and cooking water supply. About ten tons was needed, at ten dollars a ton by dog team. They paid more for ice in the Arctic than in North Carolina!

By late September snow had arrived, and Bill wrote, "I'm not quite used to snow in September, but I haven't really minded the weather so far. We are warm, comfortable, and happy. Life at Point Hope is really great. God has been surely good to little Shirley and me. Of course I miss North Carolina, but I have no desire to be anywhere else at present. Here the Church is just everything in the community. As the Church goes, so goes the village. It is a great responsibility, but also a rare privilege."

After two months of winter weather, Bill's November letter showed a more human reaction: "Don't let the moths eat up my tuxedo, 'cause three years hence Shirley and I are going to dress up and really have a party. We're going to get a head of lettuce in one hand and a bottle of fresh milk in the other and walk down the street, look for a watermelon, touch all the trees we see, and maybe climb a few. Then we'll stand on a busy corner under the hot sun and watch people and cars go by!"

With the onset of winter, Bill began building up the nucleus of an Altar Guild, and the village women started cleaning candlesticks and other altar adornments for the upcoming Thanksgiving-Christmas season. He and Shirley sang in the choir (Bill was present strictly for support; he was not known for his musical talent), and they also held Monday afternoon parties for the children attending Sunday School. He initiated Wednesday evening services in Browning Hall, followed by dancing to old time country music played on an antique victrola, and games. He wanted to offer the people as many activities as possible outside their dark, cramped homes during the winter months.

Bill and Shirley acquired Eskimo names. His was *Ungahyuliksi,* meaning "Minister," and Shirley's was *Ahknowruk,* meaning "white woman." "I was glad to be able to shed the title *Father,* which hangs a little heavy on my brow." Bill tells of the first time he heard his new name. It was after the funeral of Peel's foster mother, the oldest person in the village at eighty years of age. They processed from the church to the whalebone-fenced graveyard, Bill and two village dogs leading, followed by fifteen men pulling a sled with the casket. It was covered with a bright oilcloth and a wreath made of ribbon. All the people followed in a long line. They managed to dig deep enough through the frozen crust of ground, but it would be the last burial until spring. After the service, each person threw a handful of earth on the coffin. Leaving the graveyard, Bill noticed a new Maltese cross carved from wood over the grave of an old man who died last spring. "I asked who made it and the people pointed out Lennie. I told him it was a beautiful piece of work. Lennie said he had made the cross because the old man did not have any son to do it for him. Then he apologized for just putting the words *Until the Resurrection* on the cross, he said he just couldn't get *Day* to fit in the small space. Lennie walked on toward the village saying, "good bye *Ungahyuliksi.*' And then I noticed the widow of the old man sitting by the grave, rubbing her fingers over the cross with tears in her eyes."

Bill was learning much from the Eskimos, and he was particularly impressed with their attitude toward death. "I believe that the Eskimo concept of death and funerals is the most Christian of any I've ever known. The people are certainly sad, but they are also convinced of God's loving care and His plan for the future." When someone died, all the women in the family and their friends gathered to prepare the body for burial. The men built a plain casket from plywood or some other material that they got from the village store. It was a communal sharing of mourning. Only at the end was it Bill's turn to hold a simple service.

Bill's detailed letters to his family became widely circulated among his parents' friends. His mother carried them with her on her travels throughout the South, reading them to the many Womens' Auxiliaries she spoke before. When Bill became aware of the interest in his mission work, he began to tailor some of his letters to a larger "family." He also began to request help for things that were needed for his people and the church. This type of personal solicitation was considered questionable practice in the minds of some church people in Alaska. National Church policy stated that no individual priest or mission could solicit Outside funds, but money was always scarce because the National Church never allotted what the Alaskans considered adequate for missionary work. One problem was lack of understanding about the size of the Territory and the enormous costs of travel, supplies, and the like. The other was that there simply was never much money available on the national level, first because of the Depression, and then because of World War II. Bill never requested money, but only mentioned equipment that was needed or projects he would like to start, a gray area here, especially when his pleas went to his mother, who then used his letters to obtain help. Womens' Auxiliaries were anxious to do something in a personal way, and although this support system began in the South, it quickly spread all over the country and became a vital component of Bill's ministry.

Bill's first requests were for athletic gear: several footballs, softballs, baseball bats, volleyball nets and balls, and horseshoes. "I got in a baseball game in Kivalina—we played with a reindeer hide stuffed with moss and an old stick for a bat, but we had fun, young and old. I distinguished myself mostly by falling down several times!" Bill enjoyed these times because he was an athlete, earning letters in baseball, football, basketball, and track at boarding school and college, and he needed an outlet for his competitive nature. Also, he sensed from the start of his mission that he came closer to these people outside the formal church activities.

In a letter written a month later, Bill is more subtle. "In what price range do altar hangings run? That is a great need here; the only adequate hanging we have is a green one. We would not want anything very fancy, but something to show the seasons [of the church year]. Our mission has a little money to spare if the prices aren't too high. Also, if you hear of anyone wanting to put old hymnals to a worthy use when they are buying new ones, we could use plenty of them."

Thanksgiving was a big feast time for the Eskimos of Point Hope. Like other Americans, they used the national holiday as a day of celebration and of giving thanks to God for all their blessings. The Arctic Coast is a long way from the New England coast, site of the original party, and the food and activities were different, but the spirit was the same.

The native feast began at the hall in the late afternoon. The whole village was there, seated in families on the floor. The white colony didn't care for *muktuk* ("whale skin"), so they joined Bill and Shirley at home for ham, sweet potatoes, mince and pumpkin pie, and ice cream. The Gordons went back and forth from the house to the hall between courses.

After the feast the villagers held games of skill and endurance; contests that included the finger and arm pull, jumping to kick an object suspended above the floor, and other athletic feats such as walking on hands. Then followed native dancing, which told stories handed down from ancient days; the orchestra made up of five men who beat on large drums fashioned of seal intestine. Others chanted in rhythm, while dancers vigorously stamped their feet, with most of the movement done by their hands, clothed in white gloves. The festivities lasted until morning, but Shirley and Bill excused themselves early because Bill had to leave the next morning for Kivalina.

Peel Tooyak assumed charge of the mission in Bill's absence. Moses Melik's daughter, Ella, was to live with Shirley until he returned. Bill had complete confidence in Peel, who had worked with Archdeacon Goodman for many years. He would conduct church services, reading sermons that Bill had composed, and he and Shirley would begin rehearsals for the annual Christmas pageant. Bill had quickly discovered that Peel was a remarkable man, who would be of immense help to mission work on the Arctic Coast. Bishop Bentley agreed, and plans were already underway to ordain him a deacon in the coming year.

Bill's companion on his trip was Antonio Weber, who provided twelve dogs and a sled. The trail, running along the ocean beach, was in good shape for the first twenty miles and the two men covered it in four hours. But the next ten miles were torture, through soft knee-deep snow up and over Cape Thompson. They finally made the other side and a little igloo about seven-thirty that night. It was filled with blown snow so they had to shovel it out before moving in; then it was not high enough to stand in, or long enough for lying prone. Bill cooked supper on a small gasoline stove while Antonio fixed the dogs for the night, feeding them some walrus meat they had picked up along the way, a little old and smelly. Then they bedded down on the snow, on top of a reindeer skin, in sleeping bags. It wasn't the most comfortable night Bill ever spent. He admits now that although he thought he was a strong athlete, he was no match for the strength and endurance of the Eskimo people.

Following this first dog team trip, Bill wrote to his former college cross country coach that he found his running trails great preparation for mushing. He added, however, that the old hill and dale course never offered knee-deep snow or quite so many clothes. Bill's mother wrote him that the reason for his good physical condition was the number of hours he spent walking off demerits in high school!

The two men started out again about nine the next morning and found a better trail behind the ice cakes the wind had blown up on the beach, but it was still pretty rough going. Antonio spied a red fox and soon they added it to the sled load. They covered about fifty-five miles that day, and got to Kivalina schoolhouse about eight at night.

Bill held a service the following morning, and in the afternoon officiated at his first wedding. He recalls, "I was very conscientious at the time and felt we had to do everything as it is spelled out in our prayer book. I insisted that this couple (neither spoke English) say each word of the complicated service. I particularly remember how we struggled with 'I plight thee my troth.' There was also the problem of rings. No one in any of the villages had any. I finally sent out word to my faithful women's groups that I needed a good supply of plain wedding bands."

A second service and three baptisms followed in the evening, ending with a private communion service for an old blind man in his home, and in between the formal gatherings Bill visited all the people.

One can't help wondering how Bill was able to do so much in one day. "He doesn't just walk, he runs!" comments one of his long-time priests. "But everyone feels he takes plenty of time for them; he is genuinely interested in the people, and concentrates totally on the person he is talking with."

Antonio and Bill left Kivalina for Noatak, a village and potential outstation the bishop had asked him to visit, early Monday morning. Noatak is an interior village, "and they actually have trees here—what a sight!" Bill exclaimed. "Thousands of Christmas trees and not one at Point Hope—that is life! I'd take one along, but we already have too much stuff on the sled. Their homes are log cabins scattered along the high bluff above the Noatak River.

Bill and Antonio received a warm welcome. Mrs. Calhoun, the wife of the schoolteacher, and her son were Episcopalians (Everitt, her husband, was later to be ordained a priest by Bill), and they took the two men in. Bill was amazed to find thirty-four baptized people in this small place. He visited them all that night, and was overcome by their warmth. It was the first time anyone from the Church had come to see them. Sixty-one people attended the service Bill gave, and he appointed two of them official leaders of the group, promising to return on a regular basis beginning in March.

Everitt Calhoun, at that time not a member of any church, was considerably less awed by Bill's visit. "A native came to our door, said 'a white man's coming to see you . . . I think he is the preacher.' I thought, 'Oh-oh, that's that kid from Point Hope.' I told my wife, 'Get busy, we're going to scrub for that guy.' So we got out cans of chicken and some fresh fruit we had left, and he finally shows up. Something about him, when he walked through the door, I thought, 'No, we won't offer you a drink,' because all I had was grain alcohol. Next day I took him to see one of my students, pretty sick with TB. We both knew he didn't have a chance. But Bill did somethin' I never thought of doin'. He said a prayer. They thanked him. The following morning the kid was gone."

Bill was homesick for Shirley, so he stayed in Noatak for two days only. On the trail back to Kivalina they found other Eskimos already in the little shelter and he and Antonio crowded in with them. They offered Bill some *quok* ("frozen raw fish") and

Eskimo ice cream *(okkutak)* for dinner. "They actually had two varieties, chocolate and vanilla! The essence is reindeer fat. Frozen into one kind were some blueberries; and in the other, frozen raw fish. I just took a little of each, for it is a great delicacy. For white man's food, we used our gasoline stove. Try cooking outdoors when it is below zero."

On the trail the next day, Bill heated beans for lunch and some froze before he could eat them. He also had to blow on the fork to warm it up enough so it would not freeze to his tongue. The temperature was about zero, while a strong wind increased the chill. The sun had left the Arctic Coast altogether, not to return until 5 January, turning already short days into perpetual twilight. While Antonio was melting ice for water, Bill looked up and saw a red fox dashing by. He yelled, Antonio dropped everything, grabbed his rifle and dropped the animal with one shot. The fur was valuable and Antonio would receive a little needed cash revenue. (In a subsistence culture, money was needed mainly for gasoline and a few food staples like flour and salt.)

Back in Kivalina, Bill decided to take an extra day to visit the reindeer herders' camp before heading home. Both he and the dogs were pretty tired, for they had covered more than 200 miles in that week over some rough trail, so he hired another team and young Jimmy Hawley (later to be ordained a priest). They left early the following morning and after an all-day trip along an ice-covered river they found that the herd had gone in the opposite direction! They were forced to backtrack. When they finally found the herders, Chester Seveck, the chief, took Bill into his tent, dried his clothes, and fed him a fine supper of reindeer meat. Afterward, they had a Holy Communion service in the tent which eighteen herders and their families attended. "We sang lots of hymns and our voices resounded against the hills around us, for we were quite a way inland, in the shadow of a great cliff. It was crowded in the tent, and I had to push a dog out of the way occasionally to move, but the service truly made my trip worthwhile."

After the others went off to bed, Chester and Bill had a long talk. Chester was considered the best reindeer man in Alaska. His herd at Kivalina was the only one in this section that was increasing, and when asked why, he replied, "Every day when I get up I pray and I say, Lord, today I put myself into your hands; you are my guide; show me what to do; and I will do it." Chester then challenged Bill to a few cribbage hands, and beat him soundly. When they finally went to sleep, Bill was flanked by three dogs, one pup sleeping right on top of him.

Bill's trip back to Kivalina met with near disaster. He and Jimmy Hawley were sliding smoothly along the ice, until they hit an overflow in the river; the ice broke and dumped them and the sled into the water. Fortunately it wasn't deep, but both men got their outer clothing wet. The water quickly froze, their parkas becoming as stiff as boards. They continued on quickly until they reached the warmth of the Swans' home that evening.

Bill and Antonio got back to Point Hope about midafternoon after thirteen days on the trail, covering 425 miles. Shirley and Bill had a joyous reunion, realizing how much they meant to each other. Shirley had been desperately lonely. Bill called her over wireless radio whenever he could. She wrote, "I have just come from the soldiers' quarters where I was able to talk to Bill on the radio, a marvelous invention! I didn't realize he spoke so strongly southern! I know I shouldn't be so foolish, but I miss him terribly."

Bill arrived back to discover that Mr. Sams, the schoolteacher, would be leaving on the next plane three days later—a sudden development. He was ousted from his position by the Point Hope Eskimo Village Council because they disapproved of his living with an Eskimo woman, as well as for selling some of his supplies to village people; and they complained to the Bureau of Education. There was no replacement due, so the Commissioner asked the Gordons to fill in. They not only became teachers, but also inherited all the associated work—lighthouse keeper, reindeer herd supervisor, village radio operator, and health aide. It would now be necessary to live in the schoolhouse, much closer to the village and the day they moved was the coldest of the year so far—fourteen degrees below zero. The thermometer stayed there throughout the holiday season.

Bill's Christmas letter to family and friends was full of enthusiasm about the many church activities as well as the chal-

lenge of the new job, but the bombshell came in one paragraph
squeezed between the telling of holiday events. "... maybe some
of you might be interested in the arrival of another infant. We're
expecting a little one late in July. There doesn't seem to be much
doubt about that, though we have no medical confirmation. It
makes us very happy, but Shirley is bearing more than her share
now. Maybe this is the long awaited boy in both families, though
we'll settle for a girl. We haven't made any definite plans, but
we've agreed this would be no place for a baby to be born. It
seems that it would cost about as much for Shirley to go to
Fairbanks ahead of time for the arrival and wait around as to go
home for the whole thing. So as far as we know she will leave
here early in April for Longview. It pains me muchly that I won't
be present, but I don't see how I can."

Bill adds in a personal note to his mother, "The day we came
down to the schoolhouse Shirley began to be sick to her stomach
constantly, and finally had to give up and go to bed before
Christmas. She has been there ever since, and has great difficulty
keeping anything in her stomach. As long as she stays in bed she
feels pretty well." Bill adds with his usual optimism that he is
sure she will be up before too long. In fact, it was to be six long
weeks. Shirley knew nothing about pregnancy, nor had she ever
been around babies. Her only sister was just three years younger
and she had no recollection of her as an infant.

Shirley writes almost nothing about this miserable period: a
time of total darkness, the worst of the Arctic winter, the supreme
isolation and the misery she must have felt—the longing for her
warm childhood home and her mother's plain good food. Shirley
says that with what she knows now, she would not have had to
stay in bed. But she did not know what else to do. The village
women seldom had pregnancy problems so they were unable to
give her advice, and the nurse from Kotzebue told her via radio
to eat soda crackers.

Christmas was truly a great day, with 210 villagers coming to
Church, all wearing new parka covers used to keep the fur clean
(sewn from bright floral cotton for the women, more conservative
colors for men) over their fur parkas and new *mukluks* (boots
made of reindeer hide with sealskin bottoms). The Gordons put

a little tree—an artificial one left by the Archdeacon—on a living room table and surrounded it with gifts from their families, books, woolen clothing, and a much-treasured radio. Bill gave Shirley a small dog sled carved of whalebone and ivory which he purchased in Kivalina and she presented him with a watch band of carved ivory with walrus etched on the links.

An Army chaplain had arrived a week before Christmas to visit the soldiers, and brought along an enormous turkey, so Bill and Shirley joined the Army group for a truly festive Christmas dinner. Meanwhile, the villagers held their feast next door at Browning Hall, and everyone joined them for a Christmas pageant, complete with spotlights, a manger, costumed actors, and a choir. Then up came Santa Claus on his sleigh, laden with presents. The actual giving out took about three hours because Shirley and Bill had purchased gifts from the local store for everyone in the village. The school gave candy to each school child and the village people gave presents among themselves, ranging from a sack of fish to an outboard motor. Antonio's wife gave Bill two fresh fish she had just brought back from the Kukpuk River, and Moses Melik presented him an ivory bracelet with a cross carved on it. He gave Shirley an *ooloo,* an Eskimo woman's knife with a blade rounded like the outside of a half-moon, and an ivory handle (they are used to scrape the flesh off animal skins). The day concluded with Eskimo dancing that lasted until midnight, and then Bill took a tired but happy Shirley home via Antonio's dog team.

The following morning, as Bill was preparing to go up to the church, Antonio came to see him, presenting Bill with the beautiful parka cover his wife had made him for Christmas. ''I told him that it was his, that his wife had made it for him, but he said that was all right—she could make him another one, and he smiled and went out. Antonio had noticed that I did not have a new cover for Christmas, so he gave me his own . . . a very cherished possession. Talk about a man giving you the coat off his back! I've seen him around the village every day now, with his parka and no cover. He has become a firm friend.''

Christmas Day ushered in a week of festivities. Every night the people gathered in the school for some sort of celebration—singing and dancing, feasts, plays, gift giving. It ended on New

Year's when, at midnight, the Army fired a three-gun salute and everybody shouted.

It was a trying holiday for the Gordons because Shirley was having a difficult pregnancy. As she struggled to keep down a little soup or Jello, she and Bill had an agreement: Every time she ate something Bill read her a chapter from one of her Christmas books. Shirley celebrated her twenty-first birthday on 3 January and Bill stayed up late the night before baking her his first cake. He says it was not a masterpiece, but it was edible, with toothpicks for candles, and it got them in the spirit of the day.

Looking back on the year, Bill is philosophical, "My plans are indefinite. I just came here for a year, so I do not know what the future holds. At least we both know we will never regret coming. Life has been full of inspiration and opportunity for real service in a new land. I wish we could work things out so we could stay a few years, but that seems unlikely with a baby in the family. I'll stay on 'til the Bishop and I work out something, and Shirley will join me here or somewhere else in Alaska."

Chapter 3

Traveling Rough Arctic Trails

The Gordons look back on the six-week period that Shirley was in bed as a special time in their lives—one of the few when Bill was never far from her side. He was solicitous: bringing her special foods, reading out loud whenever he had a moment. But his letters during this time sound harried: his abundant energy was being strained to its limit. Shirley's lengthy stay in bed was getting to him—not only the increased workload, but also his deep concern over her health. Bill always found it difficult to deal with weakness—his own, and others—and this made her confinement all the more difficult for him.

Bill enjoyed teaching, however, and felt that he really got to know the forty-two children in a way that would have taken him five years as a mission priest. He admits that he would have been lost without Peel to help him with the school work. "He may be having a little trouble with arithmetic, but he can beat me on the reading 'cause he can revert to Eskimo. Imagine trying to explain a Pullman car, double decker bus, subway, or the Statue of Liberty to children who have no conception of anything like that. Peel and I gave a party for those students with perfect attendance, and we played everything from boxing to pin the tail on the donkey. One little boy pinned the tail on me, at the opposite end of the room from the donkey—much to the children's delight."

The Gordons were right at the center of village life in the schoolhouse. People were continually knocking on their door to use the wireless, to obtain some reindeer meat, for advice, and for medical help. Since there was no doctor or nurse in Point Hope, and the nearest hospital was in Kotzebue, Bill found himself in charge of all medical emergencies—from malnutrition to tooth extraction.

This side of Bill's work undoubtedly reinforced the decision he had made in his first year in college. In boarding school, he was smitten with the idea of becoming a medical missionary, perhaps in Africa. But as he struggled with chemistry and math at the University of North Carolina, he was urged to consider the ministry instead.

Bill's life became more and more entwined with those of the villagers during those winter months of 1944. "It is quite a responsibility to have a whole village dependent on you for everything. I have been letting the people have a little of the excess coal the school has here. They have gotten very few seals this year, so with little seal oil to burn, they have been suffering terribly from the cold. I wired the Territorial Board of Education for permission to sell five tons, and have been rationing it out to the neediest cases."

Although Bill was feeling indispensable to the villagers, he was also aware of their need to take on more of the mission responsibility themselves. At their annual church meeting, Bill asked Peel to introduce the idea of supporting the mission to the extent of paying for the coal and lights for the year. "This is a slight step toward independence, and I believe they will do it. I hope it carries on to something more. That is a big need here—all Eskimos have had too much given them by the Church and Government." (They voted to do so.) A year later, during a severe winter of food shortage, Bill was proud of an offering of one hundred eighty dollars from the coast villages to the Presiding Bishop's Fund for World Relief—"a real sacrificial challenge to our Mother Church."

At the same time, Bill was the worst offender, with his constant pleas for Outside help. With his usual unbridled enthusiasm, he wanted to help "his people" in any way possible. At first, it was items for the mission, but during the harsh winter of 1944 he began asking for clothing and money for the lay leaders who were having difficulty making a living as well as working for the church.

Bill's relationship with the Point Hope people was by no means a one-way street, however. A headstrong, impetuous young priest just out of seminary could have found no greater supportive Christian group than the Eskimos of the Arctic Coast. Converted to Christianity barely a generation earlier, their faith nurtured by four strong clergy, the entire village belonged to the Episcopal Church. Christian beliefs and practices were an integral part of their daily lives.

The people taught Bill much about their ways. Kivalina leader, Daniel Norton, describes how the people initially reacted to Bill: "The first time I saw him, he looked like a young boy. The people see they have to help. They had to teach him lots about winter, had to teach him about not to travel when the north wind is blowing. They taught him how to hunt. When the right wind comes you must hunt. I would take him to fish. When he travel by dog team, someone always go along."

By end of February, Shirley was feeling better. She was still weak, but she was out of bed a good deal of the time and was gaining a little weight. Sig Wien dropped in on them often, as he flew his coastal route, bringing fresh vegetables each time. Shirley says she used to dream of lettuce and tomato sandwiches, and then Sig would appear with the makings. The villagers kept her amply supplied with seal liver, once they heard it was one of the few foods she could eat. (The Gordons say it tastes like calves liver, only better.)

Shirley's lengthy illness appears to have strengthened her faith, or at least she now spoke more openly on the subject. Bill was wrestling with some problem and Shirley asked him if he had prayed. They had a prayer about the matter, and "the whole thing just straightened out beautifully."

Shirley was also having a struggle over the decision as to where to have their baby, and their plans changed frequently. They considered asking a doctor to come down from Barrow, they thought of the hospital in Nome, Shirley even considered returning home by ship. "Going home would be the most logical thing to do," she confided to Bill's parents. "I don't want to leave, I just can't imagine being away from Bill, but he won't consider my staying here. It has been a year this month since I left home,

and that is the longest I have ever been away. Two weeks was
the most before. I am as much concerned about learning to care
for our child as I am about the actual birth. Mom will be a blessing
there. I don't even know what is to be done." In a brief letter
to her own mother, Shirley added wistfully, "Am hoping for some
female companionship here next year. Anyone with experience
in child rearing would be most welcome." Bill and Shirley had
obviously made up their minds that they would not leave Point
Hope. Their year-end letter from Bishop Bentley said he would
like them to stay on for a while. He was pleased with progress
so far, though he had not forgotten his promise to transfer them
after a year if they desired.

In March, Bill made his spring trip to Kivalina. Shirley was
feeling all right, so Bill left the school in her care with instructions
to call Peel if she became ill.

Antonio had not returned from a hunting trip, so Bill traveled
with Mark Kinneeveeuk and his ten dogs. This trip they went
around Cape Thompson on the sea ice instead of toiling over the
portage, Bill's Waterloo before. They spent the night in the same
little igloo; abandoned and full of snow, but adequate. Bill had
hip mukluks made to cover his knees, and some reindeer skin
socks. He had also borrowed a sleeping bag from the Army and
traded the army boys a crate of potatoes for some of their
concentrated food.

They left their shelter at six-thirty the next morning, after rising
two hours earlier to feed the dogs, prepare their breakfast, and
pack the sled. The weather worsened and they made the ten hour
trip to Kivalina in a blizzard—no mean feat because of the almost
total lack of landmarks, the all-white landscape, and the ever-
present wind. In Bill's absence the schoolhouse had burned to
the ground. "That took my hotel and church at one stroke—
quite a blow." So Mark and Bill spent the night with Milton and
Martha Swan in their little fifteen-by-fifteen foot igloo, along with
their two children and eighty-five-year-old blind grandmother.

Martha Swan, a saintly woman, says, "He always stay with us.
He asked for caribou skin and sleep on the floor because we have
no beds at the time, we only had wooden bunk." Martha's grandmother slept in one corner of the tiny house, Martha and Milton

in the other, the boys in a bunk, and Bill by the door. "We eat mostly *ugruk* ("seal") meats. I didn't know what to cook for him because I don't know how to cook for white people. Hotcakes, he likes sourdough hot cakes. And fish." Martha's pan-fried Kivalina trout became renowned throughout Alaska in later years as Bill's favorite food. Martha says, 'Just boil trout some-times, sometimes fry them. I have only small frying pan. I still have it."

From Kivalina, Bill and Mark moved on to Noatak the following day, finding the going hard in deep snow, and they missed the trail through the hills. "I assumed that Mark knew the best way, but he got a little confused, so we made our own trail over every mountain in the Noatak range. When we finally got over them about eight P.M., we hit about three miles of waist-deep snow. I had lent my snowshoes to Antonio, so I had none, and Mark had left his at his hunting camp. We had some wade!" They made it to the old Noatak Reindeer Corral about nine-thirty, where they put up their tent inside one of the deserted buildings and used their gasoline cooking stove for heat. It was twenty-two below zero that night.

They arrived in Noatak the next day about noon, and had a warm welcome. However, Terence Driggs, the lay leader appointed by Bill, had been hired as a reindeer herder and was away from the village. "We can't blame him, for he must support his family, but it is too bad we cannot pay these men enough to make up for the time they spend on Church work. Now we have no competent leader. God will provide."

This loss marks the beginning of Bill's uphill struggles to develop and maintain native leadership in the villages. Until now he had been supremely blessed with the support of Peel Tooyak in Point Hope and the Swans in Kivalina, as well as Terence in Noatak and Upickson at Point Lay. (The Gordons encountered older Eskimos, like Upickson, with only one name. This had been their custom, and it was the schoolteachers who introduced the use of the first name since they thought it easier to call upon "Mark" than "Kinneeveeuk".)

God did provide at Noatak, in the person of a woman, Marie Stalker, an informal arrangement since no woman lay reader could be "official" according to Church Canons at that time. Her daughter, Bertha Jennings, tells of life in Noatak during that period, describing the idyllic setting: protected from the winds of the coast by the Noatak hills, and sheltered from the north by the Brooks mountain range. More mountains lay to the east and like a highway, the Noatak River ran due south to the coast. Their homes were made of logs, the roofs were of sod, and the one room inside had wood flooring. Their water supply came from the near-by river, and fuel for cooking and heating was no problem because of an ample wood supply. Life was not quite the struggle for them as it was for their Arctic coast neighbors. They still had to work hard for their food, but their diet was much more varied. Fish was basic: grayling, trout, smelt, and even some dog salmon (salmon returning to spawn and die). The people used large dippers of woven twigs (like a snow shoe, only rounded) to net the fish, and in the fall, they froze large quantities to see them through the winter months. There was also a greater variety of birds, small game (rabbits and squirrels), and caribou were nearer, although the numbers were scarce at that time. The real delicacy was Dall sheep *(Ovis dalli),* found in the mountains.

The Noatak women collected wild potatoes, onions, and celery, and preserved them in seal oil. Since seals were all important to their diet too, the Noatak people traveled to the coast to hunt them, taking their tents, and spending much of the spring and early summer living on the beaches.

From Noatak, Bill moved on quickly to Kotzebue for his first visit to about fifty Episcopalians there. It was a difficult two-day walk through deep snow blown on the trail along the river, and the overnight shelter cabin was crowded with ten Eskimos. "We were lucky to get sleeping space by the door!" Bill adds, "The scenery was beautiful, with a blue sky over snow-covered rolling hills as far as the eye can see. I love the Alaskan out-of-doors more and more."

Bill's visit to Kotzebue was the first official one by an Episcopal priest, and the people seemed glad to see him. They remained faithful, despite little attention. Most of them went to either the Friends or Roman Catholic services, but they were still loyal Episcopalians, even in the face of some active persecution. Bill appointed a leader to hold services in a home during his absence and he promised to return soon, adding another outpost to his responsibility.

The trip home was even harder. They had planned on only an overnight stay with the Swans in Kivalina, but the weather turned bad—"the coldest I have yet experienced, and a forty-mile wind blowing sand-like snow which beat against the sealskin window. No one ventured out, and the shortage of fuel kept us almost shivering." The next day was no better, and the third showed little improvement. Bill began to get impatient and slightly hungry. They had just enough food to get home on, and Milton was short, too.

Making brief forays about the village, Bill visited the people, and discovered that none of them had much food left. Two families—one a widow with two children, the other, a man in the final stages of TB, with a wife and children—were literally starving. Normally the sick and elderly are cared for by everyone else, but there was little to spare now. So Bill went to the little store and took items to both families; then he left some money with Milton to tide them over until spring.

Mark and Bill reached home on the last day of March, after being gone fifteen days, completing eight hundred miles of travel by dog team in eight months of visitations to all his outstations, from farthest north Point Lay to Kivalina, just south of Point Hope, Noatak inland, and Kotzebue at the southern end. (He also covered a thousand miles by plane, and one hundred sixty by boat.) He concludes, "It has been a great time. I have been away exactly forty days from Point Hope. Shirley deserves most of the credit for carrying on here at home. She is the heroine of the tale, not me, for she had the courage to stay home. She did a great job in my absence."

Bad news awaited Bill on his return. A doctor had arrived by dog team from Kotzebue while he was away and stayed for a week. He examined 230 people in the village and his results were sad; twenty active cases of tuberculosis that needed bed rest, and eight other probables. The biggest blow was that Peel had one of the advanced cases and was losing ground. "We are just heartbroken about his case as well as the others. The congested conditions under which all these people live only add to the contagion.

"I am sure the hard work Peel did while serving the Archdeacon in his last days surely aggravated his case, and I feel the Church owes him much at this time. However, as far as I know there is no provision for such a situation. Positively we cannot just cut him off. For the present I pay him his regular salary and he will continue to do the interpreting, but nothing else. Maybe some great-hearted soul will heed the cause of a worthy need in His name and come to Peel's help financially for a couple of years.

"Peel takes it all humbly and patiently, but I know how hard it must hit him, too. He will hate to be idle. He insists on doing so many things. I am doubly grieved, for our great plans for his ordination must now be postponed or forever closed."

Then Bill ends with the familiar note of optimism, "But we must not forget our many blessings." This phrase is typical of him; perhaps it was ingrained in him since childhood. Regardless, he had plenty of innate positiveness to help him over the rough periods.

It is April, and the Gordons' first Easter period at Point Hope, also their first whaling season, which lasts through May. Before this yearly event began a generation ago, Eskimo women prayed to the new moon for success for their whalers. If their prayers were answered, Alignuk, the moon, would send a whale to the household. Today they pray to the Christian God who controls all creatures of the sea, but something of the old ritual remains in the dance each Wednesday before Easter; a dance performed for centuries before white whalers appeared in their ships. A piece of whale meat—a huge, black, slimy lump of tail left from last year—is thawed during the night and women scrape away yellow scum before it is eaten raw. The captains are served first, then the crewmen, then the wives.

In the following weeks, the men spend hours preparing gear: New sealskin floats and sprucewood paddles are made and tested; guns are oiled and repaired; harpoons, boat hooks, and butchering knives are all cleaned and sharpened. Bombs are refilled with fresh black powder. Older women of the village sew new skins of bearded seal for the *umiaks* ("boats").

The old men watch the weather to decide when the boats should be taken onto the ice to open water. Dog teams take the boats and gear, and camps are set up right on the ice. In the early days, no cooking was allowed, or even a shelter. Today, old men say the new generation is soft; they have some hot food cooked by younger women, dry clothes, and shelters of ice blocks. The hours of idleness and waiting are passed in story telling or long discussions, or just in a sleepy stupor.

From the ice or the fragile skin boats, the forty to fifty foot bowheads look like submarines as they surface to breathe. Before launching the boat, the whaling captain says a prayer and then they paddle toward where they think the whale will surface again. All the boats try to be first, since each boat at the scene of a kill gets a certain portion of the whale, the amount depending on the order of arrival.

The lead boat is driven right up on the slope of the whale's back, so the harpooner can drive the shaft deep through the tough outer skin. When the harpoon bomb explodes, the craft is thrown off its side. The captain has to be careful not to tip over or become entangled in all the rope attached to floats and the harpoon. This maneuver must be repeated a number of times, often with other boats joining in, before the whale is finally theirs. Whales and floats frequently disappear under the ice, never to reappear, and scores of whales move on through the leads, pursued unsuccessfully. Bombs can go off prematurely, killing or wounding men, and the fragile boats often capsize, spilling occupants into the icy water where survival is questionable.

The boat that makes the first strike takes the lead in bringing in the whale: a long, hard pull. At the moment of reaching the shore ice, there is silence while one of the men gives another prayer, thanking God for their safe arrival. The flukes of the bowhead are the first to be cut off and carried immediately to the village. They belong to the captain of the boat that made the first strike and must be given to the community at the whaling feast. The butchering then begins, with the women lighting the cooking fires, boiling the strips of skin as long gashes are cut to mark each crew's portion. The whole job takes up to twenty-four hours, and dog teams hauling tons of meat race back and forth to the village storage pits.

Every part of the whale is used except the bare skull, which is returned to the sea, a custom from the distant past. Drumheads are made from the skin of the liver and lungs. Children make balls out of a rubbery substance in the head. Net sinkers come from the ribs, woven baskets from the strips of baleen, vertebrae are fed to the dogs, and jawbones are set up as monuments at the feast grounds.

This was a good year. In the first week the men caught two whales, bringing in about thirty-five tons of meat for the village. There was still another month before the whales moved up nearer the Pole, so there was hope that by that time enough meat would be stored in the ice cellars to meet the needs of future lean days. "Our Father has been good to His children in the past months," Bill writes, "and we are very grateful to Him for His gifts. Here, with everyone dependent on hunting for existence, the gifts of God in nature are real to us."

The three-day Whaling Feast, *Nalukatuk,* usually beginning the second week in June, is the high spot of the year in the lives of the Point Hope people. The great rivalry during the hunt continues throughout the feast. There are games, dancing, and singing, with the climax being the *Nalukatuk* or blanket toss. Forty or fifty people stand in a circle, grasping a large walrus skin, and toss a person into the air, often fifteen or twenty feet above the skin. It takes courage, and it is difficult to stay on one's feet. Eating orgies take place between events, the food consisting of delicacies such as raw whale kidneys, the tongue and heart, skin *(muktuk),* as well as Eskimo ice cream, flour soup—made of flour boiled in seal oil—and coffee, biscuits, and beans.

The whaling season was over in mid-May when Shirley was seven months pregnant, and it was time for her to leave. She faced a long, hard trip back to Longview, Washington, by herself, where she would stay until the birth. The most difficult aspect of leaving was the separation from Bill, their longest in their year of marriage. He flew with her as far as Kotzebue, where he planned to stay a few days before traveling north to Wainwright to visit the families he had met when he first arrived the year before. He became stranded for ten days because of bad weather, and the waiting severely tried his patience. Most of the Episcopalians had gone to fishing and hunting camps, so he had little to do, and he missed Shirley terribly. His letter home sounds unusually pessimistic: "I'm getting rather tired of wandering round. I'd like to settle down and stay home for a while, but I don't see any chance, with the visit to my northern outstations and time to be spent in Kivalina. We have more people in these places than we have at Point Hope and they deserve attention. Point Hope, with Peel, can get along fairly well without me. [Obviously, neither Peel nor Bill had expected Peel to retire!]

"Responsibility gets me down sometimes. I have quite a bit on my still young shoulders, and occasionally the decisions to be made awe me. Right now I'd like more than anything to do some of the silly, careless things Syd [Syd Alexander, his closest friend from summer camp and college days] and I used to do without having to think about the consequences. I've had to grow up very fast here. I realized that the other day when I got a letter that made me awfully mad and was quite unjustified. My immediate impulse was to write a curt reply that would have cleared me and put the other guy in the bad, but I soon realized that wouldn't do any good. I can remember a time I'd have written and mailed the thing and thought about it later. Guess I'm getting to be pretty meek!" Such a statement will cause disbelief among all those people who were to work under Bill in the years ahead.

Once Bill reached Wainwright by plane, he was grounded again because of poor weather. He had been away from Point Hope for one month, to do what amounted to about six days' work. Such is Arctic travel, and there is nothing one can do about it. One learns patience. As the Eskimos say, "there'll be good weather some day."

Bill had not heard if Shirley reached Longview safely: "I am somewhat concerned, because she is such a little girl. However no braver or better one ever lived, and I love her more and more as I miss her more and more. It is hard for you to realize what it meant for her to be the only white woman in the village. She is the most isolated one in the Arctic, for at all other places where there are white women, there are at least two. She comments on her unique position, but I never remember her complaining about it, and you would have thought she was leaving her birthplace when you saw the way she hated to leave Point Hope. With any sort of encouragement I would have asked Bishop Bentley for a transfer when I knew about the baby, but she wouldn't hear of it. She knew where my heart was, and in her own way decided that was where I should stay for the present."

Peel was steadily growing weaker; he took to his bed the first week in July. "I cannot comprehend his leaving us, though the possibility of it has been before us for some months. I never anticipated such a sudden decline. His faith humbles me. He says God knows best, and does not complain about his lot. I celebrated the Holy Communion for him and his family, and my heart surely was in that service. Peel read the Epistle in Eskimo—a word at a time, and followed each response clearly as he does so faithfully in all our services. He even led a little in the Communion hymn we sing in Eskimo. I cannot conceive of Point Hope without Peel, and it is hard to understand the passing of a man so essential and useful in the work of the Kingdom, but I must share Peel's own faith in the matter, and as God has provided Peel, he will provide another."

Bill had an additional blow when he learned that Upickson, his leader at Point Lay, had died from tuberculosis of the kidneys. And then on 28 July, Peel died. "I'm going to be lost without him—he left a place that is unfillable, for he was the combination of a unique character and long years of training. He did so many things out of the line of duty, as well as being my contact with the thought of the village. He is irreplaceable as interpreter too, for there is no one here who can approach his method of preaching while interpreting. Now I am completely on my own in the Arctic; much of this year has been spent in continuing things that have been developed in the past, but with Peel's passing, I'll have to reorganize our whole set-up on my own lines. God has given me a tremendous challenge, and I hope I can prove worthy."

The funeral service for Peel Tooyak was led by Bill, with the whole village present. For him, the ceremony evoked intense emotion. It was an impressive sight as the men of the Alaska Territorial Guard, fifty strong in full uniform, escorted the body, with the casket covered by the flag, from the church to the cemetery. It was their last tribute to their faithful lieutenant. Bill headed the procession in his vestments, with the Guard pulling the casket on a sled behind, followed by the rest of the villagers. "Peel is dead, but I am confident that his soul, buoyed by his simple faith, has received a warm welcome from the Father he loved and served so well."

Bill considered Peel, only forty-three years old, an irreplaceable loss to the Church with his death occurring just as he was about to be ordained the first native deacon on the Arctic Coast. Yet Peel's most significant contribution may have been the seed he planted in Bill's mind: a yearning for an ordained native ministry. Some of Peel's last words to Bill were about his son, Enoch, as they discussed the possibility that he would go away to school and then enter missionary work. Bill carried through this plan by sending the boy to the Episcopal boarding school in Nenana. Tragically, in the summer of 1949, Enoch was drowned on a boat trip.

The weeks ahead were difficult ones for Bill: adjusting to work without Peel, awaiting news of Shirley and the birth of their child. He turned with a vengeance to a new project, dismantling an unused mission storage building. He would take the wood and nails by boat to Kivalina for use as a chapel. With that project completed, Bill had time to worry about Shirley again. "I do hope things are all right, and my wonderful wife has everything she needs. It will be a calamity if the baby isn't born before I leave for Kivalina in ten days, for there is no radio there. I know I'd go crazy."

The long-awaited wire arrived on 7 August—"Shirley Lewis Gordon arrived August fifth Seven pounds both well." Shirley follows this with a letter to report, "The baby is now a week old. I just naturally started calling her 'Paneen' and I think it will stick. She is the most wonderful baby in all the world and looks so much like her daddy. We are so anxious to get home!"

His mind more at ease, Bill turned back to his work, to two busy weeks before his upcoming trip to Kivalina. Visitors descended, the first being a Navy PBY plane, with a crew of eleven, which was escorting two ships to the new Naval Petroleum Reserve east of Barrow. A doctor on board helped Bill with some of the sickest in the village—a small boy with pneumonia and an old man who had had a stroke the night before.

Sig Wien brought in the second visitor, Major Marvin (Muktuk) Marston, in charge of the Alaska Territorial Guard. To greet his arrival, the Guard was mustered for attention at the air strip. Bill says, "I could see Sig Wien was having a hard time keeping from laughing because we had been issued 1917 metal helmets, long overcoat-type parkas, most of which were too big for the men, and shoepacks, the smallest being a nine and one-half, while the biggest foot in the Company was a seven and one-half. So everybody's toes turned up like Laplanders." This Guard was a part of the Eskimo militia set up under Alaska's territorial governor to be the eyes and ears of the Army during the war years, the outer line of defense. Bill's military training equaled his medical training, and he remembers with some amusement the drills. "Since many of the men speak little or no English, when I give the command, 'Column left march,' some go left, some go right, and some just go home!"

To cap an already hectic week, the supply freighter arrived Saturday night, the last week of August, once again landing everything on the south beach. "We had the same captain as last year, a very impatient man, and since everyone was working on the unloading, it was out of the question to call a halt for Sunday service at the church. So at noon I held it on the beach. It was an impressive setting as we gathered there among countless packing cases by the frigid Arctic Ocean."

The next few days had to be spent putting everything away, including a new double bed and a baby crib, a gift from Bill's family. The food supplies went into the basement storeroom, which looked like a miniature supermarket with racks of shelves. Because it was well insulated, the temperature stayed between thirty-four and thirty-six degrees. The Gordons kept a kerosene lamp burning during the winter months, although occasionally it would flare up and cover everything with soot. Crates of oranges could be stored for a few months, potatoes would last six months, and even the sixty dozen eggs would keep almost that long. Bill says that after about three months the eggs developed a distinctive taste which they got used to and when they left Point Hope they found fresh eggs tasteless. He adds that their greatest food disaster occurred when Paneen was a three-year-old, and tore the labels off of many cans, leaving them in the dark as to what was inside.

The first year Bill and Shirley were at Point Hope, they used the food Bishop Bentley had ordered, based on what he thought two people would need for a year. Not only did they have his choices, but since many things were not available during the war years, the grocery company in Seattle took the liberty of making substitutions. So they were stuck with some unusual items, like a case of pickled pigs feet. They also inherited food supplies left over from Archdeacon Goodman: exotic English specialties, since he was a gourmet.

Each spring Bill would send an order to the Standard Oil Company in San Francisco for their annual supply of gas and petroleum products. Because it would take an interminable time for them to send a bill, delaying shipment another year, Bill enclosed a check, but with the amount left blank. Someone at the company must have been impressed by Bill's trust, because they developed an advertisement, used in newspapers all over the West Coast: "See how much this missionary trusts our company, and we in turn make sure our products are shipped to him on time for them to face the dark, cold winter months."

Just before his Kivalina trip, Bill received sad news from Shirley—she was anemic, and it would be another two months before she and Paneen could come home. Heartbroken, he flung himself into preparations, loading his building materials, and sailing with the store launch and barge on 20 September. Daniel Lisbourne, whom Bill had hired to help maintain the Mission buildings, accompanied Bill. They had a fine trip down on the quiet ocean, arriving about twelve hours later. The teachers, Eunice and Dan Stalker, (brother-in-law of Marie Stalker in Noatak), were living in the Friends Mission House while rebuilding the school building and store, so Daniel and Bill used sleeping bags in the schoolroom, taking meals with the Stalkers.

They and several Kivalina men, worked ten hours a day for eighteen days, breaking only for an hour at lunch and dinner. It was a race against the weather; they were determined to finish before winter closed in—and they succeeded.

Epiphany Church was thirty-nine feet long and eighteen feet wide, with a storm shed and storage place on the front about ten feet square. The only thing new in the building was the insulation and part of the roofing. All the rest of the lumber had been used before.

In late October it was time for Shirley's return with the baby, but the precise date had to be flexible. Because of the scarcity of seats for travel during wartime, civilians were often "bumped," even on a moment's notice, and sometimes during the trip, in out-of-the-way places. Shirley had to stand by in Seattle, waiting for the first available seat. In the 1940s Pan American was the only airline flying from Seattle to Fairbanks, leaving at eight-fifteen, A.M. and arriving at six-thirty in the evening, with two or three stops en route. (Today it takes less than four hours by jet.) She and the baby got as far as Whitehorse, Canada, the first day, but were then forced to spend the night, sharing a hotel room with another woman passenger.

Bill decided to surprise Shirley in Fairbanks. "It was a joyful reunion for us and my cup truly ran over. Paneen, of course, is wonderful, even more so than I had imagined. They say she looks like me, but I think she's pretty just the same, and such a good baby—she hardly ever cries, and lets us sleep *most* all night. Shirley is already putting me to work feeding her, etc., and I'm catching on, but I'm trying not to get too proficient. Girl babies aren't exactly a new thing for me, but having real responsibility for one is unique. Shirley is even more beautiful than ever, if that is possible. I always thought she was pretty wonderful, but now she's just perfect—life is too good."

Shirley adds a hand-written P.S. to Bill's letter: "Have never been so happy! Anxious now to be on our way. And Paneen *doesn't* keep *Bill* awake very much."

The joy of the reunion wore a little thin as the Gordons were forced to wait for twelve days before obtaining seats on a plane; the Army and Navy were using all available civilian aircraft. They stayed with Bill's seminary friend, Al Jones, priest in charge of the Fairbanks Mission. During this time, Bill had a number of good visits with Bishop Bentley who seemed satisfied with his progress.

Bill preached Sunday night on his work at Point Hope. He was nervous speaking to a congregation that included the Bishop and Mrs. Bentley, but it was successful. After more than a year in Point Hope, it felt strange to be in a town with restaurants, cars, street lights, and lots of people. It was a nice change to go to a restaurant for a meal, and go to a movie, but they were anxious to get back home. It was almost Thanksgiving, and the day after Bill had to leave again.

The Gordon family took off for Point Hope on 20 November with their friend Sig Wien as pilot. As they approached Kotzebue they were told not to land, or they would be quarantined, unable to leave. A diphtheria epidemic had hit Nome, Shishamaref, and Kotzebue, and doctors were taking every precaution to keep it from spreading. So the plane went on to the village of Noorvik where they all spent the night in the schoolhouse, Paneen ensconced in a drawer.

The plane finally reached Point Hope on the following afternoon. Shirley knew she was home at last because a thirty-five mph wind was blowing. The wind escalated to seventy-one mph the following day. The temperature was just above zero. But their home was warm and snug, and they were glad for the new stove Bill had installed in their upstairs bedroom, crowded quarters now, with Paneen's crib as well.

The diphtheria epidemic hung like a cloud over the Gordons during the holiday period, bringing constant concern over its spread, but they also mourned the disruption of their mail service. Since planes could not travel from Kotzebue, that meant there was no mail for the entire month. In mid-December, they had still received no letters, although the quarantine had been lifted. Now the problem was a shortage of planes, and with the accumulated backlog, it could be months before they received any Christmas gifts. Furthermore, Bill had to postpone his visitations to Kivalina and Point Lay because of the epidemic, and when it was finally lifted, Christmas was too near to allow for a trip.

Meanwhile Bill and Shirley were busy preparing for the villagers' Christmas, wrapping the usual several hundred presents. Shirley did most of that, so Bill helped with the housework. "Seems like we spend a lot of time on household routine, but maybe we'll get used to it. Tuesday I did the baby's washing for the week and had quite a day of it! That young lady has surely changed our lives in many ways. Had over sixty diapers to do, so wash day poses quite a problem—our water is presently stacked in snow blocks on the back porch and it takes a lot of snow to make a bucketful!

"The big job is melting enough snow on the kitchen stove, so I've had a continuous procession from the back porch to the kitchen—bringing in small chunks at a time, squeezing them in a ten-gallon vat and various other buckets and pans. You should see me in my boots and undershirt—not very clerical, and not in the seminary curriculum, as I recollect!"

Cold windy weather kept people housebound over the Christmas period, so the Gordons saw little of Mrs. Kimble, the new schoolteacher. She kept close to her home anyway and although Bill reported that she was an experienced teacher and the village children seemed fond of her, she was not a companion for Shirley. The Army boys, however, less than a hundred yards away, provided good times for both Gordons.

In spite of lack of mail (bundles were scattered from Kotzebue to Barrow, left behind because of wartime priorities or weather problems), Bill and Shirley had a wonderful Christmas. The village had its usual festivities, and the Gordons had traditional Christmas dinner with the Army. One package had come by boat the previous summer, so they had some gifts to put around their tree.

Christmas Eve was one of the loveliest nights Bill had ever seen. "The moon has been full and it's hard to describe it rising over the white mountains, shining down on the snow-covered ground here. Sometimes it seems almost as bright as day. Last night the Northern Lights were gorgeous—great bands of snaky green and white light all across the heavens in multitudinous patterns—the most beautiful ones I have ever seen; and I saw some remarkable ones on the trail last winter. 'Not even Solomon in all his glory was arrayed like one of these.'"

On 8 January Bill left with Antonio and his dog team for Point Lay. They had to plan on a week's travel inland each way because it was too dangerous to go around by Cape Lisburne this time of year—the ocean ice might move out at any time, and northeast winds blowing off the cliffs sometimes pick up sled dogs and travelers and blow them around. Bill was away for seventeen days, longer than expected. Then the first week of February he left for Kivalina and Kotzebue, returning on 28 February. Shirley carried on alone at the mission, with some help from Mrs. Kimble and the Army men.

Shirley began a diary again on the first of January, a leather one purchased Outside, intended to cover her exciting life at Point Hope. Instead it is a private litany of deep loneliness and depression while Bill was away on extended travel during the months of January and February, 1945. It ends abruptly in early March upon his return, and when the dark, cold winter days are over.

The diary starts on New Year's Day with happy comments about their New Year's dinner with the Army and Mrs. Kimble, and then her birthday party on the third. A week later, Bill left for Point Lay with Antonio Weber in the worst weather in weeks, leaving Shirley and the baby alone in the mission house. From then on, her entries were brief cries of lonely despair. She also worried constantly about Bill as she endured some of the worst weather they had yet encountered. Thirty mile per hour winds and temperatures below zero imprisoned her indoors. The gales blew snow drifts against the house, and cold air through it. The generator faltered, and then stopped so Shirley was left with an oil lamp and candles in the twenty-four hour darkness.

Paneen was little company—in fact the baby cried most of the time, and kept Shirley isolated from adult companions. She was teething, Shirley thinks today, or perhaps the obnoxious fumes from the balking generator were affecting both of them. Shirley soon lost all interest in housework and became deeply depressed. Daily diary entries speak of taking the next airplane out. "I give up, I'm not a 'brave' girl. I can't take it and I'm leaving!"

Bill returned from Point Lay almost three weeks later after a difficult trip in the wind and cold, but left again for Kivalina after ten days at home. This time an Eskimo girl moved in to stay with Shirley and the two had fun making pastry and sewing dresses. This respite did not last long, however. Bill did not call in by radio on a regular basis, and as the days went by, Shirley became angry over his silence. When he did reach her it was by radio from

Kotzebue, which was to her an unexpected extension of his trip.
She writes that she was bitter. "He asked if everything is o.k. here.
O.K.! There is no place to run, so I stay. Paneen cried all night.
How long?"

During Bill's first absences the year before, he contacted Shirley
by wireless almost daily, except when he was actually on the trail.
And for those times he gave her specific itineraries. Now it seemed
as though Bill felt Shirley could handle the isolation, especially
with the baby to keep her company, and there was no need to
be constantly in touch. He had to be about his business, and she
had proved herself competent to do hers. Also, he counted on
Mrs. Kimble to give her some feminine companionship. He had
sadly misjudged the situation; the schoolteacher not only stayed
to herself, but she lived more than a mile away in the midst of
terrible winter conditions. And although Paneen was a comfort
to Shirley, no mother was as unprepared to care for an infant,
and she needed Bill's support for baby care alone. It was almost
more than could be asked of anyone.

However, life became bearable again for Shirley when Bill was
forced to end his travels with spring breakup in April. Then he
started on a new project—building up his own dog team. He
decided that after two winters of tutelage under the best Point
Hope men, the time had come to start traveling on his own. His
reason? It was too expensive to hire teams. But anyone who
knows Bill Gordon recognizes that he had to undertake this Arctic
mode of travel alone to prove to himself that he could do it and
to demonstrate to the Eskimos that he was one of them.

In a letter to his family in late July, Bill describes a harrowing
experience in his usual understated fashion. He did not want to
worry them, he says today. But he admits now that it was a risky
and foolhardy undertaking. Bill attached a second-hand outboard
motor to the fourteen-foot mission boat which he renamed *The
Tar Heel.* "I waited almost a week for good weather—we had
a south wind and too many waves. Finally, I got away at nine
o'clock P.M. I wanted very much to reach Kivalina on Sunday,
hence the late night departure. With daylight both night and day
now, it is wise to take advantage of good weather when it comes.
However, I did miss my sleep.

"I went alone for there wasn't much room, and there was no one around to go anyway. I got wet from spray after about an hour out, and that was the worst part of the journey, for I remained soaked all the way to Kivalina. The ocean water temperature stays around thirty-eight degrees year round and the air was about forty-five degrees. A fairly strong breeze from the north came in, bounced the boat about, and built up too much surf to go ashore comfortably so I stayed out the whole way. I got to Kivalina at eight-fifty Sunday morning, with nine and one-third hours actual running time—not bad for eighty miles. The trip would have been fun except for the wetness and the sleepiness."

Bill then waited again for the weather. "Tuesday night the wind from the north stopped so I put some canvas sides on the boat to keep out the spray, and about one A.M. I started for home, again traveling at night to take advantage of the favorable weather. However, a few miles out the wind started coming from the south. Gently at first, but increasing, and it got kinda rough. I stayed close to the beach—my boat rides pretty well—and things were o.k., though I had to be on the alert all the time to keep the boat on an even keel. I got around Cape Thompson about 8 A.M. and figured that I was on the home stretch, though the water was rough. *The Tar Heel* was pretty seaworthy, and the canvas sides were holding out the spray. Then, about two miles past the Cape my motor quit, and it wouldn't start again. I had to use my oars to keep off the beach, and once when I hastily pulled them in to check the motor, a big wave tipped the boat and took one oar overboard. I didn't see it 'til it was quite a distance away, and then I couldn't go after it with the one remaining oar, so I had to let the boat wash up on the beach. It washed perfectly, and I took off the motor and pulled the boat up without anything getting wet.

"I found a soft spot on the ground behind a little sand hump where I lay down for a nap. Then it started raining and I had to pull the boat up and tip it on its side for a shelter. I had brought along a sizable piece of canvas for protection, but I had used that for the sides of the boat, so I only had a narrow strip left. I put this over the floor boards, put them under the shelter of the boat and spread my sleeping bag on this for a bed. The waves were too big for me to try to launch the boat again so I settled down to wait. I stayed at the Cape about thirty hours—until three o'clock Thursday afternoon. An airplane passed over soon after I landed and I hoped he saw me and reported to Point Hope that I was o.k. He did not. While I was asleep, a boat from Kotzebue via Kivalina came by, but they didn't see me either, so they also had folks a little worried about me.

"I slept most of the time I was at the Cape, for it rained continuously. My shelter didn't keep out all the wet, but it helped. Thursday, about midafternoon, the wind let up some and the waves died down, so I cleaned the carburetor on the engine and launched out again. But the motor refused to start. I worked quite a while and then gave up. I saw I was drifting toward Point Hope with the waves and current and thought I could make it that way, but I watched a landmark and discovered that I was drifting about a mile every two hours. I was twenty-two miles from home and I couldn't row for I had only one oar. I decided to give the motor one more try and this time it fired, running at half speed on one magneto. It quit again just as I got around the lighthouse on the Point—I was aiming for the north beach, where there was more shelter from the high waves.

"The wind was now blowing me back out to sea, and I was barely able to make headway by paddling with my one oar. I could see a small boy standing on the beach watching me, and I was wishing with all my might that he would go find someone with an *umiak* to come rescue me. But he just stood there, thinking, I guess, that an adult was capable of taking care of himself. I was finally able to move close enough so I could jump overboard and pull the boat onto the shore. I was surely glad to get back after forty-seven hours from Kivalina, and the people seemed glad to see me. The trip wasn't too strenuous, and was an interesting experience."

Bill made this hazardous journey because he didn't want to be dependent on others for summer transportation, yet he had no experience in handling boats, in spite of years at summer camp. Again, since his "dinghy" was similar in size to *umiaks*, he also wanted to travel the Eskimo way—no thirty-eight foot launches for him! It was particularly irrational to shove off onto the frigid

Arctic water when the engine was not working and the boat had one paddle. In fact, the entire trip was one only a headstrong, impulsive person would even consider.

Just six days later, the mail boat the *Nanuk,* arrived at Point Hope, bringing the second- and third-class mail that had accumulated during the year. Bill decided it was necessary for him to go on with it to Point Lay for a summer visit. Shirley agreed that this was the time to go—the weather was good and Mrs. Gaddie, the District nurse, was keeping Shirley and Paneen company.

When they reached Point Lay, Bill found Tommy Knox, the lay reader, critically ill. He was not expected to live more than a few days, so Bill had a service of Holy Communion in his tent. "I am glad that I could get here in time; Tommy and Peel are among the most spiritual Eskimo men I have met and it seems hard to understand why they should be taken from us while they are still so very useful and necessary in the Lord's work. Tuberculosis is a real curse of these native people, and it hits me mighty hard to see them dying and not be able to do anything about it. There is a proposal now before the U.S. Government to make a substantial appropriation for TB hospitals for the more than 4,000 estimated cases in Alaska, and I can think of no greater need for the Territory. I only pray that our leaders are not so shortsighted that they reject the plan."

The following day, Knox died. "Tommy was conscious to the last, and he went very peacefully. He knew the end was near and was ready to commit himself into God's hands. His last move was to cross himself just before he passed on."

Following the funeral service, Mrs. Knox came to Bill to thank him for everything, saying that it was a great comfort to her to have him there. "Her words surely made my trip here worthwhile, for it means a great deal to me to be able to help my people. I am so different from them in so many ways that it is hard to get close in times of need, but I am sure that the language in the Spirit of God is universal."

Although Bill was impatient to return home, the weather was poor, and the *Nanuk* became marooned by ice at Barrow. He was forced to wait another week before he could be picked up, a waiting time that was hard on him because he would be absent over Paneen's first birthday. This was to be the beginning of many children's birthdays Bill would miss. For him, as for most clergymen of that era, his priorities in life were God, Church, and then family. Today, many of his successors state, "God, family, and then Church." Shirley, and later the children, accepted the fact that the Church came first for Bill. But this acceptance did not lessen their feelings of disappointment, nor the consequences of a frequently absent husband and father.

Shirley spent much of her spare time in the summer and fall refurbishing the mission house, and she wrote detailed accounts of her efforts to Bill's family in October. "You should see the lovely room I am sitting in! Bill has finished painting and I have hung most of the pictures and made new curtains. The walls are light blue and the ceiling is pale ivory. Bill hid the exposed wires and put in sockets so we can use table lamps. I wonder if they make thirty-two-volt electric irons?

"Now we have a washing machine, a vacuum cleaner, and a radio. We get good reception and can hear Seattle, San Francisco, Los Angeles, even Philadelphia, and Richmond (180 miles from Bill's home) on long wave. We want a refrigerator—strange as it may seem—and Bishop Bentley recommends a kerosene model." Shirley rambles on, sharing her dreams for a waffle iron and toaster, a couch-bed and table and chairs. She draws a diagram, showing the Gordons exactly where she has placed their gift of two chairs, a small couch, a rocker, two tables, and her sewing machine.

But their big news was that they were expecting another child in May 1946. This time Shirley planned to go home with Paneen in February, with Bill joining them on furlough in July. He had to wait for relief in Point Hope, and Bishop Bentley thought it would be early summer before he could get someone.

Bill's letters home were also full of news about Paneen. "She is a real handful. She is walking quite a bit now and jabbers 'Daddy,' 'Baby,' and 'Puppy' all the time—her favorite words. She loves the dogs, and every time I come into the room she wants to be lifted to the window to see them. She is in ecstasy when I take her outside to them.

"You should have seen me bringing Paneen home on my back

under my parka," Bill says. "I hope none of my parishioners saw me, for that is generally considered a woman's job. Paneen likes to travel that way, and it is surely easier than carrying her in my arms. It was twenty below zero but Paneen didn't seem to mind it. There was a time when I would have thought anyone taking a sixteen-months baby for a walk in that temperature was crazy, but you get used to the cold here. Paneen is mighty cute in her parka made of rabbit with fur inside, a cover of green plaid, a hood lined with beaver and trimmed in wolverine. She insists on calling me 'Bu'—a corruption of Bill, and that is the first thing we hear in the mornings—much to my disgust. She tries that a while and then switches to Da-da, and then I can't resist. Tomorrow will be Paneen's first Arctic anniversary, and she has stood the year remarkably well. She is so strong and sturdy and active, one of the happiest babies I have ever known, and I can't imagine how we ever got along without her before. Her little brother or sister will make our home more lively I'm sure, but if he doubles Paneen's joy he'll have to go some."

Bill had other "youngsters" on his mind—training his dogs took a lot of his time, and his first trip with his own dog team was almost his last. He started the day after Thanksgiving, in 1945. Today he says, "I still wisely realized that I could use some help and was glad to know that Jimmy Hawley planned to return to Kivalina with his dogs that same day so we could go together. But the Eskimo dance kept us both up late that Thanksgiving night. I was all ready to leave early, but Jimmy never showed. I finally went down to the village and found he was just getting up. I told him I would start out by myself since the first twenty-five miles of the trail was along the beach north of Cape Thompson and was clearly designated. He would certainly catch me, with his faster and better dogs before I reached the Cape.

"I took off with my ten dogs and Jimmy never did catch me. By the time I arrived at Cape Thompson, I had gained a lot of confidence. Too much in fact, and I decided to go around the Cape, about ten miles out on the ocean ice, since there was no beach there. I expected to be able to see because there was nearly a full moon. It was clear and about ten below zero. I pulled out on the ice and went just a short way when I realized that the rising moon was blocked by the high cliffs and I was in total darkness. I had great difficulty going over the huge ice cakes that were pushed up by the wind into pressure ridges and I had to let the dogs pick their way.

"Also, the ice constantly shifts in and out with the winds, leaving thin spots, and one needs to see the ice to tell by its color just how thin it might be. In the darkness I could not see much of anything and after I had gone about three miles my dogs and sled went up over an especially high pile of rough ice blocks. When we came down on the other side, I heard a cracking sound. The front of the sled had broken through a thin area and was caught under the ice, while the dogs had gone across it and were strung out on the other side. I went forward to try to lift the sled out, but when I put my extra weight on the ice, the whole pan gave away, and I sank up to my neck into the frigid water. I thought at first I could just climb out, but the ice was too thin and it kept breaking off. Finally, I pulled myself behind the sled and pushed down on it, forcing the bow up onto the stronger edge. I called on my dogs and they started to pull, hauling the sled and me as I held onto the runners. I let them drag me lying down for about a hundred feet until I was sure I was on strong ice again. I was soaking wet, but my sealskin boots and pants and heavy fur parka gave me some protection, although they froze right away.

"I still had about seven miles to go and I knew I had to keep moving, so we started on up and down those difficult ridges again, and all along I wondered whether I was coming to another thin place. Three of the dogs became tuckered out and I had to unharness them, so I was down to seven, and it took me four hours to finish the trip.

"The last hundred yards along the beach were tortuous because I had to walk over a foot of snow that had been glazed over. With each step my feet would break through and I could not bend my legs because my pants were frozen solid. I finally reached the abandoned igloo at the south of the Cape about ten o'clock, but the wind had blown the entrance full of snow. I climbed through the seal intestine window on top, got my gas stove going, and found some dry clothes. [Fortunately only part of the sled had submerged.] Then it took me an hour to unhitch and feed the dogs. They are so important to travel here that they get first attention. So it was after eleven when I fixed some coffee and ate a sandwich [frozen], pilot biscuit, and dried fruit. I was glad to get into my sleeping bag that night!"

The next day Jimmy Hawley came around the Cape. He had wisely camped on the other side, a little startled Bill wasn't there too. When he came across the open area, he wasn't sure that Bill had actually made it. They went on to Kivalina together and the Swans took Bill in. Martha dried off his clothes, and cooked him a number of hot meals during his three-day stay.

The day before he left, Milton Swan told Bill that he needed to go to Point Hope, and would go along with him. "I took that as he said it, and never thought much about it. We made the trip with two dog teams and no great difficulty. It wasn't until years later that I realized that Milton did not need to go to Point Hope at all. He was simply concerned about my own welfare and the dangers I might get into, so he went along to watch over me. But he was gentleman enough and understanding enough to not say to me, 'You dumb white man, you don't know about traveling by dog team, you need someone to watch over you.' It was typical of the wonderful caring and love of that man that he would take about five days out of his life when he critically needed to be out hunting and trapping to escort his very inexperienced *Ungahyuliksi* home."

Point Hope was quieter over the Christmas period of 1945 because the Army finally pulled out. But the quiet was broken just before Christmas when a typhoid epidemic broke out in Kotzebue—eight cases and two deaths. It began to spread to nearby villages so the Government nurse, Miss Keaton, was sent to Point Hope to vaccinate everybody. A new pilot, Bill Peterson, came to take her home, but the weather turned bad and he became a guest of the Gordons for a week. (Their house had a continuous flow of stranded guests.) Bill writes, "I believe there was the hand of God in it all, for on Tuesday two young boys here came down with serious throat infections which the nurse diagnosed as diphtheria, although none had been reported in the area. She immediately got on the radio and asked for vaccine to be brought in. Some was found in Fairbanks and an Army plane made an air drop. More villagers became ill, but we didn't lose anybody. There would have been no hope if she had not been here, and we are very thankful."

One of the highlights of the Christmas period was the traditional dog race, which Bill and his team entered for the first time. "It made everybody in the village feel better because I finished last! Herbert Kinneeveeuk made some comments about various dog teams as prizes were given out at the Christmas party, and he said something about my dogs which made everyone laugh. I asked what was so funny; he said my dogs were too fat. He is certainly right, as no one here considers a fat dog in any shape for real serious work."

Bill's performance improved only slightly over the next two years. He explains, "I could have done a whole lot better, but the race trail went right by my house, and the dogs always wanted to turn in there and go home. So, I asked Shirley to come out, stand there with a broom, and sort of encourage them to keep on going. I was doing fine up to that point, but my leader, Jerry, started to turn in. He had a habit of jumping out at people, even me once in a while. So, when we came to Shirley, Jerry took a little lunge at her. She lost her nerve, fled to the porch, and all of my dogs followed her! By the time I got them off and on the trail, I had lost a lot of time."

Another year at Point Hope was over, and Shirley left for her family's home in February of 1946 to await the arrival of their second child, while Bill stayed behind to continue his solo dog team trips, including the longest one of all—thirty-five days to Barrow and back. He would join Shirley in July for his first six-month furlough, the allotted "time off" after three years, given to all Episcopal Church missionaries at that time. Before Shirley left, however, they talked of the future. "Bishop Bentley flattered us by asking us to come back to Point Hope after furlough. Neither Shirley nor I thought we could commit ourselves to another three-year term, since two children will present some problems. But we told the Bishop we would be willing to come back for two years, and then be transferred to another Alaskan post a little less isolated." Neither of them had an inkling of how the events of 1947 would change their lives forever.

Chapter 4

Roots of His Faith

The Gordons' return to Point Hope on 21 December 1946 was more difficult than ever because of the continued uncertainties of air travel, the extreme cold, and a new baby. Billy (William Jones Gordon III), the much hoped-for boy, had been born on 14 May and was now seven months old, while Paneen was a handful at two and a half. The most grueling part of their trip was en route to Fairbanks. They were delayed in Seattle, had to spend one night at Annette Island in Southeast Alaska, and three days in Whitehorse, in the Yukon Territory, where the temperature was forty-five degrees below zero. "It wasn't so bad until the hotel radiators froze up one night; then we had ample preparation for the Arctic!" Bill adds his most characteristic comment: "Christmas is moving in on us so it will be a close race. We'll take whatever comes and make the best of it."

When they finally arrived in Fairbanks, they encountered another challenge. There were two babies—one four months and one three years old—who had to go to Kotzebue. Their mother had abandoned them in Fairbanks and someone in Selawik, a village near Kotzebue, was adopting them. The babies needed a caretaker on the flight and the Department of Public Welfare offered to pay Bill's fare if he would assume the responsibility. Bill would have agreed in any case, but the seventy-five dollars he saved about paid for his 120 pounds of excess baggage.

Everyone arrived safely in Kotzebue. Bill and Shirley spent the night there and got home to Point Hope just as it became light (but no sun) about eleven o'clock the following morning.

They raced against time and Shirley got all 260 gifts for the
villagers wrapped for Christmas while Bill caught up on Point
Hope affairs and prepared his annual holiday newsletter with a
report on his six months' furlough. He began by mentioning brief
visits to their family homes on the East and West coasts, the first
opportunity for parents to meet "the other half," complete with
two children. That, plus a comment about one week at the
beach takes one sentence; all the rest is devoted to the work he
accomplished. Bill could never be content with six months away
from his job, or even with doing nothing for more than a week.
And doing nothing, for him, can take place only at a beach.

"We got in the General Convention [triennial meeting of the
National Episcopal Church], and then I spoke ninety-nine times
on Arctic Alaska, ranging from Washington State through Iowa
to Rhode Island and all through the South. It was a strenuous
schedule, but I thoroughly enjoyed it, particularly because I met
many old correspondence friends for the first time. I was impressed at the very genuine interest shown everywhere in the work
that the Church is doing in the field, and let no one say that
the Episcopal Church is not missionary-minded. Maybe we are
shortsighted until we know, but once the facts of the story are
revealed, our people are quick and generous to give of themselves
and their substance."

Shirley writes to her family after the busy holidays: "Surely
was good to arrive here before Christmas, tho' I began to doubt
if we'd make it. And then there was so much to do, I almost
wished we hadn't—but it is grand to be back. Things are very
pleasant in my redecorated house and the table was pretty for
Christmas dinner—we brought along a turkey from Fairbanks.

"Right now Billy is in the play pen on top of the day bed—
opened partially. It makes a perfect place for him off the cold
floor. Paneen really enjoyed Christmas this year. She saw Santa
dress in our living room [Bill preparing for the village Christmas
party]—even stuffing in his big fat pillow, but she doesn't seem
to be disillusioned.

"Paneen has a crib in the office now [Billy took over her former
spot in the Gordons' bedroom], but has learned to climb out of
it and we find her in our bed 'most every night when we go up.

Yesterday was a nice day and warm, so Paneen spent about two hours outdoors playing with the puppies in the snow—she loved it and didn't want to come in for dinner. Cold doesn't seem to bother her very much.''

Eunice, a new young Eskimo helper, came in six days a week to assist Shirley, which made life much easier. Her frequent letters this year reveal her contentment, with her home, her children, and even the isolated village life. She coped well with Bill's lengthy absences, commenting more casually on his journeys. Bill called in via radio regularly, and Shirley knew more of his plans. Their communication had improved so much over the previous year that one can only assume some form of confrontation occurred, although neither remembers it today.

Shirley was more relaxed with Billy, and found companionship with Paneen. Together, they tried to grow narcissus bulbs on one of the window sills, but Bill commented, "You should see Shirley's flower garden now—the big question is whether maturity or Paneen will get them first!''

Everything was going smoothly. Then, on 29 March Shirley wrote a terse letter to her parents: "Mom and Dad, A second plane is coming tomorrow so I'll get a real letter off then. Bill's father died of a heart attack last Wednesday. The funeral was yesterday. It is a terrible shock. He had never had any trouble. Love, S.''

Bill's mother wrote more about her husband's death to Shirley's parents: "Will was visiting in the hospital on the afternoon of 19 March when he had a heart attack and was put to bed. After a cardiograph examination, the doctors assured us he would get well with sufficient rest. On the 26th, I stepped out of his room and returned a few minutes later to find he had suffered another attack and was barely living. I am so glad that William and Shirley and the children were home last summer, that we could have the family reunion, and be so happy together. I have felt deeply for the children who are far away, yet in a way it is easier, than to be where one misses a familiar presence all the time.''

Bill was greatly shocked and saddened. He wrote to his mother: "How you have been in my thoughts and prayers during these days. I knew Daddy was not strong, but I never remember his really being sick. If the time has come for God to call him home then I believe he would have wanted to go this way, and how much richer the heavenly fellowship must be as my father finds his place there.

"I have tried to tell myself that Daddy would not want us to grieve for him (as St. Paul says 'as of one without hope' [1 Thess. 4:13]) because if any mortal man on earth ever had the heavenly vision and hope my father did, and now God must have a higher and better purpose for him there, but I cannot help feeling the separation and grieving for the loss of his presence—not only among us his family, but among the many thousands who have felt the touch of his presence through the years. If there was ever a man on earth sent from God and one who lived by and for the things of God, that man was my father, and always and forever the vision of the high calling that he has shown me will be a guide and a power, for he has proved to me that it humanly can be done to live according to all the things that Jesus has taught here on earth.

"I keep reminding myself now that if the things I believe and preach to others mean anything then they must mean something to me, and I am comforted as I think of an illustration that I used recently of traveling with another dog team here in the Arctic and having that team pull on ahead and out of sight for a while. But all the while I know where that team is going and I can see some of the tracks it has left, and I know that come nightfall I will be at the shelter cabin and will find my fellow traveler and friend there ready to greet me with a warm fire and shelter. Such a one has just gone on a ways ahead and will be waiting for us when we arrive. Surely that is true of our Daddy. He has gone on ahead and higher, but we are on the same trail and he has left us some very clear tracks to follow and just as surely when night falls for us, we will find him there waiting for us.

"Shirley and I read the burial service together at ten o'clock yesterday morning, and we were certainly there in spirit with you all. I rejoice again in the wonderful words of St. Paul with the magnificent promises he gives to those of us who have the hope. How I longed to be there at my place by your side in the family circle. You have done so much for me that it is very hard for me to be away when I might be able to do a little for you.

I considered trying to get out and come home as quickly as I could, but after thinking it over, I realized it would be some time before I could get there, and the money might be better spent for some other need.

"Shirley and I have been talking of the many things we have to be thankful for. The wonderful six months there at home—Billy's arrival and his baptism by his grandfather—the opportunity for Shirley and the children to know Daddy and him to know them. God in his own way must have had a very definite plan for us all.

"I now hear an unexpected plane overhead; I am going to close this abruptly and write more later so that you can hear something from us as soon as possible. How you are in our prayers, my mother, ever and always.

"Much, much love to you all from us all,

"Your son, William"

In the same mail, Bill printed a hasty note to his oldest sister.

Dear Nancy,

I just have a minute while a plane is here, but wanted to write a note to you. Of course, I'm not thinking too clearly about everything yet, for the shock is still fresh, but I feel that I ought to do something now. Mother and Grace will need a home, and I am somewhat inclined toward our coming out and finding a church in North Carolina so they can live with us. Then I'd be able to repay in some way the great debt I owe Mother. I believe the Church will relieve us from our commitments here, under the circumstances and it won't be too big a blow to me. Of course, I'd like to finish my term at Pt. Hope, but I have largely made my contribution here, and it would ease our minds a lot to have the children some place where they can get proper food and medical care. Wish I had more time, but I'll write more in detail later.

Bill

Bill reacted to the family tragedy in typical fashion: he had to do something quickly, impulsively. He was already too late for the funeral, and the cost of a trip to North Carolina was well beyond his or his family's financial means. His youngest sister, fifteen-year-old Grace, who was the only child home at the time of his father's death, recalls that their mother, an unemotional person, showed few signs of grieving over her father's death, but cried as she read Bill's letter. She wrote back instantly, telling him that he could not come home; that if he left Alaska she would feel that she had lost them both. She felt so strongly that his work was where God was calling him to serve at that time.

In the weeks ahead, Bill was forced to work through his grief with Shirley at Point Hope. He was helped by a letter from his close friend, Syd Alexander, describing the wake and funeral for him. As was the community custom, the casket remained open at home, and available for viewing day and night because of the many local people on mill shifts. "Flowers were everywhere, and as many as forty people came by to pay their respects between twelve and two A.M., coming off the late shift. Many more came in at the crack of dawn, before going to work at eight o'clock. He was very much loved." Syd also described the funeral, the large crowds composed of everyone in the small town of Spray as well as friends from miles around.

William Gordon was only sixty-five years old, his hair still black, but Bill says his father worked himself to death. Ministry was his vocation, avocation, and recreation for eighteen hours almost every day of the year. (The son was to emulate the parent in this way.) Preacher Gordon ministered to the entire town, although two-thirds of the people he dealt with were not Episcopalians. He was also a learned, well-read man, who had graduated Phi Beta Kappa from the University of North Carolina, from Sewanee Seminary, and then the Episcopal Theological School with high honors. He kept in touch with the outside world, knew many leaders in the Church, and always carried a well-worn, much-read Bible. His friends and coworkers knew of his intellect, but say he was not a polished preacher; rather he was a good teacher and could talk theology with anybody.

William Gordon's schedule left little time for his family; he was seldom home for meals and dinner consisted of a bowl of shredded wheat late at night. When he did come home, he often brought all kinds of people with him for food or comfort. Besides the family demands of seven children; his widowed mother (she died in 1935) and sister "Miss Bettie" had a home across the street. They had lived with him throughout his college and seminary years, and were very possessive. There was always tension between the two households which neither William nor Anna could resolve, but the children, particularly Bill, were the beneficiaries of much unconditional love from two more strong family women.

Bill remembers his father as being kind, loving but not naturally exuberant. He had twinkling blue eyes, a warm smile, and a teasing sense of humor. "He was not a disciplinarian, but he could reason, and that was tough to deal with," Bill reminisces. "I'd get exasperated when it seemed to me he was being too patient; however things usually worked out his way. He taught me what love is all about. He never talked about judgment or wrath. He wanted only what was best for me. But I was not close to him— he was home so seldom, and I didn't feel it easy to talk to him."

William Gordon always spoke a simple message: "God loves you—He cares." And this would be followed with "Here am I, Lord, send me!" He expected this same commitment from others. Bill's sister Nancy's husband, Sandy Dameron, gives the perspective of an outsider brought into the fold. "It is unusual that two people of such strong faith and dedication could come together and have all seven children be good examples of what such an environment would produce. I've never seen a whole family who put their complete trust in a higher power the way they were taught to, and live their lives accordingly."

Nancy claims it was not that easy, that as a teenager, she rebelled. "I'd get so upset—I'd think I'm never going to pray about anything else as long as I live. And then I realized that I couldn't accept everything our father said because he was human and could be mistaken. So I had to make up my own mind." The children were allowed to make mistakes as some went through this stage of independence, then found their own way back to faith. Of the six girls, two became missionaries (Laura to Brazil and Jocelyn to India). Almeria became a Christian Education teacher, and she, along with Mary Irwin, a nurse, spent some time working in Alaska. Nancy was also a nurse. Grace claims to be the black sheep, but she taught school in North Carolina for two years and is now an active layperson in her Episcopal Church. Grace was born when her mother was forty-five years old, and when asked by his other children why he picked her name, William smiled, replying, "It means Benediction." Bill had become used to sisters by then. When Laura, the third daughter was born, three-year-old Bill asked if they could send her back and get a pony.

Grace, as a four year old, ran about swatting flies during the family morning prayer services, and she has a vivid memory of her confrontation with her father over smoking. (Cigarettes, cards, liquor, and dancing were not accepted by Preacher Gordon.) He told his youngest he would meet her after school in the kitchen to settle the issue. She expected to be grounded, or at the least, receive a severe tongue lashing, but all he did was to tell her how much he loved her. "It makes me cry even now to think of it," Grace reflects. "It was the heaviest punishment I could have had."

Bill, who often told his friends, "I have six sisters and each of them has one brother—me," was the recipient of much love and a "you can do no wrong" upbringing throughout his growing years. However, he says he also felt the sense of vocation to "serve my fellow man. That's what you did with your life. It was not spelled out, but it certainly permeated the atmosphere at home. There was no pressure on me to become a priest, but subconsciously I was aware it was there—people just assumed I would go into the ministry."

Bill rebelled in little ways from the time he was born on 6 May 1918. He arrived, a ten-pound baby, before his mother could get to a hospital, and she claimed that during Sunday services he slept while she played the organ, but the moment it was time for the sermon, he began to cry. She told friends he was a stubborn little boy. When she confined him to his room until he said 'thank you' to someone, or apologized for something, he never would, so she inevitably gave in. When Bill was four, she wrote, "He is always interested in camping, cars, and sports, and at home he is a great tease. At this time his only ambition is to be a man who drives a car. [In 1922 driving a car was the equivalent of flying a plane today.] He also does not care very greatly for Sunday School, sometimes telling me on Saturday night that he does not feel well. He is unconscious of the sweetness and depth of his devotional life as he daily gives thanks at mealtimes, repeats his Bible verses, and prays so devoutly himself."

Both Bill and his sisters agree that it was a good decision to send him away to school when he was fourteen years old. A close family friend made it possible for him to receive a full scholarship to the Virginia Episcopal School in Lynchburg, an exclusive boys institution. Once there, he thought he could get out from under parental authority and shed the "goody-goody" image attached to preachers' sons. "I wanted to be something virile, like a fireman," Bill recalls, "and I was deliberately getting demerits to impress the new guys."

In the middle of his first year at the school, the headmaster wrote in a letter to Bill's father: "I am sorry not to be able to write encouragingly about William's general attitude. He does much better school work than is usual for a boy who gets so many demerits. I do not know what kind of a disposition he displays at home, but he is quite surly in his attitude here. He is so unpleasant as a waiter that we will have to relieve him of his job if he does not develop a more agreeable manner. I hope that his present lack of responsiveness is in some way connected with his physical development and that he may soon develop a different attitude. I expect that you can help him while he is at home Christmas. I hope that he will not have any left-over demerits to delay his leaving."

Matters continued to go from bad to worse, with Bill walking off hours of demerits around the football field and being grounded on weekends when students were allowed to go to school sporting events. His final act of defiance, during his second year there, was to sneak off to watch a football game while he was confined to the grounds. Of course he was caught, firmly rebuked, and threatened with dismissal. The Headmaster warned him he would hear dire words from his father, so when Bill received the dreaded letter, he kept it in his pocket as he paced out more demerits. He finally found enough courage to open it, and read his father's words telling news of family happenings only. The very last sentence was: "We love you, son. Your mother and I expect great things from you. We look forward to your coming home for Christmas. Daddy"

Bill says today that this letter literally changed his life. If his father had taken him to task, he might have continued to be rebellious, but his antics were obviously getting him nowhere, except around the football field, and Bill decided it was time to begin to live up to his parents' expectations.

He tried hard to avoid any demerits at all in the next semester, and he was dismayed when his report card showed one. Determined to wipe the slate clean, Bill approached the stern, somewhat frightening headmaster to ask if he would remove the one 'black mark.'

"Did you really deserve that demerit?" Headmaster Mattfield frowned at the sixteen-year-old boy.

"Yes, I did," Bill admitted.

"Then do you think it would be fair to you and the school to remove it?"

Bill wanted to sink through the floor of that dreaded office. The mark remained.

During his final two years at boarding school he became Big Man on Campus, receiving better-than-average grades, and earning four letters in sports: track, baseball, football, and basketball. He was captain of the baseball and track teams his senior year, and state champion in the mile run. In his spare time, he waited on tables and was delivery boy for a laundry and dry cleaner. He was also struggling with his own theological beliefs. His brief letters and cards home during this time reflect the big change.

One post card to "Daddy" gives the scores of his latest ball games, and Bill concludes with "we had a right hard snow here Sat. nite. Still on the ground. And it has been awful cold. Love, Wm." The North Carolina boy found Virginia more wintry than home. Another states: "I made the first touchdown of my career. Getting rather cold around here. What ever happened to my driver's license?" A letter to his father on the parent's birthday, starts out, "We won the first game the baseball team has won in three years. I got two hits. I hope you enjoy your birthday to the fullest extent and have many more. I know my dad is the best any boy has and I thank you for all you've done for me and hope I can pay some of it back."

When Bill's grandmother died during his junior year at school, Bill wrote his mother: "I can't get over the calmness of Daddy and Miss Bettie during these days. I only hope when I get in a like position I can put it all in God's hands like they do. I know Memie was such a Christian and lived such a marvelous life that we ought not to be sorry. But I don't see how we can get along without her influence." This was closely followed by another letter which must have surprised Bill's parents. "You know I really think I've decided what I want and am led to do. In chapel this morning it just came to me. . . . I should take a medical course and then go to Liberia or some place that does not have a Christian church doctor. I've had a lot of ideas before, but this is really the first serious thought I've ever had and I really mean it. I really think that's what God wants me to do and is leading me to. I don't think I would ever make an outstanding minister. I can't get up and talk very easily in public and the medical profession has always appealed to me. I'm missing you all and please pray for me."

The family apparently wrote immediately of their support, because Bill's letter a week later says, "I thank you for your letters, Mother and Miss Bettie. They give me a greater assurance that I have made the right choice and help me keep in the Way. Daddy, I certainly need everybody's prayers, for a lot of times I just don't see things right and I know I've got sins to be forgiven and I'm really not worthy to go into God's service." Bill had reached a compromise between his ingrained desire to serve people and his continuing rebellion against following in his father's footsteps. He also had a deep concern over his ability as a speaker, one which was to haunt him for the rest of his life.

Going to college at the University of North Carolina in 1936 was a foregone conclusion, made possible by a National Church scholarship designated for the three North Carolina Dioceses— $150 a year each. The bishops involved decided to combine the money, and Bill was the first recipient of $450 annually for four years. He lived in the Chapel Hill Church parish house, helped print church bulletins, wash windows, and perform other chores to earn his room.

True to his earlier decision, Bill took a premed major the first two years (seeing much of his friend, Syd Alexander, who later went on to become a doctor), but he had a tough time with science courses earning low grades. Finally, the Dean of the Medical School called Bill into his office and bluntly told him to take a closer look at his future plans. Bill wrote his parents, "I had a long talk with Dr. MacNider and he said it was obvious to him that my main idea was the ministry, and medicine was just a sideline or a means to an end. He used my YPSL [Young Peoples Service League] work last spring and grades in some studies to point out that my heart was rather there than in medicine."

Bill says today: "That sealed my commitment to seek the priesthood—my personal commitment, instead of going that route because others wanted me to." He was still not ready to take on the serious responsibility of service to others, but again he compromised. His college life, along with Syd's, was full of fun, pranks, and mischief. At the same time, through his commitment to teach Sunday School in return for his room at the Rectory, Bill became involved in the Young Peoples Service League, a Diocesan-wide organization, and one which Bill helped spread throughout the South. He became treasurer his sophomore year, then president for his final college years. He pulled in Syd, purchased a 1930 Chevrolet for twenty-five dollars, (Bill called it *Anesthesia* because it put everybody to sleep), the Bishop paid them four cents a mile for gasoline, and the two covered 10,000 miles on weekends as they worked for the youth group in the southern states. Bill showed innate organizational skills as the League grew and he planned their itineraries, meetings, and retreats. He also made many friends among members of the Women's Auxiliaries, where he and Syd spent weekend nights. During later years in Alaska, these women became his staunchest supporters.

All was not work on these travels, however. Syd Alexander relates many stories of their good times together. One weekend however, ended in near disaster. They were scheduled to speak at a YPSL group in Winston-Salem, and decided on the spur of the moment to spend the night at their nearby summer camp. It was in the dead of winter and everything was closed up tight. Then Bill remembered a window with no lock next to the third floor fire escape. As he jumped from the steps onto the roof over a second floor porch, he slipped and fell to the ground. Syd was only a premed student, but he knew enough to see Bill's arm was broken. He lifted him into the car and rushed him to a hospital twenty-six miles away.

Syd recalls that he and Bill had little spending money in college, not even for movies. The big date was to go to the coffee shop for a cup of hot chocolate. Bill never did join a fraternity, although he had many invitations—it was lack of money. "But mine practically adopted him, and we spent a lot of free time there. Bill was very attractive and everybody fell in love with him. He always had a girl or two around him. At one big YPSL convention dance he had three girls—each thought she was his date! He was a clever operator. I can't recall all the foolish things we did, and some I can't repeat. College times were fun, a carefree interlude before we had to grow up."

On Graduation day in June of 1940, Bill received the following letter from his father:

Dear Son,
    On this your graduation day, I want you to know that I thank God for you, that I am proud of you and that you are a joy to us all.

    I believe your college years have been very fruitful and that their full meaning will become clearer as the years go on. You have truly fought a good fight, have unselfishly, nobly, and admirably kept faith with us in endeavoring to live under those conditions required by limited financial resources. You have done an outstanding piece of work among the young people [of YPSL] and you have made up in friends in that field what might have been lost in wider contacts and friendships in the college world.

    May God bless you and keep you and so fill you with His Holy Spirit that in years to come it may be truly said, here was

a man sent from God for such a time as this.
Ever yours—gratefully and lovingly in Christ.
     Daddy

With the arrival of spring weather at Point Hope, Bill's thoughts
returned more to his job and village life. In May, he took his last
dog team trip to Kivalina before summer breakup and Shirley
went along for the first time. Wisely, she did not mention her
plans to her worry-prone family until she returned. Then she
wrote, "I've had quite a thrilling experience since leaving home
at noon on Tuesday. We had to travel all the way to Kivalina on
the ocean ice—which might seem fine if you think the Arctic
Ocean freezes like glass. However, it is a mass of pressure ridges—
high piles of large blocks of ice. What places might have been
smooth ice had water standing on them, and the dogs often
floundered through enough to cover their bellies. I was glad to
be perched high on top of the load. Bill wasn't quite so lucky
and was drenched to his waist—once stepping in a seal hole while
trying to keep the sled and me from turning over. He did a
remarkable job and I was only dumped twice. There wasn't much
choice of a place to fall—in the water or on ice as hard as cement.
I think I'm glad I fell on the ice—it just added to my bruises. I'm
stiff and sore and black and blue from bouncing along, trying to
stay on the sled.
     "The weather was beautiful when we left Point Hope, and I
wanted to wear just a sweater, but Bill made me put on my jacket
and snow shirt [Shirley's was white calico]. I was glad I had it
because the sun went behind clouds, the cold wind began to blow,
and it was raining before we made camp at the abandoned igloo
beyond Cape Thompson. We had covered thirty-eight miles in
ten hours when we stopped there for supper. The place was full
of snow [as usual], so we pitched our tent on the beach and spent
the night. It was really comfortable in a double Arctic sleeping
bag placed on caribou skins on the sand.
     "The next morning it was still raining, but we started out
anyway. It rained all day, and though the trail was much better,
this was the hardest part of the trip for me. My parka was soaked
through before we reached Kivalina at seven-thirty last night. Bill

says the trip was the worst he's had in twelve visits to the village, but it really was fun for me in spite of the rigors.

"I was not worried about the children—there are two doctors and two nurses in Point Hope at the moment, studying the diet of the people. I also have two excellent Eskimo babysitters— Carmen and her sister Uskiwana."

During the summer months, life settled back into a happy routine, with Shirley coaxing some lettuce plants in the small greenhouse and Bill rewiring Browning Hall so he could use a new electric victrola, as well as a movie projector, introducing films to the villagers.

Then their peace was interrupted by two unexpected events. Bishop Bentley was elected vice-president of the National Council of the Episcopal Church. He would leave Alaska to be head of all overseas work.

Bill wrote in his newsletter: "Bishop Bentley's particular gifts and ability, so ideally suited for work in this Great Land have made him one of the most loved and admired men in Alaska today. He has been a wonderful Father in God, and a true friend, guide, and inspiration. His influence and vision led me to the Alaskan field; our whole life in Alaska has been permeated by his influence. Just as surely as our God provided Bishop Rowe and now this His servant, He will again provide a man who will lead us onward in our eternal quest for the Kingdom of God here. Do pray that the House of Bishops will be guided to a man, who like David of old, will be of His own choosing." Prophetic words about an extreme youth taking on leadership, spoken by another youth who had not the least thought that such an august Body would even consider him.

On 6 August Paneen put on her parka to run down to meet Carmen, Shirley's new helper. Shirley continued with her work, and only looked out the window to see what progress they were making. She saw Carmen running up the steps with Paneen in her arms, her overalls soaked with blood. Four dogs from Bill's team had broken loose and two jumped Paneen, biting her on the legs.

Bill was away, so Shirley sent Carmen for Mrs. Alexander (the new schoolteacher), while she undressed Paneen and wrapped her in a sheet on the couch. She was afraid the child was going into shock because she was dead white and her teeth chattered visibly. With the schoolteacher's help, Shirley cleaned Paneen's wounds with green soap solution and sprinkled them with sulfanilamide powder. One bite could have used stitches, Shirley thought, but she didn't feel up to causing the child more pain and by the time Bill returned home the following day, Paneen seemed all right.

Two days later Paneen started running a temperature, so when pilot Pete Peterson came to Point Hope the next morning, Bill sent Paneen and Shirley to Kotzebue to see the doctor. By then her temperature was 103 degrees, but given sulfa and hot, moist compress treatments, Paneen recovered quickly and they returned home a week later. In a letter describing the scary incident to her parents, Shirley added that while in "the big city," they gorged themselves on fresh peaches, cantaloupes, celery, carrots, and oranges. She also assured them that Bill had strengthened the dogs' chains so they would not be able to get loose again.

Bill's life was made immensely easier that year because of a new acquisition—a Jeep. Previously he was almost helpless in the summer with no means of transporting anything except by human backs, a critical problem when the annual supply boat arrived. No one argued about the need for the Jeep, but the circumstances surrounding its acquisition caused a good deal of controversy.

Bill's friend, Dr. Syd Alexander, passed the word among his friends and soon they had contributed not only enough to buy a Jeep, but extra funds for parts and maintenance. It was a gift useful not only to Bill, but to the entire village. The Jeep was immediately put to work doing everything from hauling coal and other freight dumped on the beach (for the school as well as the mission), to hauling ice and transporting heavy sod blocks for the villagers as they winterized their homes.

Neither Syd nor Bill anticipated the uproar Syd's thoughtfulness would cause. Someone on his list of contributors asked the National Church if the solicitation had been authorized by them. The associate director of the Overseas Department reprimanded Bill, who stood firm. He said that if the Church sent out any kind of directive harmful to Syd, he would have Bill's resignation the next day. The associate director backed down and nothing further happened.

While Bill and Shirley were preparing for another winter in the Arctic, the political wheels of the National Church had begun turning. The House of Bishops was to meet in Winston-Salem in early November to elect the third Bishop of Alaska. It was not necessary that he come from that District, but in light of its uniqueness and particular challenges, the selection of someone already familiar with the area would be advantageous. But Alaska was at a point in its development where many of the trailblazing missionaries were retiring, and a shortage of funds had not allowed for many replacements. The most eligible and popular priest was the Reverend Warren Fenn, in charge of the Anchorage parish, but his health was not good. The parish of Sitka was vacant, the priest in Juneau had just resigned, the one in Ketchikan had just arrived, and Al Jones in Fairbanks was not planning to remain. That left the Reverends Henry Chapman of Anvik, born there of missionary parents and fifty-two years old at the time; Jennings Hobson of Tanana; Wilfred Files in Fort Yukon; Ed Turner in Seward; and the veteran Mervin Wanner in Valdez, who had greeted Bill on his way north on the boat.

In mid-October, Bishop Edwin Penick of Bill's home Diocese in North Carolina, wrote Bill's mother with what "may seem like a strange request, but I know I may rely on you in making a confidential inquiry. It is possible that when the time comes next month at the House of Bishops to nominate a successor to Bishop Bentley, I may feel moved to place Bill's name in nomination. If I should do so, the Committee on Nominations will want some biographical data that might not be immediately available." He then asked her if she would answer an enclosed list of questions and give him permission to present them, should Bill's name come up.

The questions were wide-ranging, including Bill's school grades and extracurricular activities. "This is important," the Bishop wrote, "as it denotes leadership. It would include athletic teams, contests won or lost. The spirit of the athletic field sometimes becomes the spirit of the missionary field." Another question asked how well Bill worked with others, and did she know how he was regarded by his fellow workers? "I am sorry to say so, but churchmanship may have something to do with this election. Is Bill impatient or intolerant towards those who differ from him?" How Anna Gordon responded to Bill's churchmanship is not known. Although Bill had been in Alaska for four years, he had had little or no contact with any other areas and priests beyond the Arctic Coast. He did have a friend in Bishop Bentley, however, who knew of his extensive work among native lay leaders in the outstations. Bill and his parents also had a number of long-time friends among all of the bishops from the South.

Mrs. Gordon did write Bill, telling him of the questionnaire and the possibility of his name coming up. Al Jones also wrote, saying he'd heard of the possible nomination. "I thought that was a very wild idea at best," Bill says today, and he put the idea out of his mind. It never occurred to him that he would be considered for the office. He was twenty-nine years old; in the last forty or fifty years no one under thirty-five had been elected. Only Bishop Tuttle of Wyoming had been consecrated some months after his thirtieth birthday, and he was the sole priest serving the Utah, Wyoming, and Montana area at the time. So Bill went about his work for the coming year by starting on a dog team journey to Kivalina on 6 November, the day before the election was to take place.

Bishop Bentley comments on the election of his successor: "The Church had to find someone to replace me in Alaska, someone who, if possible, knew something about the field and had proven himself able to do that work. Bishop Frederick Goodwin of the Diocese of Virginia and an old friend, had visited us in the summer of 1947. He was keenly interested in Alaska and he wanted to see something of the Eskimo work on the Arctic Coast. So he went to Point Hope, spending several days with the Gordons, and was delighted and charmed by what he found there. When he returned to Nenana, he made the suggestion that Bill Gordon might make a good replacement for me. I said, 'Yes, he would be. But he's so young.' I thought about this. I confess I had other, older, more mature people in mind."

When the convention began and the matter came up, another bishop asked Bentley to tell them who in Alaska he thought might make a good bishop. He was a bit awed by being called on to offer an opinion on his successor, but nevertheless he got up and recommended Bill. Bishop Tucker of Ohio then made the formal nomination and Bill was elected on the first ballot. "I feel the Holy Spirit surely guided the House when it elected Bill Gordon," Bentley says. "Physically, mentally, and spiritually he was prepared in every way to hold that post and to meet those responsibilities."

On 9 November Bill wrote his mother from Kivalina. "How I wish I could talk to Daddy and you. This overwhelming news reached me here at Kivalina on the night of the seventh—at the time of the election I must have been asleep in the old abandoned igloo just south of Cape Thompson. The Kivalina radio has a nightly radio schedule with the Kotzebue Hospital, and I was waiting to send word to Point Hope of my safe arrival when I got the messages.

"You can imagine my feelings to have this come upon me so unexpectedly. Shirley was at the school and I talked to her a minute or two on the radio, but I can't recall what I told her except that I would come right back to Point Hope instead of going on to Noatak as I had planned. That night I prayed and I thought, and all I could see was my tremendous unfitness, unpreparedness, and inadequacy for any part of such a job."

Bill's first reaction was to refuse, but it was a decision that required serious consideration. He wired Bishop Sherrill, the Presiding Bishop, that he was away from home and could not make a decision until he returned to Point Hope and talked to Shirley.

Shirley was astounded that Bill would even consider not accepting the election. If they believed at all in the guidance of the Holy Spirit and the minds of the House of Bishops, then the decision was almost out of their hands. Yet Bill was undecided. He had been happy in Point Hope and the contrast with his life and work and that of a bishop was a sharp one. Bill and Shirley talked and prayed together, and "it came to both of us that we must accept the election, realizing fully our own complete inadequacy for the task, falling back on God's unfailing promises and the guidance of the Holy Spirit to fill in the emptiness in ourselves." Bill wired his acceptance.

"I just cannot bear to think of leaving it all here," Bill wrote to his mother. "I have been touched by the reaction of our people. They are not demonstrative or emotional, but Milton Swan's 'I will be lonesome when you leave us' carried a wealth of caring and feeling. Of course, I will not be completely away from it, but life can never be the same, I know. This new work will mean a tremendous change for my own family, and a real sacrifice for them. I will necessarily be away from home even more than I have been at Point Hope, and I realize only too well how much of the work to come will be Shirley's as well as mine."

Of Shirley, Bill says today, "actually, it should have been her choice, since it disrupted her life more than mine—much of the care of the children, of being home by herself, involved her. But the utter simplicity of her faith and how it applied to our life was very clear and evident in accepting this decision."

Shirley knew little of what was involved in being a bishop's wife, having recently joined the Episcopal Church and being only twenty-four years old. Most are much older, their children grown up by the time their husbands are elected, and they have long been active in parish and diocesan life. But Shirley is intrepid, and had no doubts that Bill was the right man for the job.

"This does mean we will spend the rest of our lives in Alaska which pleases us both. [Episcopal bishops are elected for life.] Looks like I've hitched my wagon to a star."

Bill returned to Kivalina and Noatak to complete his twelve-day fall visit, and he had plenty of time to sort out his thoughts while mushing on the trail. It was hard to look at where he was headed; so much was unknown. But he pondered at length over the events that had brought him to this turning point in his life. If National Church headquarters had had their way, he would probably never even have come to Alaska!

"I kind of drifted into Virginia Seminary from the University in September of 1940—a natural continuity. Most North Carolina boys going into the ministry were sent to Virginia, but those who hadn't too much Episcopal background went to Sewanee." Bill's grades at college were only a little above average, but he could pass any Christian theology exam with no effort on his part and his work with the YPSL was a definite plus. So there were no worries over obtaining a full scholarship. A letter from the Dean to Bishop Penick stated, "Although we have twice as many applicants as we can take next year, we shall certainly find room for him, if I have to throw someone out."

Of Seminary, Bill says it was more like a prep school. They were required to live in dorms; there were about seventy-five students at that time, and only seventeen in his class. "I wasn't stimulated or challenged by the studies there, issues raised in class were not pertinent, although they did try to shake us up, and into a sound theology." Bill slid through as effortlessly as he could, earning money by working in the bookstore and manning an air raid switchboard in the basement of the nearby Masonic Temple. He made about $1,000, so his social life was not curbed by financial needs. However, because of wartime conditions, any travel and all vacations were cut to the bare minimum, and students worked in the summertime as well.

In the fall of his senior year, a representative from the National Church came to the seminary to talk of the need for men to go to Alaska. That seemed like the other end of the world to Bill, but he was intrigued. He still harbored vague dreams of missionary work. The alternative was to return to North Carolina, the sphere of family influence, and become Bishop Penick's "fair-haired boy." So Bill applied for a position in Alaska.

Church headquarters sent a personnel man to interview Bill in November and they turned him down; the reason given was "too young." Bill accepted the verdict with equanimity, bought himself a used car and received a church assignment in North Carolina from Penick. But the seminary dean, knowledgeable about men and missionary work, insisted the National Church send down someone in the Overseas Department. On Christmas Eve, while he was working at his air raid switchboard, Bill received his letter of acceptance for Alaska. For a few moments he thought it was too late; he had purchased the car and Bishop Penick was counting on his taking over a small church. It did not take long to decide, however, and at two A.M. on Christmas morning he called his parents to share the news. After that, the days became a blur: graduation on 16 January, ordination as a

deacon on 24 January, and his train trip to Seattle in late February.
Bill knew his shortcomings as well as anyone, when he took
the time to think about them, and this he did now as he and his
long-time friend, Mark Kinneeveeuk struggled against icy winds
upon their return to Point Hope. It was here on the Arctic Coast,
not back in Seminary, where with the guidance and example of
these deeply committed Christians Bill's personal faith was
strengthened. The Eskimos were a kind and simple people, with
a down-to-earth religion that they practiced unquestioningly in
their daily lives. They were Bill's teachers on every aspect of life
and they molded much of his theological thinking and leadership
concepts for the crucial years ahead. There was Peel, the Swans,
Tommy Knox, Peter Koonoyak, Sam Rock, and others who lived
the lives of the saints; but there was also Antonio Weber, who
taught him in a much different way.

Antonio was among the few who did not regularly attend
church, although he was a devout Christian. "Through Antonio,
at some point I realized that God wasn't primarily interested in
the people who actually sit in God's house; that there were other
ways of indicating God's care and a person's devotion to Him.
Antonio understood God's gifts, he was a man who knew who
he was, and what his talents were. He was a born teacher and
taught me all I knew about dog team travel. But it was his way
of helping me which was a wonderful object lesson—he gave me
the gift of his own knowledge in a way that I could take it and
use it myself. It wasn't easy, either; he didn't play games with
me or ease up, nor did he ask too much. And he never once
shamed or criticized me."

The weeks following Bill's return were filled with upheaval and
uncertainty for the Gordons, but they still took the time to enjoy
to the fullest their final holiday season at Point Hope. Bishop
Bentley sent word to Bill to come to Nenana for a conference
as soon as possible, but winds gusting over sixty miles per hour
combined with the zero degree temperatures kept Bill on the
ground until 2 December. "It wasn't too unusual to watch fifty-
five gallon oil drums rolling over the tundra because of the gale,"
Bill commented as he waited impatiently.

The Gordons kept busy answering a stack of mail from friends and relatives, brought in on the last plane before the big blow. Many were from North Carolinians who sent good wishes: "You could hardly have been otherwise, with such a Father and Mother." "How I wish your father might have been spared to see this happen. But there may be just as much rejoicing in Paradise."

One lengthy letter stands out from the others, written by Evangelist J.J.D. Hall, a longtime friend of Bill's father. He wrote, "I tremble to think of one so young taking up such a terrific burden, but God surely can give you the strength. What I am interested in knowing is what you are going to do about doctrine and practical life. On every side the Church is giving way, in my judgment, in the fight against sin and the devil. We must have strong men to stand up and defend both the Bible and the Church. If not, surrender the whole thing and go out to play. There is no reason I know of why you should not be an outstanding prophet of the Lord. Your home training certainly should indicate that you can do it and if you do not, there will be a terrible reckoning at the Great Day of Judgment."

Bill was also faced with numerous decisions about his consecration, the myriad details concerning a ceremony that basically came from the Anglican days of Henry VIII. Since Bishop Bentley's experience with the service was limited to his own, Bishop Penick took over all the preparations. The date posed no problem since it had to be as soon as possible after Bill's thirtieth birthday, and 18 May was chosen. The place was also easy to settle on. North Carolina, of course, so that friends and family could attend easily (leaving Alaskans "out in the cold," which they were used to at that time anyway). A large enough church had to be selected, however, and the Church of the Good Shepherd in Raleigh was Bishop Penick's recommendation.

Bill became stubborn when his former superior began discussing the Bishop's traditional ring. Bill had never worn a ring, and strongly disliked the idea of starting now. "If I have to, the smaller, the better," was his reluctant reply, and he wanted it to be given him by the Young Peoples Service League. In "high church" ritual, Episcopalians will kiss the Bishop's ring, which is often the size of a quail's egg. But Bill got a small one, large enough only to accommodate the Seal of the District of Alaska. After his consecration, he seldom wore it, carrying it in his pocket when he went on more formal church visitations.

In addition to the ring, there was the matter of a set of vestments, a gift from the priests of Alaska. Bishop Penick suggested that Bill consider a long woolen cape "to be worn over his robes, especially on outdoor occasions. Don't worry, I am not talking about a cope, or any other Anglican robes. I have found that a long black loose cape, with lots of cloth in it, and many folds, has been one of the most useful articles in my ecclesiastical wardrobe." It is easy to guess Bill's reaction to this suggestion!

Other concerns on Bishop Penick's mind while the Gordons were still at Point Hope included the printing of invitations and the number to be printed. "That will depend upon the length of your list. If we start with 150 Bishops and 100 to the clergy and other officers of the Diocese of North Carolina, you can see the list will be long. Your mother writes of her desire and intention to cooperate in every way. I shall probably pester her a good deal about details."

Bill's immediate concern was his meeting with Bishop Bentley in Nenana, and he wrote his mother afterward that those three days "will remain one of the really happy memories of my life. Bishop Bentley was wonderful to me in his attitude, comments, and actions, and it reassures me a great deal that he has confidence in my ability to do the job." Bishop Bentley went over the work of the Church in Alaska, beginning in Ketchikan, the gateway to Southeast Alaska, telling him things that would be helpful. Bill knew almost nothing about the rest of the District, evenly divided between white and native parishioners. He had met three or four of the clergy and had a little exposure to the churches in Fairbanks and Nenana, as well as his four months in Seward. But the rest was a vast unknown and he was appalled at the enormity of the task.

Bill found a young cousin, a layman just out of the Marines, to take over the Point Hope post for a year, and on 13 January 1948 the Gordon family flew with Bill Peterson in a twin engine Cessna to Nenana. They took only belongings of immediate need, leaving some heavier items to follow on the boat the following summer. Most furniture would remain behind since it was Church custom in Alaska in those days that all rectories be furnished with Church property. The Gordons had moved into an almost empty house at Point Hope except for the coffin and 900 detective novels, so they decided to leave behind most of their own purchases, taking only the crib for Billy.

Shirley did not stay long in Nenana, flying south for a visit to her parents in March. Bill joined her in mid-April. Meanwhile, he tried to learn more about the administration of the District on his own because Bishop and Mrs. Bentley had left for New York the day after Christmas.

Eighteen May, twelve days after Bill's thirtieth birthday, came all too soon. Memories of the momentous occasion vary—from Paneen and Billy who have none because they were relegated to the church lawn to play during the lengthy service, to Bill's youngest sister, Grace, who was mainly overcome by the large numbers of photographers and other members of the press milling about. This also was one of Shirley's strongest memories. She was deeply annoyed by what she considered a rude invasion of their privacy at a precious family moment. *Life* magazine sent a whole crew, saying they intended to run a full story on this young, handsome family, thrust so suddenly into a job of enormous responsibility. While they used only one picture, some southern newspapers carried large spreads; Bill was the youngest bishop ever to be consecrated in the Anglican Union (meaning all of the British Commonwealth at that time), beating out Bishop Tuttle by three months, and he looked even younger than his thirty years. Bill reflects today that there was a lot of comment throughout the Church and beyond, about the youthfulness of the new Bishop of Alaska—and serious doubts as well.

Susan Chapman, wife of Henry Chapman, the priest at Anvik and also a former member of the North Carolina Diocese, was among the few from Alaska present, and she wrote a more detailed description of the event for her friends back home.

"The weather is of great importance to a consecration with its long outdoor procession. Yesterday was absolutely ideal, with sunny skies and balmy air. Crowds were at the door of the large old stone Church, smiling and greeting one another. Inside, marble columns supported carved stone arches leading to the sanctuary. Graceful wood beams formed the vaulted ceiling. The altar was ablaze with candles. The reredos [screen behind the altar] was of deeply carved white marble. In front of it the red gladioli were colorful and stately.

"Soon after taking our places, I saw someone smiling a greeting. It was Mrs. Bentley. I looked more closely and saw Miss Bessie Blacknall. Across the aisle from the small Alaska delegation, and just under the pulpit sat the Bishop-elect's wife and mother, his five sisters [one was in Brazil], and aunt. The church was crowded, with 1100 people in attendance.

"The procession was impressive: The choir in pure white, the large number of clergy wearing red stoles, and the ten bishops in their red robes with white rochets. The third crucifer, the one who preceded the bishop-elect, was from Bill's home church in Spray and he carried the wooden cross that had been used there in the services conducted by Bill's father.

"When the time came for the offering, Bishop Bentley told of recent serious budget cuts and how Alaska had been affected. He said the offering for the day would go to provide a priest at Nenana. The offering amounted to well over eleven hundred dollars.

"The service was a most inspiring one and I shall always be thankful I could be present. Our new Bishop bore himself with quiet dignity and simplicity, and I am sure with a deep sense of dedication."

The service was led by Presiding Bishop Henry Knox Sherrill, and assisted by Bishops Penick and Bentley. Bishop Goodwin was the litanist, and the other bishops took some part in the two-and-a-half-hour ceremony. The only lay person involved was Syd Alexander. The sole Alaskan was Al Jones from Fairbanks, representing Alaska as presbyter. The Reverend Warren Fenn of Anchorage had been chosen first—his parishioners in particular were unhappy over Bill's selection due to his age and the fact that they did not know him at all. Unfortunately, Fenn suffered a serious heart attack just before the consecration.

Bill himself remembers little of the details of his consecration, although the presence of one of the guests among that throng made a lasting impression. It was the headmaster of the Virginia Episcopal School when Bill was a student there. The older man was living hundreds of miles from Raleigh at the time, and Bill was amazed that he made the effort to come such a distance. "I guess," Bill reminisces, "he wanted to make sure that the bishop-elect and the obstreperous boy were one and the same person!" Otherwise, Bill was almost overcome by the awesome feelings and sense of deep responsibility emanating from the solemn words of the centuries-old service. For an impulsive, rambunctious young man, the questions posed by Bishop Sherrill must have been a little frightening:

Bishop: Are you ready, with all faithful diligence, to banish and drive away from the Church all erroneous and strange doctrine contrary to God's Word; and both privately and openly to call upon and encourage others to the same?
Answer: I am ready, the Lord being my helper.
Bishop: Will you deny all ungodliness and worldly lusts, and live soberly, righteously, and godly in this present world; that you may show yourself in all things an example of good works unto others, that the adversary may be ashamed, having nothing to say against you?
Answer: I will so do, the Lord being my helper.

The sermon, given by Bishop Thomas C. Darst, retired Bishop of the Diocese of East Carolina, was equally strong in its wording. At the conclusion, he addressed Bill personally, acknowledging his brief ministry so far, but one filled with meaning and purpose in a lonely, barren outpost. And because he had proved to be such a faithful, loving shepherd of a few children of God, the bishops were calling him to a wider service. They were placing a great responsibility on his shoulders, but they were sure he was worthy of their confidence. The bishop reminded Bill of the words of St. Paul to his son in the faith, Timothy: "Let no man despise thy youth; but be thou an example of the believers, in word, in conversation, in charity, in spirit, in faith, in purity" (I Tim. 4:12).

The service concluded with the laying on of hands by all ten bishops, and a picture records a complete circle of red-robed patriarchs hovering over the kneeling young man. The expression on Bill's face looks like that of a scared little boy carrying a precious and heavy load on his back. No wonder Bill does not remember the details of the day; these church leaders, indeed everyone in that church, and all who were to read the press accounts, would be watching him carefully in the months and years ahead as he took on what must have seemed like an impossible task running the enormous, and impoverished, Missionary District of Alaska.

Chapter 5

Battling the Wilderness

Immediately after his consecration, Bill, anxious to start work, hurried back to Alaska. Shirley and the children remained behind, spending time in North Carolina and then in Washington with her parents. Bill's first duty was a major challenge: a two-month summer trip on 3,500 miles of the treacherous waters of the Interior via the forty-foot, five-ton mission boat, *The Godspeed*. This was a real test for him, his only experience with boats having been short trips in the small ones at Point Hope. Testing seemed to be the pattern of Bill's life, beginning with his coming from North Carolina to Alaska with no cold weather experience at all; being assigned to the Arctic Coast during his first year and having to learn to travel by dog team; then being elected bishop when he was still somewhat inexperienced as a priest. There would be more testing in the years ahead.

Bishop Bentley had been making this summer journey on the Tanana, Koyukuk, and Yukon rivers to visit the missions and fish camps for over twenty years, as had Archdeacon Hudson Stuck before him, mostly using a twenty-four-foot open boat called *The Discovery*. It was powered by a ten-horse outboard motor. A canvas cover over the bow gave minimal protection from the elements. Mrs. Bentley usually went along and they camped out in a little tent on sandbars along the way.

Bishop Bentley had long dreamed of a more commodious craft and he designed *The Godspeed* himself, having it built in Seattle in 1947. It was named after one of the boats that brought the settlers to Jamestown in 1607. A sturdy, comfortable vessel that could navigate in only two and one-half feet of water, it had two berths in the forward cabin, a lavatory, and a galley in the aft cabin with a small oil-burning range, a sink, table, and locker seats with ample storage space for foodstuffs. A small pump drew water directly from the river.

The boat was powered by a 115 horsepower engine and had four fuel tanks, sufficient to provide the boat a cruising range of 1,000 miles. Unfortunately for Bishop Bentley, he had only one summer on *The Godspeed* before being called to New York.

Bill knew he would need help, so he signed up a college student, Bishop Goodwin's son, to be his crew, and made arrangements to follow the FAA* tugboats that traveled the rivers, at least until he got acclimated. The pilot of one, *The Taku Chief,* was Jim Binkley, who with his wife, Mary, were in Bill's first confirmation class in Fairbanks. Jim watched for Bill as best he could, and they became close friends. One wonders just how much Bill did follow these tugboats, though, because he often commented on passing them as they were docked, of moving on without waiting. He never was a good follower!

Bishop Bentley had drawn detailed charts during his many summers, carefully outlining the proper channels and marking the danger spots. Had Bill followed them exactly, he would have had little trouble. However, his ship's logs for the summers of 1948 and 1949 are filled with brief comments about running aground, usually while trying to take shortcuts. "Stupidly, I took a shallow-looking slough—full of snags and about two feet of water. Tried to go through and got stuck hard. Spent two and one-half hours getting off. Lost an hour there." Then, "lost some time clearing the bar in front of Anvik . . . lost time on two false sloughs—scraped another sand bar and got water pump clogged." Bill's patience was severely tried by dead-end sloughs and meandering river channels.

Bill also comments on the day his stern line somehow fell overboard and wrapped about his propeller shaft. It required making many dives into the icy cold water over a forty-minute

---

*The CAA (Civil Aeronautics Administration) was changed by an act of Congress in 1955 to the FAA (Federal Aviation Administration). To avoid confusion, FAA has been used throughout the book, regardless of date.

period to cut it free. Far more embarrassing to Bill was becoming ensnared in another object. Late one evening he was in a rush—as usual—up a slough near Allakaket and got tangled in fish net, with serious results to the net. Again he had to take a lengthy swim to clear himself.

Bill's log for the first summer is chatty and contains a number of incidents and personal comments. The following year, it becomes "business only," simply recording facts about the weather, distance covered, stops made, and gasoline consumption. The latter was a major concern, especially the first year, when Bill was unsure of how many gallons he was using, or where he would be able to resupply his tanks. On both trips he made frequent comments about high waves, treacherous currents, and driftwood. Large logs and branches carried by the swift water could dent the hull or damage the propeller. In 1949, a late breakup left ice in many areas when Bill first set out, and he had to keep a sharp eye out for floes. Small streams, where he wanted to camp overnight, were often frozen tight.

Bill visited eight missions and twelve smaller outstations during both his two-month trips, but, because the people left their homes for fishing camps in the summertime, he had to make many more stops, including any old-timer's cabin he passed. He stayed for two or three days at the bigger villages, but most other visits were far briefer, some for only twenty or thirty minutes. Bill's terse log the second summer sounds as if he was in a constant hurry, but he always had time to carry away mail people wanted sent, to take grocery orders to the next outpost, or to supply some necessary item from his own supplies. He was given fresh salmon everywhere he went (so many that he says he has had his fill of fish for life), and an occasional most welcome pie. Otherwise, his food consisted of canned goods because of the lack of refrigeration.

At one fish camp stop, Bill held a service on a bluff overlooking the river. "It was a setting unmatched by any cathedral and I was reminded of the many times that our Lord preached out-of-doors to his listeners." Many babies were baptized during those two summers, a few people were buried, and marriages were frequent. "Just below Steven's Village we stopped for an hour to marry

a couple in a tent. A pleasant memory was the wonderful smell
of fresh spruce boughs that had been cut to line the floor—almost
like incense!''

During his second summer trip in 1949, Shirley, having sent
Paneen and Billy down to Seattle to her parents, accompanied
Bill for the first three weeks. Bill took that period more slowly
and both enjoyed not seeing another person for days as they
cruised through the beautiful wilderness. The log reads: "The
regular crew of the boat consisted of the Bishop and Mrs. Gordon.
The Bishop's duties were those of pilot, engineer, and dish dryer,
while Mrs. Gordon was in full charge of the galley and such
extracurricular tasks as sounder [ascertaining the depth of the
water with a long pole] and deck hand.''

Shirley left the boat at Allakaket, where Bill picked up Dr.
Edward H. Dunn from the Ft. Yukon Episcopal hospital. Doctor
Dunn stayed on board for the rest of the journey, treating illnesses
at every stop they made. He was often left behind, somehow
catching up, or being picked up later as Bill had to hurry on.
In his log, Bill makes frequent references to airplanes—a number
stopped to bring him mail or passengers, and he takes an oc-
casional side trip via air, once returning to Fairbanks for several
days. The log concludes: "Thus ends the summer trip of *The
Godspeed* for 1949 and probably the last trip of the craft for the
Episcopal Church. She has done well." The boat was sold to Jim
Binkley, and the funds were put into an airplane.

Today Bill says, "I think that if I could do one thing over again
in my life as Bishop of Alaska, I would choose that summer trip
with *The Godspeed*. Unfortunately, I did not appreciate the
priceless opportunity of being in the wilderness all those weeks.
We could go for days and never see a person; there were beautiful
fresh water streams, animals everywhere, the glories of Alaska's
eternal summer daylight, and an uncanny sense of being the
master of the world which, of course, I was not. Then there were
the fascinating old-timers I met all along the way, but never took
enough time to get to know better. They were some of the finest
people I've ever met anywhere."

Upon Bill's return from his first trip on *The Godspeed* in mid-
August 1948, Shirley and the children flew back from their

summer stay with families and they moved directly into their new home in Fairbanks. Bishop Bentley's original plan was to build one structure to house both the bishop's office and residence, but Bill was concerned about combining the two, because of children present. So a house was purchased with some of the Bishop Rowe Memorial funds, and an office building would follow. Meanwhile, two rooms in the parish hall of St. Matthew's Church would serve as the District Office.

Their new home, at 903 Kellum Street, was built in 1937 by Noel Wien, brother of Sig and founder of Wien Airlines. The plain white clapboard house, with three bedrooms upstairs, provided ample space for the immediate future. Another bedroom and bath on the ground floor were converted into an apartment for Bill's secretary. A large living room, dining room, and kitchen were also a major change from the Point Hope bungalow. Fortunately for the Gordons, it was fully furnished, having been occupied by an Air Force family who left their furniture behind.

All of the Gordons faced great changes following their years at Point Hope. It was like Christmas for Shirley, rediscovering the benefits of civilization. Bill spent most of his time learning about his new job. He got a three-months crash course from Bishop Bentley's long-time secretary, Mrs. Lois Cox, who had already sent in her resignation. Bill also had to learn to preach all over again. On the Arctic Coast he had become relaxed over this undertaking, his great concern since boarding school days, because while talking through an interpreter, he had thirty seconds to a minute between each two or three sentences to think about what he wanted to say next. Bill adds, "I am thankful that I gave my first sermons at Point Hope, where the Eskimo language was limited to about a thousand words. It helped me to simplify my vocabulary, keep my sentences short and my message brief and to the point." Another valuable lesson learned from the Eskimo people!

The Gordon children question whether Bill ever felt at ease in the pulpit, but his style always has been relaxed and folksy as he relates a few of his many anecdotes from his years in Alaska. He has never written out a sermon, relying instead on brief notes scribbled on scraps of paper. He paces back and forth, twirls his glasses by a stem, and has people mesmerized with his charm, wit, and storytelling.

Fairbanks was still a small frontier town in 1948. Its gold dredges worked full-time, two military bases were an ongoing part of the community, and the University of Alaska was developing slowly. The narrow streets were unpaved, saloons and log houses dominated, and long-time residents confide that a tough group of gangsters exercised control over certain aspects of town life. Army base construction brought in a lot of summer workers, but winters, with four hours of daylight and temperatures dropping to thirty, even sixty degrees below zero, were left to the old-timers. Social life was important then, especially bridge clubs and square dancing.

Shirley initially had little time for fun in Fairbanks, when Bill put her to work as his secretary. The job included letter writing and all the District bookkeeping and arrangements for mission staff members coming to town for various reasons. Shirley and Bill had had frequent drop-in visitors during their stay at Point Hope, but now their home became a full-fledged hotel (there was only one real one, expensive and seedy).

Fortunately, Wilma Butler, Mrs. Cox's replacement appointed by the National Council, arrived in January of 1949, moving into the apartment in the Gordon home. Wilma and Shirley became good friends; the new secretary provided companionship during Bill's frequent trips, and she was an excellent built-in babysitter.

Bill found his work more of a challenge than he had anticipated. There was a shortage of nursing and maintenance staff at the Fort Yukon Hospital, and vacant spots at Tanacross, Tanana, Fort Yukon, and Point Hope hung over his head too. He felt strongly that he himself ought to minister to those places, but that would have left him no time for any of his many other responsibilities. "It is heart-rending to see critical work that needs to be done, with no one to do it."

Meanwhile, Father Fenn had to leave immediately for a year's complete rest, and he was not expected to get well enough to return to an active parish like Anchorage. So Bill was busy looking for a man to take his place.

Later Bill received the further bad news that the priest on

furlough from Tanana would not be returning, but at least the
Reverend Robert Reid, the new man for Nenana had arrived (his
salary was paid out of the offering taken at Bill's consecration).
The man on furlough from Fort Yukon had also returned, and
the church in Fairbanks, which had burned down in 1947, was
rebuilt. Living in the Arctic wilderness, however, always keeps
one on the thin edge of survival, and just when Bill felt good about
developments, tragedy struck. Ice from heavy spring flooding
severely damaged the hospital at Fort Yukon the summer of 1949,
the school building of the Nenana boarding school burnt to the
ground in December of that year, and Robert Reid was to meet
with a tragic death just one year after assuming his post in Nenana.

Also in early 1949, the National Church sent Bill the bad news
that severe cuts had to be made in all missionary budgets. "We
are heartsick," he wrote in a monthly newsletter, "not only that
these cuts have been made, but also that hoped-for appropriations
for a relief priest at Point Hope were deleted. Alaska has been
hard hit, but no more so than any other field. We must not blame
the National Council for this action. The fault lies in the fact that
the Church just simply has not provided the necessary funds
to carry on our missionary work, even to hold the line on a
minimum basis." Bill then urged the workers in the District to
send in news of projects in their area, so that the Church Outside
would know what was going on in Alaska. Bill himself had begun
a massive effort to sell subscriptions to the *Alaskan Churchman*
all over the country, using his Point Hope mailing list to reach
those people he knew were ready to give to a worthy cause. This
little District magazine was to become a major source of funds
in the years ahead.

Bill concludes this first staff newsletter with a strong message
about the work of the Church in Alaska: "As we start a new year,
I hope we will all seriously consider the work we are called
to do here. So often we are kept so busy both physically and
mentally with everyday material problems that we lose sight
of the real reason for the existence of the Church. We are here
to minister to the souls of the men and women and boys and girls
in the Territory. We are here to build churches and buildings and
add numbers of baptized and confirmed persons to our rolls only

in so far as these things enable us to minister to the souls of men. "There is more than enough materialism in the world today. We of Christ's Church must set our eyes on higher things—on far-off goals. Certainly we must concern ourselves with practical matters, but surely we must beware lest these practical considerations blind us to our real purpose in serving the Cause of Christ.

"We can impress once again on our people that their bounden duty is to follow Christ and to worship God every Sunday in His Church. This is very important. The habit of regular worship has never been popular in Alaska. Our churches will never stand on their real strength until we have a band of loyal and devoted people who feel a greater loyalty to their Church than they do to their business. We must have men and women willing to take responsibility in the affairs of the church as their own concern— responsibility for serving and supporting the church in its every phase.

"Our task is not easy; our earthly resources are limited, and our workers are few. But we are not alone. If we trust in our own strength to do God's work we shall surely fail, but if we 'in all our ways acknowledge Him, He will direct our paths.' "

Ideally, missionary bishops would spend less time on personnel and financial needs, and concentrate instead on the spiritual opportunities. But Bill was living in the real world. He was still deeply concerned about the situation at the Fort Yukon Hospital. "Doctor Dunn is splendid—I cannot praise him too highly—but we have just two nurses there now, the maintenance man is so unwell that he cannot do much, and there are grave personality difficulties among the staff. The hospital is practically full of patients, and the government wants to add a twenty-four-bed tuberculosis ward at their expense, and pay us a per diem for the patients we care for. But we cannot accept the offer unless we can staff it, and now we cannot even staff the twenty-seven-bed ward we have."

While Bill's life was full of difficulties with people and budget funds, he was also flying commercially between a number of the missions and churches. He began a hectic schedule at the start of the year, returning to the Arctic Coast, then going down to Anchorage, up to Fort Yukon, and even to Nenana. He was troubled by the delays he encountered with public transportation, as well as the extremely high cost. "Every time I take a trip I am more convinced that I need an airplane of my own. I feel I can do twice the work in half the time and expense this way. Then maybe I might be able to see something of my family, too."

Bill took his first flying lesson on 1 March 1949 at the Alaska Flying School in Fairbanks. No shove in this direction was necessary, but Bill did have two good friends who prodded him on: Bill Peterson, the Gordons' Arctic Coast flying friend, and Fred Goodwin, another son of the Bishop of Virginia and also a Wien Airline pilot. Fred's cousin had wrecked a Piper Supercruiser, a three-place aircraft, and needed to sell it in order to pay repair costs. The price was $1,500, a bargain according to Fred, so Bill bought it with some funds given him by supporters in the States who were interested in "creative" ministry. (Money from the sale of *The Godspeed* went to the second plane.)

Bill was ready to solo after ten hours of instruction at Weeks Field (just a block and a half from his home). Now all he had to do to get a private license—and carry passengers—was to accumulate thirty-five flying hours, then prove his proficiency to a flight instructor. He did some flying around Fairbanks, practicing landings and takeoffs, and made a cross-country trip fifty miles down the Tanana River to Nenana to conduct a little business as well as get in some more time.

Easter was approaching, and never, to Bill's knowledge, had the congregation at St. John's in the Wilderness, at Allakaket, had an Easter Communion Service. He was determined, if the weather was any good at all, to make a visitation there. It was a rather risky cross-country flight for an inexperienced pilot, "but I was young, somewhat brash, and supremely confident. But not so much so that I did not consult with a pilot friend, Johnny James, whose parents operated a roadhouse at Hughes, a former gold camp on the Koyukuk River below Allakaket.

"Johnny told me he would be going back to Hughes in his own Stinson plane, and I could follow him that far. So, on a fine Saturday morning we took off and flew west to Tanana for refueling. Then he pointed out Bear Mountain, about 4,500 feet high and 100 miles to the west, suggested that if I aim so many degrees to its left, I would hit Hughes without difficulty. From Hughes all I had to do was follow the Koyukuk River seventy-five miles on north to Allakaket." Johnny James wanted to visit with friends, while Bill was in a rush, as usual.

So much for following someone else. The terrain Bill traversed was heavily wooded and hilly, devoid of human habitation. The river leg was easier. The Koyukuk and the Tanana are the two largest tributaries of the Yukon and the former extends far north of the Arctic circle, to its source in the Brooks Mountain range. Allakaket is a unique settlement 500 miles north of the junction of the two rivers, just above the Arctic Circle. The village is actually two—the Eskimo homes on the north bank and the Indian families on the south. Eskimos had come up the Kobuk River from the Arctic Coast many years earlier, and although traditional hostility existed between the two, the need to trade necessities brought them together, and over the years the peoples have grown into a close community. They have long shared the mission church, which in earlier days required two interpreters at every service.

Archdeacon Hudson Stuck, a British priest who was in charge of a church in Texas, when in his forties, left it to become a priest in the missionary District of Alaska. Archdeacon Stuck established the mission and school in Allakaket in the winter of 1906-07 after Bishop Rowe visited the gold mining camps just to the north, and determined that these people had been impacted by outside influence and needed help. The Bishop appealed to the church home office for a priest, but received no response. He turned next to the Brotherhood of St. Andrew, with the same result. At that point two women came to his rescue: Deaconess Clara Carter, who had been in nursing-missionary work a number of years already, and her companion, Miss Clara Heintz of California. (Yes, two Clara's!) Other women followed these two brave trail blazers, so that Allakaket was unique as the only mission ever staffed solely by women. They were paid little, including living expenses, and were almost 1,000 miles from Fairbanks by river, or between a five and ten-day trip by winter dog team.

The mission is noted, too, for its picturesque log church with a steeple and cross on top. A bell is inscribed with the words,

"O YE ICE AND SNOW BLESS YE THE LORD; PRAISE HIM AND MAGNIFY HIM FOREVER." The compound buildings sit high on a bluff above the river where Bill set down his plane, after just three hours and ten minutes of flying time from Fairbanks. Miss Amelia Hill, R.N. had arrived on the Koyukuk in 1922. She was the nurse for the entire length of the river, served as postmaster for Allakaket, and conducted regular services for St. John's in the Wilderness. Miss Bessie Kay arrived in 1933 to teach school and help with other village activities, including tagging furs during trapping season. In summertime they had an immense vegetable garden, its produce feeding everyone for months. The people called the ladies "Miss" and they also used this formal title between themselves for the sixteen years they lived together.

Bill discovered that half of the village was down with the flu, but they had a happy and moving Easter Communion Service the next day and he baptized several children. Then he visited twelve homes where the people were too sick to come to church, and walked across the frozen river ice to the Eskimo families. An elderly woman said something in the Koyukon language. The interpreter laughed and translated for Bill: "She said you are not too lazy to get around." It was a very affirming and warming tribute, and more than made up for the difficulties and risks of making that first cross country flight.

Three months later, Bill obtained his pilot's license. Now he was qualified to carry passengers, with a grand total of about forty flying hours to his credit. On the following day he took off on his annual visitation to the missions centering around Fort Yukon. Flying northeast over the wooded hills behind Fairbanks (only in Alaska would a 5,000-foot-high range be called hills to distinguish them from our 15 to 20,000-foot-high mountains), he easily found the largest native village in Alaska on the banks of the Yukon River at its most northerly point. The 300-mile-wide basin surrounding Fort Yukon looks like a gigantic pizza pan: flat, uniform in many respects, including the height of the dense stands of spruce trees. The one outstanding feature is the wide river, cluttered with sand bars, meandering aimlessly between high banks the entire distance. Winter temperatures on this Interior plain can easily drop to sixty or seventy degrees below zero, but summers are hot, with tomatoes and other warm-weather vegetables blooming in eighty to ninety degree heat.

The outpost was established by the Hudson Bay Company, a complete, well-built post for Canadian soldiers and traders in 1847, when the Russians still owned Alaska. The United States then usurped Fort Yukon after its purchase of Alaska, and the Episcopal Church inherited the mission work begun by the Canadian Anglican Church in 1862. Anglican Archdeacon Robert McDonald had translated the Bible, the Anglican Book of Common Prayer, the Hymnal and other devotional literature into Takudh, the Canadian dialect of the native tongue. But, since language varies greatly between the Indian tribes, these translations in Fort Yukon were of no use to missions farther down the river.

When Bishop Rowe reached Fort Yukon in 1898, he was most impressed with the depth of the Christian faith among the Indian people. He laid groundwork for building a hospital there, as he had done in seven other camps and towns, and brought Archdeacon Stuck to run the mission.

Stuck, who later led the first expedition to the top of Mount McKinley, made regular visits to other villages within a 1,000 mile radius, either by boat in summertime or by dog team in the winter. He was ably assisted by a group of strong native lay readers, living evidence of the strength of the legacy left by the Anglicans. Two men were ordained deacons: William Loola in 1903 and Albert Tritt in 1925.

On Bill's visit to Fort Yukon, he held services at St. Stephen's Church, a large log building with an organ and electricity, all a gift from a New York Womens' Auxiliary. The altar hangings are of white moose hide with a multicolored floral design in beadwork, made by the village women in thanksgiving for the end of World War I. Next Bill visited the hospital, a two-story log structure with a modern solarium wing for TB patients, beds for twenty-eight patients, X-ray equipment, an operating room, and a clinic. Its electrical plant served the other mission buildings as well.

This entire compound had come close to being wiped out in a severe flood during spring breakup that year, a natural disaster that often hits villages built on river banks. When the ice is late in going out and the river is higher and swifter than normal, the water carries massive ice cakes along with it as it overflows into the settlements. At Fort Yukon, huge chunks of ice up to seven feet thick and thirty feet square swept through on 13 May, destroying twenty cabins and damaging all the others. Water, two feet deep at ground floor level, knocked out the hospital generator, almost destroyed the organ, and damaged the beautiful altar hanging. All the hospital patients were moved to the second floor, while the villagers fled to the one small hill east of town, where the Air Force and Red Cross dropped them tents, blankets, and food. At the time of Bill's visit three months later, life was back to normal, with few signs remaining of the disaster. It had taken most of the summer to remove mountains of mud and build twenty-three new homes, this time farther back from the bluff.

With passenger Wilfred "Shorty" Files, priest-in-charge of Fort Yukon, Bill quickly made the rounds of the nearby villages that had once been so hard to reach. He flew almost 800 miles in four days, using fifty-five gallons of gas. By boat it would have taken him two weeks, and 400 gallons of gas.

Bill was the first bishop in the history of the Episcopal Church to use an airplane in regular visitations, and the National Church had a lot of reservations about small plane flying. In fact, at one point the Presiding Bishop wrote him to encourage him to give up flying because it was too risky. Bill wrote back, saying that if he would persuade the Bishop of New York to travel by Greyhound Bus instead of driving his own car, then he would consider giving up flying. He heard nothing further. Bishop Bentley, however, sent a letter of approval and support, ending it with the comment, "Keep an angel on your wing."

Bill's enthusiasm was tested during his first full winter of flying. Battling thirty to sixty degree below zero temperatures while refueling—heating the engine with a plumber's firepot, removing and warming the oil—all for only four hours of daylight in which to fly did nothing to dampen his spirits. At Christmas time he planned to cover as many unmanned missions as possible. He wrote his mother: "I will leave Fairbanks on the morning of 26 December and fly to Tanana for a Christmas Communion. On the 27th I'll go on to Rampart, then Minto, Steven's Village and

Allakaket—a day at each place. All this depends on the weather, and there is a fair chance that extreme cold or snow will keep me grounded some of the time. Shirley is almost wishing for bad weather and I'm tempted to wish likewise—I do want to be here for her birthday—but I realize how much a service will mean at Christmas to our Indian people.''

Surviving the winter without problems, Bill took a bold step: selling the little Supercruiser, and with funds from *The Godspeed,* he purchased a new Piper Pacer (7360 Kilo). It was a faster plane, which could accommodate four people, although at times, especially during winter when passengers wore parkas, Bill claims "It was a friendly fit, and I expected to see our outlines on the doors outside.''

With great self-confidence, many more hours of flying experience, and a faster plane, a number of "incidents" began, ranging from forced landings to a crash. Bill's first accident occurred when he set out to visit his two sisters after Christmas in 1952. Almeria and Mary Irwin Gordon had come north to spend a year serving at empty mission posts, and were winding up their stay on the Lower Middle Yukon, where the church had missions at the three remote Indian villages of Anvik, Shageluk, and Holikachuk (later renamed Grayling when the site was moved).

"The weather turned favorable on New Year's Day, so I took off from Fairbanks and flew southwest to McGrath on the Kuskokwim River and refueled. The next 150 miles would take me across the McGrath Mountains into the Yukon Valley and to Anvik. I had no way of knowing what the weather was like ahead. I found the area covered with patchy low fog, and by the time I was within thirty miles of Anvik, it was solid overcast. I had to start back, but about fifteen minutes later, I spotted a little hill poking up through the clouds, some breaks along its side, and I could see a river down below which I knew was either the Innoko or a slough running from the Yukon into the Innoko, near the village of Holikachuk. So I let down through a hole, planning to fly along the river. Unfortunately, the fog was much lower than I had anticipated, and it was impossible to follow the tight bends. So I landed on the ice and taxied a while, looking for some familiar landmark. I had been this way twice by boat, but it looked different with the frozen river and snow-covered landscape. As I was taxiing around a curve, I came to some open water at the entrance of a small stream. There was no way I could stop, so I kicked the plane rudder sideways, but it slipped into that hole and broke the left ski in half.

"There I was. It was about zero degrees, not terribly cold, but not exactly warm either. And I wasn't at all sure of my location. Nobody knew my whereabouts since I could not file a flight plan and it would be some days before anybody looked for me because Shirley would assume I was in Anvik and my sisters would assume I was still delayed by weather.

"I decided to walk down the river a ways to see if I could spot any familiar landmark, but after going about a mile, I decided it would be wiser to stay near the plane where I had a sleeping bag and some emergency food rations.

"Then I thought about my radio—a long shot at best, since the only frequency I had was for airport towers and FAA stations, and the nearest facility was 125 miles away, across the mountains at McGrath. Its range was about twenty-five miles, and it wasn't any frequency that local people would normally listen to.

"Still, I decided to give it a try. I radioed, 'This is Bishop Gordon, and I am down on the Innoko River somewhere near Holikachuk, either above or below the village.' I added a description of the terrain, realizing there was about 1 to 10,000 chance that anybody would hear me.

"About two hours later, just as it was beginning to get dark, I heard a dog bark and then a man's voice. I let out a yell and somebody called back. In a few minutes, a friend of mine from Holikachuk, Walter Maillelle, came over the river bank with his dog team. I thought he was coming in from his trapping camp, and I asked him if he could take me into the village. He said, 'Sure, that's why I'm here. I'm out here looking for you.' Then he told me that everybody in the village was gathered in the *kashim* (the community hall) for a New Year's Day feast and dance except Willie Galilie, who was home because his wife was very sick. He was fooling around with his radio, just switching the dial at random. All of a sudden he heard the word Holikachuk, and he listened and he heard my message. Within fifteen minutes, ten dog teams were out ranging up and down the river, and Walter had come right to where I was, five miles above the village."

Bill enjoyed the village feast before hitching another ride to Anvik to visit his sisters, then returning to Fairbanks to seek help in retrieving his downed plane. He prevailed on Gordon Charlton, the newly-arrived young priest at the Fairbanks church, and a flyer himself. They flew in Bill's new Cessna 170, now ready to fly after having a more powerful engine installed.

The two pilots hit bad weather, a snow storm this time, but Charlton was able to land on the river ice, next to Bill's crippled plane. Bill put the new ski and a strut on quickly, and then took off following the crooked little slough below the level of the high banks and tall trees until he gained enough speed to climb higher. They met back at Holikachuk and planned to fly to Anvik in the two planes, but the weather was bad again. Bill told Charlton, "It's all right, you just follow me," and he took off.

"I followed him," Gordon, now a bishop in Texas, says, "but he was already out of sight by the time I was in the air. He just figured I was behind him and didn't wait to be sure. So I went back, because I wasn't about to fly in that poor weather alone. Bill did get terribly impatient and he pushed weather badly. He wasn't going to be weathered in if he could avoid it. He was always looking ahead to his next plans, and weather was a major complication."

Intimate knowledge of the terrain, after only four years of flying and boating, saved Bill's life this time, as it was to over and over in the years ahead. Seldom consulting his maps, he was not much of a navigator. He followed rivers and mountains. Bill has been known to say, "Well, my IFR [Instrument Flight Rules] is 'I Fly the River.' " Bill's second daughter, Becky, who was born shortly after this episode, says today, "I was really shocked, when I learned to fly, to discover that you are supposed to use maps, keep a record of your mileage and fuel consumption."

Shirley flew with Bill on one of his early trips to the Arctic Coast. Bill says, "We knew that the weather in Kotzebue might deteriorate. I figured I could get across most of the Interior, since the weather seemed to be good in between. We flew for about two and one-half hours over high scattered clouds until the cloud deck began to thicken, so I let down and started following a little winding river. The visibility got worse and worse until we were flying into a real whiteout. Suddenly Shirley said, "I think I see a rotating beacon!"

"I told her, 'You're crazy—the nearest rotating beacon is in Kotzebue, and we must be at least seventy-five or eighty miles away.' I knew we were coming up on Selawik lake, just this side of the coast—a large, white expanse that I could not possibly cross without any dark references for visibility. At that point it was like flying inside a pail of milk. Shirley kept insisting that she saw the occasional flash of a beacon. So I turned toward it and there, to my amazement, was the village of Selawik with a rotating beacon off the end of their airfield. The visibility was half a mile or less, and I very thankfully landed there. We discovered that the light had been installed just two months earlier."

The Gordons' Arctic Coast friends always looked forward to their flying visits. Shirley went along whenever there was room in the plane and she could leave the children, which was seldom. In his sermons, Bill often tells of giving Milton Swan his first airplane ride. "I was going from Kivalina to Noatak and I needed somebody to interpret for me in Noatak, so I asked Milton if he would go with me. He somewhat reluctantly said that maybe he would, but he obviously had doubts. And so I said to him, 'Milton, you're a man of great faith. You believe you're in the Lord's hands. And you are also the kind of Christian who is ready to go whenever the Lord decides your time has come.' "

Milton's reply was, "Well, Bishop, suppose we get up over those mountains between here and Noatak, and the Lord decides your time has come. How am I going to get down?"

Bill had many close calls when he challenged the treacherous Arctic Coast weather, but his first plane crash occurred on a sunny day. He was flying two visitors from the National Church on a survey of the Missionary District work. It was midsummer and he elected to start them out in his former home territory. For many years the standard practice was to refuel planes from fifty-gallon barrels of gasoline. Since water often accumulated in the drums, pilots routinely used a chamois cloth in their funnel as a filter. Bill had accidentally left his behind at their previous stop.

"So I borrowed a funnel and chamois skin from Wien Airlines. Then we took off from the end of the runway, and just after we got in the air, I turned to pass out sandwiches to my two passengers. At that moment, the engine sputtered and quit. We were about 300 feet in the air, and in a tight turn heading north towards Point Hope. I had no option, since I was too low and did not have enough air speed to maneuver in any direction, so I kept turning, heading back toward the end of the cross runway. I almost made it, but we stalled out and ended up in a ditch. The plane flipped over on its back and right into the Kotzebue Friends' Graveyard.

"I was suspended upside down in my seatbelt, but I was able to get out with my passengers and no one was really injured. One of the men had a cut across the top of his head where he had hit the button on the dome light in the ceiling. [It bled profusely and he was taken to the Kotzebue hospital for stitches.]

"The plane was badly damaged, but we were able to right it and push it up to the edge of the airfield where I checked the gas line and found it full of water. Further inspection revealed about a gallon of water in the tanks. I checked the funnel I had used and discovered it had been left out in the rain, so the chamois was soaking wet and naturally would allow water to go on through."

On another occasion, Bill was flying a planeload of women from a meeting in Kotzebue back to Fairbanks. The weather was poor and he flew on top of a cloud deck, hitting the Yukon River just past Galena. "I thought I had it made but a southwest flow of air was blowing clouds in over the river, and I finally had to drop down to about fifty feet off the ice in very limited visibility. Then the windshield began to ice up and I had to turn up the cabin heat to top volume to try to melt enough so I could see. I had to follow every bend of the river closely, and although I knew it well, it was still a tricky operation. I finally reached Tanana, and while I was refueling, a small Army plane came in, headed in the direction I had just come. The pilot asked the FAA about weather and they suggested he talk to me, that I had just come through. The pilot replied, 'You mean the preacher? Well, if he can get through, I sure can.' So he took off. Twenty.minutes later he called the FAA to say he was in an impossible situation and would have to turn back. He added, 'that preacher must have had a copilot!' "

On another flight returning from Kotzebue in summertime, Bill did not get through. "I was very frustrated and edgy, anxious to get back to Fairbanks. The weather wasn't good, but I decided to try anyway, flying over the Selawik Hills toward the Kobuk River where I might stay overnight at one of those villages if necessary. But the weather got worse and I was being forced lower and lower onto the hills. I realized also that I had waited too long to turn back. The only wise thing was to find some place to land, knowing that I was in tundra area—marshy hummocks— and the plane was not likely to stay upright when I sat down.

"I picked out a low hill, lined up into the wind, and landed. The plane rolled about a hundred feet and then went up on its nose and over on its back. The turning over was very gentle and I was not hurt at all. When I crawled out, I noticed that smoke was coming out from under the cowling and that alarmed me a little, since the gasoline was also pouring out from the wings. I looked into the engine and found that the battery had fallen out of its box and was being shorted out. There was no time to disengage it, so I found a pair of wire cutters and cut the ground wire.

"It was rainy and foggy, I was at least a hundred miles from Kotzebue and I wasn't on a flight plan since I wasn't sure where I was going to end up that night. So, I might be there for some time to come. I got back into the upside down airplane, found my sleeping bag, and spent the rest of the night asleep on the ceiling. The next morning the weather was better, so I spliced the ground wire back onto the battery and then stretched out the trailing antenna to my T30 radio (a newer, much improved model) to try to raise somebody. I sent out a mayday call for over an hour, and then, wonderfully, I heard Kotzebue. I told them my predicament and estimated just exactly where I was. I asked that they find somebody to come pick me up, suggesting a lake about three miles away that could handle a float plane.

Four hours later a Coast and Geodetic Survey float plane arrived, landing on the lake below me. Back in Kotzebue, I made arrangements with a bush pilot friend to return to the site for me, taking some Eskimo men to right the plane and tie it down. Obviously, it was going to have to remain there until winter freeze up, when I could put it on skis and fly it out."

For Bill, the only difficult part of the whole experience was encountering, on the Wien flight between Kotzebue and Fairbanks, the same stewardess who was on board after his accident in the graveyard. Her first comment was, "Do I have to do this for you every year?"

This time Bill prevailed on another priest to help him recover his plane. Norman Elliott was a thin, intellectual young man who was more at home with books than with airplanes or wilderness life. However, Bill asked him to take flying lessons while Norman was temporarily serving at the Anchorage church and he went north to Fairbanks with the ink not yet dry on his license. He inherited the yellow Piper Pacer (7360 Kilo) from Gordon Charlton, and following an erratic take-off from a village strip, causing Bill and several priests to dive into nearby bushes, Norman's plane was dubbed "the drunken canary."

Norman recalls overloading the four-place plane with a propeller, two skis, a battery, tool pack, and camping gear. Bill was never concerned with weight—although he did keep the balance in mind—if there was room, it would go.

Bill did the flying, landing on the frozen lake near the downed airplane. Then he took right off through the tundra, climbing the steep hill, the propeller strapped to his back and pulling a ski. "He just left me," Norman recalls, "with the tool pack on my back, the heavy battery, and a ski. I staggered up—I didn't know where he had gone—except somewhere above me. I tried putting the battery on the ski, but it kept sliding off. I would take ten steps, then bend over to try to catch my breath, then take ten more. When I reached the plane, the Bishop said, 'Where have you been?' I replied, 'If I'd been in my right mind I'd be on furlough instead of here.'

"We found we didn't need the propeller; the one on the plane wasn't that badly damaged. And we didn't need the skis, because there was only a thin layer of hard-packed snow on the windy hilltop. So, he quickly took off and flew his plane down to the lake, while I walked back—he didn't want my extra weight on board.

"When I finally returned, he had already put the tent up, fastening a rope to a bush, and had started to cook supper on his gasoline stove—a mash-like mixture of hot dogs, beans, and something else. But it was so windy, he decided to move the stove inside the tent. Then, he asked me to unzip the door, as it was getting stuffy inside, and the tent collapsed on our heads. We spent the night that way.

"The next day, just before the Bishop took off at first light, he said, 'Don't land on the river in front of Kobuk. Land on the lake behind it.' I had no idea where we were, and wasn't at all sure where we were going. All I knew was that if I flew north, I would hit the Kobuk River. My plan was to follow him, and I took off just a minute or two behind him. But I never saw him again. Finally I came to the river, and I saw tracks on it in front of a village, where planes had landed before. But there was the lake just behind it too, and remembering the Bishop's last words, I landed on the lake. The wind was blowing hard, but I finally got the plane in close to the shore, got out and staggered through snow up to my hips toward a group of villagers waiting. I said, 'Kobuk?' They replied, 'No, Shungnak. Kobuk twelve miles up the river.'

"So I got back in the plane, but every time I tried to taxi out to the middle of the lake, the plane would weather cock in that fierce wind and be blown right back into the bank. Finally I hit on the brilliant idea of starting the plane, then getting out and letting it move slowly while I steered it. Just as I got to the tail, the plane started to move. So, I clung to the fuselage, slowly working my way back to the open door. Somehow I was able to reach inside and pull the throttle back, stopping the plane. Just then the Bishop landed. Again, the famous words, 'where have you been?' And then, 'What are you doing here?' "

Norman was on a visit to Eagle with Bill the winter of 1951-52, and as Norman puts it, "struggled through waist-deep snowdrifts to an empty cabin on the trail." Once they managed to light a gas lamp, they saw a cot against one wall, and a wolf skin on the floor. Norman records in verse:

"Bless my mitre," said the bishop,
"Here's a pretty how-de-do,
For yon cot, upon my crozier,
Is not big enough for two!"

"True my lord," replied the deacon
As he dropped from off his back
All the heavy load he carried—
Both his and the bishop's pack.

The poem goes on with a lengthy discussion as to who will
get the cot, and who is left the rug. Norman concludes that the
Bishop decides to toss a silver dollar:

Skillfully the bishop tossed the dollar
which he'd taken from his poke;
Caught it in his hand, concealed it.
"Tails," the deacon cried. The bishop looked—
And then he spoke!

All night long the peace was shattered
by the bishop's blissful snore;
while the deacon tossed and tumbled
On the wolf-skin on the floor.

Bill's retort to Norman's account is that he won fairly, and,
besides, the wolf skin was a much more comfortable spot anyway.

This poem of Norman's, and his many stories, were repeated
whenever the clergy of the District gathered over the years. And
others competed to provide their own anecdotes; humor which
poked fun at their autocratic boss. And Bill had a good repertoire
of amusing tales about his subordinates with which to retort.

Bill needed all the humor from any source, because the early
1950s were years of great struggles and almost superhuman effort
on his part to garner the human and financial resources the
Missionary District so badly needed. His many former contacts
in Outside Womens' Auxiliaries and the large number of sub-
scribers to the *Alaskan Churchman,* which he insisted on editing
himself, were valuable supports for his efforts. So, too, was a film,

Light of the North, part of a series of twelve missionary movies made by the National Church in 1951. Basically the story of Bill and his flying and work among the villages, it was released in 1952 and attracted a large audience (especially since it was also shown on television). Many of the people who later came north to work in the District say the film piqued their interest. Another benefit was its effect on the Episcopal Church Womens' organization meeting at the 1952 General Convention. Each year they raised thousands of dollars from Thank Offering blue boxes, filled with pennies by Episcopal women all over the country. Many women at the meeting were shocked by the small size of the plane Bill was flying, and the dimensions of his work. So the budget that year was increased to include $8,000 to buy a new airplane for him. En route home, Bill picked up a brand new four-place Cessna 170, named appropriately *The Blue Box,* a replica of each woman's blue box painted on its side.

Other than trips to conventions, furloughs every three years consisted of one week with each family, one week at the beach in North Carolina, and then speaking engagements, as many as he could fit in, all over the country. He included seminaries and universities, churches and womens' groups; wherever he was asked, he would go. He became a much-sought after speaker, telling stories of his travels in the Far North and of the people living there. This hard work slowly began to pay off. His first recruits were seminarians and college students, young people going north to fill vacant posts for the summers or to provide Bible teaching in return for a great adventure. Many went back often, some even stayed. In fact, Bill was frequently accused by his bachelor clergymen of recruiting young women Bible School teachers in order to provide suitable marriage partners.

Students graduating from seminary began to respond to his persuasive salesmanship, too, and Gordon Charlton and Norman Elliott were among the first of many to come north to work for Bill. So was Robert Reid, who went to Nenana in 1948, and Howard Laycock to Point Hope two years later.

Bill was on a speaking tour when he got a telephone call from his secretary in Fairbanks telling him that Robert Reid, the first person he had ever ordained, had been drowned along with

Enoch Tooyok, the son of Peel Tooyok, a student at St. Mark's, and Teddy Muller, the fifteen-year-old son of the maintenance man at the Mission. They, along with another student, Thomas Tuzroyluk, had set out on a moose hunting trip down the Tanana River to the Kantishna River. They had a heavily loaded boat and when they turned across the swift current of the Tanana, a stiff breeze was blowing cross-river, making some waves. Just about that time, the outboard motor on the boat quit. This made the bow of the boat drop quickly and the water washed over it, swamping and then quickly sinking it in the silt-filled water. They all had on heavy clothing and boots or shoepacks. Thomas Tuzroyluk managed to slip off his rubber boots, and as he came to the surface, he found a piece of driftwood that helped him get to shore. No trace was ever found of Bob Reid and the two other boys, or the boat.

Thomas, an Eskimo boy from the Arctic Coast with not much experience in rivers or woody country, found himself about twenty miles upriver from the nearest habitation at Manley Hot Springs. With nothing but his wet clothes, he remained by the shoreline all night long. Then he walked up the Kantishna until he found an old fish camp and a small birch bark canoe, a vessel with which he was not familiar at all. He paddled back to the Tanana River, carefully searching both banks, but no trace of anyone was found, only two sleeping bags and a pair of shoe-packs. After paddling all day, Thomas finally reached Manley Hot Springs where he reported the tragedy.

On Bill's 1952 furlough, he had a similar call. This time the Reverend Howard Laycock, the priest at Point Hope, had been killed with three others, two adults and a child from the village, when he stalled his small plane in a turn in heavy fog and crashed on the sandspit at Point Hope. Arrangements had already been made to ship his body home to Springfield, Pennsylvania. Bill's friends, Bill Peterson and Shorty Files had helped to take care of this tragic situation. Bill flew from South Carolina to Pennsylvania to spend some time with Howard's widow and to officiate at the funeral.

These two deaths, as well as the fire at the Nenana School and the flood at Fort Yukon, were a constant reminder to Bill that his work and the lives of those who served under him were always prey to the awesome, destructive force of a harsh, cruel and unforgiving environment. Even his beloved airplane, the new joy of his life, was particularly subject to the evil whims of the Arctic wilderness.

Chapter 6

"Watch ye therefore: for ye know not when the master of the house cometh..."

One of Bill's goals as he moved into the mid-1950s, buoyed by the initial success of his recruitment and fund raising efforts, was to fill each of the twenty-seven missions with a seminary-trained resident priest. Thoughts of lay and native ministry roles that were planted at Point Hope remained dormant at this stage in his aspirations. Growing into an energetic, charismatic, and confident leader as the pieces began to fit into his overall plan, he pushed even harder, impatient when ensnared by details. As always, he was a decisive man of action, leaving behind a trail of anger and hurt feelings liberally mixed with admiration and hero worship.

A missionary bishop was in a powerful position. He had total charge of his District, responsible only to the National Church, which in Bill's case was far away and fairly out of touch. Bill thought of himself as a bishop in every sense of that authority, but he never considered himself "holier than thou." He never became pompous, nor was he on an ego trip seeking praise and glory.

Regardless, this enormous power was his, and Bill never let anyone forget that it was "my way." Because he had taken on an almost impossible job of high visibility at a very early age, Bill felt heavy pressure to run the Church in Alaska correctly. His work schedule taxed him to the limit, causing irritability and impatience, giving him little time to relax and be human, and pushing him into an unbending stand against any "High Church" practices, as well as strong opposition to gambling and alcohol.

On the latter two issues he never relented, perhaps because of his fundamentalist upbringing. "High Church" practices, which upset him considerably, included the reference to priests as "Father," the congregation's standing as the priest came up and down the aisle, certain forms of chants, and the practice of TARP (a Catholic ritual, meaning "Take Ablutions to the Right Place," of bringing order to the Communion elements before the conclusion of the service). Again, his background at home and at Virginia Seminary were the strong influences but although most of his early recruits came from the same school, later priests brought in "High Church" practices and battles ensued.

The strong leadership qualities that had been growing since the days of his presidency of the Young Peoples Service League came to the forefront as Bill now developed a team of priests and volunteers. In spite of his heavy hand on rules and policies, he placed full confidence in all new recruits, trusting them completely as he left them in isolated outposts. This attitude encouraged the new workers to risk stepping out, to grow beyond their known capabilities. His innate optimism was contagious. He never asked anyone to do what he himself could not handle, and his physical strength and courage and his endless hard work could hardly be matched by any of his young men. He inspired fear and awe, great respect and deep love, and some strong dislike.

Bill used various methods of recruiting, as attested to by the men and women he lured north. He was among the first missionary bishops to give summer jobs to college students and young seminarians. Dale Sarles and Al Reiners were two among the bachelor clergymen who came as volunteer workers and were sold on the Far North before graduation; going back was a foregone conclusion.

Don Hart, a New Englander with dreams of working among Indian people in nearby Canada, recalls that he and his wife received a call from Bill while he was visiting Don's seminary. "He was holding court," Don, now Bishop of Hawaii, recalls. "I was all dressed up in my Boston clothes, and here he was in his boots, feet up on the coffee table. We spent a fascinating two hours while he described Alaska, and where he would like us to go. He treated me as important to his work, the only one who could deal with a particularly difficult village. And here I came from a New England Diocese where the bishop didn't even know my name!"

Tom Cleveland wanted to go to Alaska while still in seminary and no persuasion was needed, but his wife, Charlotte, another Easterner, had many misgivings. She recalls, "when Tom said I had to meet the Bishop of Alaska, my response was negative. I had grown up with bishops in New Jersey (her father was a clergyman and headmaster at Groton School), and they were all big, old, and bald, and patted me on the head. Also, we had just had our first baby ten days earlier and it meant getting a babysitter.

"I went, but it was a shock to walk into the room and see a southern Greek god slouched on the couch, his feet on the table. I was terrified of going so far from home, and when he asked me what I wanted to know about Alaska, I could barely get the words out, which is strange for me. I finally asked him something stupid, like 'how cold does it get?' He told us to think about it, and write him a letter. It took us two more years (and another child) to get there, but there was never any doubt in our minds about going after meeting him."

Gordon Charlton was already assistant rector in a Houston church when Bill wooed him north. His wife's straightforward response was, "No. Anywhere but Alaska." She reversed herself when Bill wrote offering the position at the Fairbanks church, and she says she was teased that a very handsome, persuasive man could change her mind so easily.

Another young wife, who was pregnant at the time, could not be persuaded that easily. When Rick Draper told Anne that Bishop Gordon was coming to the Seminary looking for recruits, she replied, "I'm not going to Alaska. I'm going back to North Carolina. I had known about Bishop Gordon all my life—he was kind of a folk hero to the people of our parish, but I was not about to go to Alaska. Then he dropped by our apartment, and I said right off, 'You just got to know that I really don't mind roughing it, but there's no way I can tote honey buckets and have a less-than-one year old. And you have to know I'm not going to boil water every time I wipe my baby's face, either. So there's just no way in the world we could go to Alaska.' He laughed, and told us to think it over. I was miserable for the next three days because I knew Rick wanted to go in the worst way. I finally gave in. If we were ever going to go to Alaska, I guess we'd go up right then, or I'll get swallowed by a whale like Jonah and be spit up on the shore.''

Judy and Curtis Edwards needed no persuasion. All through seminary they talked of little else than going on to work in Alaska, and he put airplane sectional maps of the entire Territory all over the walls of their small apartment. Curtis wrote Bill to apply for a job in his senior year. Both their families were deeply unhappy over the young couple's decision, anxious for them to remain at a Texas church where the three grandchildren would be close. Mothers-in-law were an obstacle to Bill's recruitment efforts, as were some men who were concerned for their wives moving to such an alien, wilderness environment.

When these and many other recruits first arrived in Alaska, they discovered that Bill's charisma could be overshadowed by the autocratic, less-than-human side of his character. Dick Clarke, a young bachelor who loved camping and was determined to move as far away from Massachusetts as possible, had not met Bill prior to going north. He drove all the way from the East Coast, up the rugged Alaska Highway, and finally reached Fairbanks late one August evening. He found the District office, but no one was in sight. "I poked around, glanced in one door and saw what I thought was Bishop Gordon sitting at his desk, signing letters. I walked in and said, 'Hi, you must be Bishop Gordon. I'm Dick Clarke.' He replied, 'I know, and you're three days late!'

"Then I spent two days and nights in the hostel, with no more signs of the Bishop. His secretary asked me for dinner the second evening, and just as we were sitting down, the phone rang. It was for me—the Bishop. The first thing he said was 'Are you doing anything tonight?' I thought he might invite me out to visit, or to see the town, so I said I had no plans at all. Then came the bombshell: 'Can you be ready to leave in thirty minutes because I have a chance to fly you down to the Lower [Middle] Yukon?' I rushed to get my things together and we took off in the middle of the night [in August it was light twenty-four hours a day].

"We were headed for the mission at Holikachuk on the Lower [Middle] Yukon, but there was no place for a plane on wheels to land in the summer, so the Bishop took us to a sand bar across the river from nearby Anvik, where Dale Sarles was stationed. First the Bishop buzzed the mission house to wake up Dale—it was about three or four A.M.—and then we sat on the sand bar. I was slowly sinking into the wet sand; there was a light drizzle, and the mosquitoes were out en masse. The Bishop began to hem and haw, and rant and rave a little bit. And finally a boat came from the village. As Dale approached, the Bishop greeted him by saying, 'Mr. Sarles, I have a text for you—watch ye for you know not when the master of the house is coming' [Mark 13:35]. Then he dropped all my things on the sand bar and took off. I was on my own."

Another young couple shared the same experience, only they were dumped off at a small village airstrip, the Bishop taking off without even walking them to the mission house or introducing them to villagers. Both the Cleveland and Hart families were left in similar fashion, although Don recalls that Bill came into their village to collect Bible School students and before he left, he said a prayer with them. "I had a good feeling of his sense of caring for us," Don says, "that we were a part of a team. But then he was off, and we didn't see him again until two or three months later."

Al Reiners reminisces, "Three of us seminarians from Virginia arrived in June. We had seen the film about Alaska, and the Bishop had written to us that we would each be assigned to a village. I was hoping for one along a river, with the tall pine trees, picturesque log cabins. We were all kidding about who was going to have to go up to cold Eskimo land and get all the blubber. The Bishop greeted us at the airplane and said, 'Al, you'll be going right to Kotzebue with that bush pilot across the field.' The other two guys nudged each other and whispered, 'He gets the blubber!'

"My first couple of weeks in Kotzebue were just the absolute pits. The Bishop had rented a two-room cabin for me, which contained a table and two chairs. That was it. I had a sleeping bag and I borrowed an Army cot from the bush pilot. But there was no stove, no way to cook. It was very depressing. Also cold, and I was wearing a thin leather jacket.

"The Bishop had given me a hundred dollars for expenses, and said to write his secretary if I needed more. The trust he put in me was incredible—he gave me a great sense of responsibility, of confidence. If this man, on just the little bit he knows about me, trusts me that much, well, by golly, I'm going to live up to it. So, after a week of feeling sorry for myself, I just threw myself into work.

"Before I left Fairbanks, the Bishop told me three things about going to Kotzebue: have three services a week—Sunday morning, Sunday evening, and on an evening convenient to the people during the week. Two, be with the people, and third, to play with the children. I believe now that this is the best outline of ministry I've ever heard and I've been working on that basis ever since. Everything else one does is just trimming."

Judy and Curtis Edwards were more fortunate. After Bill flew them to their new home in Tanana, he spent the night with them in order to fly the priest being replaced back to Fairbanks the following morning. Judy did not have to contend with a sand bar arrival, but there was the Yukon River; broad, silty, flowing swiftly beneath a high bank less than fifty feet from their log house. Her five- and three-year-old daughters were off and playing along the bluff with young Indian friends within hours of their arrival (the youngest, Curtis III, was only a year old at the time). Judy, who claims she was an immature twenty-six-year-old was terrified. "I'd never seen a river bigger than one about two feet wide. I was so nervous about the children, I asked the Bishop how to deal with their safety that close to the water. He replied, 'You just teach them,' which wasn't any help at all!" "In retrospect," Judy adds, "I think he kept closer tabs on us, hopping in often that first year. I think he sensed that at any moment I might start paddling for Texas. You better keep your eye on this one, she doesn't look secure!"

The "dumping off" stories of these young people became legends over the years, with new ones added almost as frequently as someone arrived. Bill's words were the same, no matter what the situation: "The village is over there. Don't do anything for the people that they can do for themselves." Someone, like Judy, occasionally summoned the courage to ask a question. Usually it was, "But how do I run the Coleman lantern?" or "What about the stove—the wood?" Bill's inevitable reply was, : "Go ask one of the people in the village—it's the best way to start meeting them." One young man, fresh from seminary and city life, claimed he brought lots of books to read in the solitude he expected, but he never got beyond the Bible and the manual on his stove.

A former member of the National Church Overseas Department says he tried to persuade Bill to provide some indoctrination, but giving him advice was like dealing with a headstrong teenager who had already made up his mind. Bill's method worked "in many cases," the church executive says. "The men and women were able to move into such a situation, identify with the local people, and learn on their own rapidly, but painfully. Some just never did at all."

Joanne Reiners, who had worked for Bishop Bentley before marrying Al and going to Kotzebue, went to see Mrs. Bentley for advice before she left. "I asked Elvira if she had any words of wisdom for a young bride going to Alaska, and she replied no, she had no words of advice. But she did say, 'I cried when I left home, and I cried when I left Alaska, and I cried a lot in between.' It was not many months later when I knew for myself that what she said was true."

Today, Bill staunchly defends his policy. "There is no way that you can prepare anybody for living in a remote native village before he or she gets there. Through indoctrination you'd get a lot of preconceived notions that are inaccurate—no matter how perceptive a teacher is. I would always follow these new people up after a short period of time—two or three weeks [most reported it was at least two months]. Actually, I had little choice— who would train them? We had no money to hire anyone and I would have to leave them because I didn't have a few days or a week to hold their hands. Often I put them someplace where there was another priest nearby."

Rick Draper, who arrived among a later group, and was from the deep South, flew directly to Kotzebue. He was told that his predecessor was still there and would fill him in on everything.

"I was groggy from jet lag," he said. "We were met by the wife because her husband was weathered in at Point Hope. She talked nonstop for the next three days about the Bible Class books, the altar linens, a sick Eskimo woman in the hospital, the idiosyncracies of their washing machine—it was all one big blur. Then he came back and gave me a twenty-four-hour monologue on all the things I had to remember. He said, as we drove them to the airfield, 'I forgot—tomorrow night you have a healing service at seven-thirty, P.M.' I had never conducted one. Then, as he boarded the plane, he finished with, 'I shouldn't tell you this, but this has been the worst two years of my twenty-year ministry in Alaska!' "

"So," Bill adds thoughtfully, "not as many of them got quite so dumped. Some of them got kind of dumped. They turned out pretty well, most of them. Bishop Bentley sure dumped me at Point Hope! And I was much more isolated in terms of mail or radio. Most of what I learned about Alaska, I learned by doing."

Bill believed strongly that in order for these men and women to be effective in their work, they had to accept the village as their permanent home, and as missionaries they were not taking God to the village, but discovering God there. One had to be patient, to listen, and to serve rather than dominate or overcome. For Bill, the culture and traditions of the people were of utmost importance and should be preserved. A legacy from his time at Point Hope, this was a far-sighted policy, and one not generally accepted by other missionaries or government agencies.

A permanent home for Bill's new recruits meant, for the most part, a village of ten or twenty homes: one-room log houses (except on the Arctic Coast) caulked with either sod, rags, or paper. Most also had small entryways, and an occasional family was lucky enough to have an interior partition of lumber. The only larger buildings were the local store (a small trading post) the community center, the school, the church, and the mission house. Fort Yukon, Tanana, and Kotzebue were exceptions with their hospitals and FAA facilities; they also had more homes. Nenana was a notch higher, and classified as civilization because it was on the railroad. The towns and cities of Alaska posed a different situation altogether.

The village setting (again except for the Arctic Coast) was invariably on the bank of a large river, which provided access to fishing and a travel corridor. Before 1930, large steamboats run for the benefit of miners were frequent visitors, but when the gold seekers left, so did most of the boats, other than the annual summer supply barge.

The terrain beyond the river bank, where the buildings were clustered, depended on the locality. Missions along the Yukon and its tributaries were generally surrounded by spruce forests and rolling hills. Some verged on flatter swamp land, and others were more hemmed in by cliffs and higher elevations. Regardless, the isolation was total, except for some localized small boat travel, dog teams in winter, the summer barge, and the weekly mail plane. Air fields differed too, from the sand bars of the Lower Middle Yukon (mail planes used floats on the river), to primitive strips made by villagers, to the larger but still unpaved runways at the biggest villages.

Anvik, Holikachuk, and Shageluk were located about 300 miles south of Tanana, and so were not en route to the Arctic or even the villages of the Koyukuk. Church workers there sometimes complained that they were "the armpit" of the District, off the beaten track and therefore easily forgotten. Though Bill made frequent stops in Tanana or Nenana or Fort Yukon or Kotzebue en route to other missions, the Lower Middle Yukon meant a special trip, usually undertaken only once a year. Left alone for so long, some of those in charge felt they were being discriminated against, but Bill, with his busy days and tight flying schedules, denies this. In fact, he made a point of spending each Easter in Anvik, flying in daffodils to brighten the church service. He chose this village because it was the site of the first Alaskan mission actually founded by the Episcopal Church.

Living conditions for Bill's new team were as primitive as those the Gordons had faced in Point Hope, and mission houses were small, by Outside standards. The Sarles's home in Minto was two stories, built by Dale himself (other priests also built their homes). The Clevelands, in Holikachuk, had two stories too, with the one bedroom upstairs. Their twenty-four foot by twenty-four foot house was a squeeze for a family with three children. The downstairs was one large room, with the children using bunk beds in the windowless back section.

Judy remembers that the Edwards home in Tanana was an adequate size, but the rooms were all "chopped up into tiny boxes." This made heating difficult, and one of Curtis's projects was to improve on the stove and build a large living room. In spite of their small living quarters, several families expressed feelings of guilt, shared by Bill and Shirley in Point Hope, that their house was so much larger and better furnished than those of the villagers about them.

"Basic Sears Roebuck," was the description of the furniture, and of course the heating and cooking stoves were the focus of household activity. A few of the men quietly paid a villager to supply them wood, but the majority did as Bill told them, and learned to chop their own enormous stack to see them through the lengthy cold months.

Most cook stoves ran on propane gas. The tanks were brought in by boat in the summertime, but if families ran low, Bill would fly in the heavy, cumbersome cargo. Although this type was a luxury compared to Shirley's coal-burning "monster," it was a challenge to heat large galvanized cans of water. "Try to heat all the water for your family wash on a thirty-inch range," Judy recalls. "And we had no cold water (and it was *very* cold) detergent in those days."

The water was carried from the river, or in a few cases, pumped by hand. In winter, some chopped ice for melting or dug holes in the ice to take out clear water. "I never thought much about it, but the villagers threw their garbage out onto the river, close to my holes," Dale Sarles recalls. "One of my favorite memories in winter," Judy says, "was throwing out a big dishpan of water and having it freeze before it hit the ground. My damp hands would stick to the doorknob as I went back inside."

The children adapted readily to the freedom and fun of village life, although parents had a hard time getting them to bed at nine or ten on a summer night when the sun was still shining and their native friends roamed the village until early morning. In fact, Indian and Eskimo youngsters are given a free rein since there is little harm they can come to around the settlement, and they learn very early not to wander.

For adults, making friends took longer. Judy Edwards shares her search for a niche: "I remember walking past a house where three young native couples were having tea—I could see a large redheaded woman serving it. I learned later that this woman's name was Pinky; her children were the same age as mine, and all were redheads, too. I wondered if I'd ever have any friends, if I'd ever be included. I felt so strange and I felt like they were so strange—it was all mutual.

"We had only been in the village three days when I could sense there was something wrong. People were hurrying between the houses, and somebody came to the door to get Curtis because there had been a death. A young woman had been downriver in a boat and had drowned. Curtis was asked to go and get the body. As he left, he told me to go to her family's home. Well, I had never done such a thing before, and at first I told myself I don't know this family, I can't do that. Then something said to give it a whirl, so I went. It was Pinky's sister who had drowned and Pinky was there. I thought, there's only one thing we can do as women—this was a roomful of women—and that's just to hold one another. So I decided I was just gonna do it, and I went up and hugged Pinky. I think a bonding began then, because I never felt ill at ease with her after that. Our friendship developed, and it helped me become identified with all of them—got me accepted by them because I was one of them. I was never an Indian, I would never be an Indian. I had only been there three days, but I was somebody that could feel as they did."

Al Reiners recalls his first acceptance by the people of Kotzebue: "I hope this doesn't sound corny, but I had a kind of life-changing experience that summer because of the people. I was so miserable the first week, and then I finally found the woman whose name the Bishop had given me. She was five miles out of town and I just walked there. Actually it was the first time I wasn't cold since I'd arrived. She and her seven kids gave me a warm greeting. They were all in their tent having lunch and she invited me to stay. It was the best stew I ever put in my mouth.

"I'll never forget the first Sunday I had services in the school-house. When those Eskimos started to sing, it amazed me. Almost choked me up. I couldn't believe that these people, who appeared to be very primitive, could do that. I learned more about Christianity from them than I had learned in my whole life. They were very down-to-earth people, and their religion was down-to-earth—it was a deeper thing to them than I had ever encountered before. And they were kind and thoughtful. I would be out in the village visiting somebody and when I returned, I'd find somebody had brought me a keg of water—water was hard to come by on that sand spit—or a freshly baked loaf of bread."

Most of the missionary wives recall feeling like they were living in a fish bowl during their first weeks in the villages, and they had to get used to having visitors in their homes all day long. "People were constantly coming and going," Charlotte Cleveland recalls, "just sitting in the living room. I finally learned that small talk wasn't expected." This community closeness had its positive side, because whenever Charlotte or any of the wives needed help, someone would come over immediately. Tom Cleveland puts it succinctly: "If you blew your nose, everybody in the village knew it before you got your handkerchief back in your pocket." Another priest discovered his breakfast orange juice was frozen one morning, and while it thawed out, he decided to pay a visit to a bed-ridden old woman at the far end of the village. When he arrived at her home, she greeted him with, "I hear your juice was frozen."

The mission house became the gathering place, although most Indian villages also had their own meeting center, the *kashim*. In very early days this building was restricted to men, often used as a kind of sauna before the days of soap. In the 1950s the *kashim* buildings in Holikachuk and Shageluk were the most ancient, built largely underground like Point Hope homes. Archdeacon Hudson Stuck suggests that this remnant shows the impact of early Eskimo influence on the Lower Middle Yukon. Holikachuk used its thirty foot by thirty foot building as a community hall for dances and traditional potlatches.

Village celebrations were held on a number of occasions during the year. Tom Cleveland recalls the time in Holikachuk when "a man in the village shot a wolf and a wolverine, and since this combined kill brought in seventy dollars for the family, as well as two much prized pelts, Jimmy gave a wolverine potlatch. Everyone went, and the two animals were strung up against the wall, hanging by red kerchiefs around the neck. The wolverine wasn't skinned yet—just frozen, but the wolf was. People brought boxes of crackers, dried salmon, and other things placing them beneath the animals. Everyone just sat there in silence and there was no ceremony or eating. Finally Jimmy divided the food among the people and everyone went home. Apparently the people were being good to the spirits of the animals so that more of these animals would come into their traps."

Potlatches were held on very special occasions, and the fare varied considerably. Often a family gave one in honor of a birthday, wedding, birth, or funeral. In early days the people never ate together if it was a food potlatch; they brought their own plates, which were filled with food to take home, often enough for several days.

The whole community put on a feast to celebrate the coming of a special guest, like Bill. He always arrived with doughnuts and soda and contributed them to the party. The menu usually consisted of dried fish, moosehead soup, boiled muskrat, and duck, which had been sitting on the back of the stove for weeks until the flavor was pungent. Dessert, to accompany Bill's gift, was Indian ice cream, made of lard or moose fat, sugar, blueberries, and fish oil.

Indian dancing—usually with masks—accompanied the festive meal, but very few "outsiders" were ever included when Shageluk and Holikachuk put on their traditional "stick dance," which had a spiritual motif and was held only once every three or four years. This dance, which predated white man's arrival, was found in the isolated Episcopal villages of Shageluk and Holikachuk, and further downriver in some villages under jurisdiction of the Roman Catholic Church. The ceremony was interwoven with the people's early spiritual lives.

Archdeacon Hudson Stuck, writing of his journeys in the early 1900s, noted the widespread "primitive animism" and other ancient beliefs of the people along the Lower Middle Yukon, while further north they had been almost forgotten. It was difficult to decide which native customs were commemorative and symbolic, like our own folklore and fairy tales (Friday the thirteenth, salt over the shoulder, warts from toads, or Santa Claus, the Easter bunny, the tooth fairy) and which were covertly pernicious or evil. He concluded that "primitive animism" recognizes the world of deep mysteries and that there is something in man superior to himself that does not die with the death of the body.

Hudson Stuck also wrote of seeing the enormous power of the shamans, not all of them good by any means. But even in his day, their roles were already changing. They could no longer cause someone to be put to death, or help themselves to many wives in the village; however, they were still the acknowledged village leader, the spiritual person one turned to when ill or plagued with troubles of any sort.

"I never felt there was any friction or antagonism between us and them over shamanism or some other form of spiritualism," Glen Wilcox recalls. "The people felt themselves to be Christians in what they were doing. There was no feeling that they were slipping back into something that wasn't good religiously. The shaman was a person who could talk of the Holy and had a certain creativity about him. That's why he stood out, that's why he was chosen, because he was in touch with the spiritual world. The religious leader, in whatever religious atmosphere you find him, stands apart."

Many of the village elders—the leaders of the 1950s and 60s became the native church leaders and the sacramental priests Bill later ordained. At an earlier time they might have been practicing shamans. Bill believed that these leaders were recognized for innate spiritual qualities and therefore were the ideal candidates to be church leaders.

The ancient rituals and customs of the native peoples came to the fore when there was a death in the village, which was often in the 1950s and 1960s. "The process of preparing for burial was so much a part of community life," Charlotte Cleveland recalls. "We were not included in all the preparations, but I always baked food to take to the bereaved family—Tom wasn't even called upon until the church service, but we each had our parts."

Don and Betty Hart lived in the Koyukuk village of Huslia for five years, then moved on to Anchorage. While there, their five-year-old son died from a rare kidney disease. Immediately after his death, they decided to return to visit Huslia, where Andrew had spent most of his young life. "The Bishop flew us there," Don recalls, "and left us for four days. The people greeted us warmly and then the whole community put on a potlatch. There were speeches, and music and food, exactly as if one of them had just died. Our seven-year-old daughter stayed in homes of her former friends—the people really reached out. It meant a lot to see them and be with them again. They know how to cry—how to mourn. Our whole attitude toward death and dying was molded while we lived there, and I'm sure the Bishop knew exactly why we wanted to go back."

These young men and women were taught by the villagers to live in new ways; a life without benefit of supermarkets, electricity, telephones, cars and many of the built-in entertainment features they took for granted. Joyce Sarles remembers going berry picking in the fall. "I went along with a boatload of women to the blueberry field. Some of the older ladies would sit down and pick the bushes clean. They were master berry pickers. We found our cranberries right around the village itself."

"I went rabbit-snaring with my next-door neighbor," Charlotte Cleveland recalls. "And at another time Grandma Lucy, as our kids used to call her, made Tom a net to fit on the end of a deep-net pole—using the same stitching method we'd seen on the old-fashioned Maine lobster pots."

Charlotte was particularly impressed with the "tea partner" tradition practiced in Holikachuk and a number of other Indian villages. "In a village of a hundred people, one doesn't usually get invited out to dinner; the homes are too small, and families seldom have food to spare. So the tea partner scheme solves this social problem. Everyone, including our children, had a partner, and once a year we would entertain or be entertained for a two-day period. My partner was David Maillelle and I would give him a big meal at our house, enough so he could take a whole plate of food home. Then the following year, I would go to his home. It was a really special form of visiting and fellowship."

Learning to hunt and fish with the village men was an important adjunct to the priests' lives. Not only was this a command from Bill, but also fresh fish or ptarmigan, duck, and moose meat were a welcome relief from a diet of canned goods. "We got pretty good at hitting ptarmigan in the air with our twenty-two's," Tom Cleveland recalls. "Fishing was easy in summer, using dip nets in eddies, and fish traps that looked like funnel-shaped baskets. But in winter, as soon as the ice became thick enough so you could walk on it, all the men in the village got together to build a fish fence all the way across the Innoko River (a quarter mile wide, maybe fifteen feet deep in the middle) to catch whitefish which were headed for the ocean. We cut a canal in the ice, then we stuck four-inch-thick poles deep into the mud about every twelve feet. Next we'd take willow branches that people were cutting along the shoreline, weave them into sections, slip them down against the poles, and secure them with wire. It took almost two days to finish.

"The fence wasn't so tight that the fish couldn't get through, but the current moving the willows scared them, and they milled about trying to swim downstream. Holes were cut in the ice above the fence, and using dip nets, sometimes as many as three or four fish were scooped up with one dip. We just plopped them on the ice and they froze. We would spend three to five days there, then bring a huge load back by dog team. We kept the frozen fish in a cache, stacking them just like cordwood."

These clergy families also learned to fend for themselves in other ways. Glen Wilcox, who built his own mission home in Anvik, also built himself two boats—a large launch and a canoe. (River travel was important to him when he was in charge of all three Lower Middle Yukon villages.) The canoe was unusual in that it was made of nineteen Standard Oil gas cans! "I took a kitchen can opener," he explains, "cut off all the tops, flattened the cans and squared them up. Then I made a frame and covered it with the tin, soldering the pieces together. So in two days I had built myself a fifteen-foot-long canoe. Still have it, too."

The men had to learn to deal with village medical problems, as Bill had to in Point Hope. But airplane travel had increased sufficiently so that really sick people could be sent out to hospitals. The missionary families were more reluctant to ask for evacuation for themselves, however, because the cost would have to be borne by the impoverished District, and they knew that Bill himself would not come unless it was a real emergency. Some villages, like Tanana, Kotzebue, and Fort Yukon, were fortunate to have doctors and hospital facilities, and a few of the clergy wives were nurses. They could not earn money for their work, however, because the National Church ruling at that time stipulated that when a man was commissioned as a missionary his wife was, too. This was to ensure that all families received equal pay (small as it was).

Clergy families were not expected to get sick, one wife recalls, but women were evacuated for medical treatment when they developed pregnancy complications, and all went to Fairbanks to have their babies. When the children developed the usual childhood diseases, they were nursed back to health in the village.

Although Bill insisted that the men and women stay in the village in order to establish their roots there, the men left far more frequently than the women and children, either for local trips to nearby villages or for clergy conferences and other gatherings. Betty Hart will never forget their first winter in Huslia, when Bill came to pick up Don for a regional meeting. "It was the twenty-ninth of November and we were having our first real cold spell—forty-five degrees below zero. Suddenly the kitchen propane stove wasn't working right, the water pump in the cellar froze, and we couldn't keep the furnace hot enough. Frost was crawling up the walls, and here comes the Bishop to take Don to Tanana. I was pregnant, with a one-year-old daughter on my hands. I literally panicked. I was very angry and nearly hysterical—I remember yelling right in front of the Bishop. But all to no avail. Off they went, and there I was. And I had to cope.

"The next day, the Bishop's plane returned. He said he had to go to Fairbanks, and would I like to come along and stay in town with the baby while the meeting was going on? This was the beginning of my realization that he did care about all of us, but he was going to take no sass from an Easterner, and I had to do my share. I had to realize that Don belonged to him and the church and God and I was going to have to learn to get along on my own. Beyond that he was supportive."

Bill often praised the women, calling them the true heroines of the District, because they had to stay put, usually alone and under difficult situations. He had far less patience with some of the bachelor men who tended to drift to Nenana and Fairbanks for a little companionship and civilization. Following one of the earliest clergy meetings, Bill flew four men back to villages, leaving still-bachelor Dale Sarles off at Nenana to take his boat on to Minto. It was a cold, rainy summer evening and the priest-in-charge of Nenana at that time, had no trouble persuading Dale to spend the night. Trouble came when Bill was forced to return to Nenana because of bad weather. As he buzzed the rectory—his custom upon arrival at any village—Dale said, "That's the Bishop." His cohort replied, "It can't be." Dale kept insisting it was, and ten minutes later Bill walked into the rectory.

"The Bishop had explicitly told me," Dale recalls, "to go home. When he walked into the kitchen and asked where I was, my friend replied that I had gone to Minto. The Bishop said, 'Oh no, he didn't—he wouldn't have gone without his orange hat,' nodding to my favorite piece of clothing sitting on the living room couch. The jig was up, and I had to come out of the bathroom and face the music. I can't remember what he said, but I think he was a little bit amused. Of course he couldn't let me know that he was."

"I used to get quite concerned with the bush clergy who spent a lot of time in Fairbanks when I was bishop," Bill says. "They said they needed to come in to really live. Unconsciously, they saw their work being in the villages, but their living was somewhere else. I would always correct them if they were asked where they were from, and they replied, 'Boston,' or 'Baltimore,' or 'Ashville.' I would tell them, 'Right now you live in Allakaket, or Tanana, or Huslia. That is your home. That is where your roots are.' I feel the psychological significance of that was extremely important. You are from where you live. If you can put your work and your living in the same place, it makes a world of difference. Another reason I was a little upset sometimes was that I got out only once during my first three years I was at Point Hope—when I broke a tooth and the Bishop thought I should have it taken care of."

Bill frequently dropped in, unannounced, on the bush clergy along his route of flight. Sometimes he just wanted to see how things were going for them or to refuel, but he was also occasionally forced down because of bad weather. These visits were particularly hard on the bachelors; they knew he liked to find a clean house, but their housekeeping efforts were not always impeccable. At one of these unheralded stops, he found the clergyman was gone, visiting a trapping camp. Bill recalls, "I found that there was not one dish or pan that was clean, so I spent an hour washing them before I could fix myself something to eat. I made some slight comment about that when he returned. His reply was that he really didn't think that there was anything in the Bible about cleanliness being next to Godliness.

"Another bachelor priest was, likewise, a housekeeper of somewhat doubtful talent. Time and again when I visited him, his house was a mess. But then, I arrived once and there was not a dirty dish anywhere. So I went to his kerosene refrigerator to get out some milk and I found it jammed full of used dishes that had been collected over a period of many days."

Rick Draper remembers waking up at about seven o'clock one morning to the sound of a razor in the kitchen below. Al Reiners recalls being roused even earlier by the rattling of the coffee pot, and hearing Bill mumbling, "Where do they keep the coffee around here?" He had already flown for three hours. These dawn visits had become routine to the men on the Arctic Coast; Bill was always the first up and about by plane, not in the least reluctant to stop in unannounced for breakfast, which he cooked himself. But he especially enjoyed dropping in on some of the wives who were his favorite cooks. They had learned quickly what he liked to eat, and even under the most primitive circumstances, they were able to whip up his favorite coconut cream pie from canned or boxed ingredients kept handy. Joyce Sarles made a terrible blunder, however, when she was first married. She cooked up lemon meringue instead, one which Bill hated. She still recalls the look of disappointment on his face.

A new young seminarian, working in the village of Eagle for the summer, was unaware of Bill's drop-in habits. Bill flew in about midnight to pick up Norman Elliott, who had gone there earlier in the week. He found the house completely locked up, a big surprise, but he knew of a wood chute outside that opened into the basement. "It was like a tunnel going under the house, coming up in the living room," Bill recalls. "so I went down through it, found my way into the living room, went upstairs to the volunteer's bedroom and shook him awake. I asked him about Norman, and the reply was that he had gone to a nearby village with some fire fighters. So I thanked him, went back outside the way I had entered, and flew on to get Norman. I heard later that when the seminarian awoke the next day, he thought he had dreamed all this, since he knew he had locked the house up tight."

Bill's scheduled visitations to bush villages—usually once a year for two or three days—were a time of great joy for everyone, and were preceded by much anticipation. Charlotte Cleveland remembers, "everybody in the village would clean their house—the curtains washed, the floor scrubbed. And they always put on a big potlatch for him in the *kashim*. Toward the end of our stay in Holikachuk, we got a projector that ran on a village generator and the Bishop brought along a movie, and tons of doughnuts, cans of soda pop, and maybe oranges."

"We would go on Episcopal standard time when the Bishop arrived," one priest recalls. "We literally set our watch by his—if he said it was ten minutes after one, it was ten minutes after one. When he left, we reset them according to village time.

"I also remember his bringing in propane tanks along with the doughnuts—the latter were often squashed beneath the former—they were full and he'd lift them out of the plane by himself. The people admired his strength and willingness to do physical work."

Dale Sarles says the Bishop would inquire first about who was sick in the village, and who had asked especially to see him. He enjoyed visiting in their homes, and the people were pleased to have him. In most villages he went to every house and he knew the entire family by name, even if he had not seen them for a year. He also remembered who was related to whom, what children were born when, and he brought them news of relatives he had recently seen in hospitals.

One priest recalls, "he could sit down and talk about what was going on in their lives. He was comfortable with the people. He could kid them—he was one of them like no other Caucasian leader I've ever seen. I always thought it significant that one lady in the village told me that Bishop Gordon appeared to her in her dreams. I think that shows how he submerged himself into the identity and subconsciousness of the people."

"It wasn't necessary for the Bishop to stay with the priest," Al Reiners says, "but he usually did, and it was special because you saw him as just another human being—using a sleeping bag on the living room couch, shaving at the kitchen sink in the morning. . . ." Wives recall his helping to cook breakfast and playing with the children, but they seldom had to prepare a big dinner for Bill, because of the village potlatches. However, Judy Edwards will never forget the large meal thrust upon her when Curtis was ordained during their first winter in Tanana. Bill brought in all the groceries she had asked him for, "and he just left them with me while he began flying in lots and lots of people. Of course, I wanted to have a traditional dinner, but there were eighteen of us, and I was the only woman. I had never even cooked a turkey before, much less made gravy, sweet potatoes, and Waldorf salad. I just couldn't do it, especially with the small stove. So the Bishop came out to the kitchen and took over. Every time I have this meal now, I remember how he taught me.

"By the time I got to the church for the ordination service, I was frazzled. I managed to get the girls into nice dresses, but I'll never forget looking over at Lucy in the pew and seeing a large smudge of charcoal all the way across her face. It just hit me that six months earlier we had been in a magnificent church in Houston for Curtis's ordination to the Diaconate."

The Sunday morning service during Bill's visitations was attended by almost everyone in the village, and Bill always preached. He also selected the hymns (even if they had already been chosen, some of the priests comment wryly). And when it was time for him to leave, he would sit at the dining table with the priest, and his family if he had one, saying an informal prayer. This was when he would bring up his concerns or the priest's.

One clergyman adds that regardless of Bill's haste to leave, he "would stop everything to pray with the family, and it was always personal and informal. It was obviously an important part of his ministry and it meant a lot to him and to us. I don't think I've ever had another bishop in my home, or pray with me that way." Another says these times were special to him, and he learned much more about informal praying than he had ever known before.

"It was his way of communicating with us on a personal level," another suggests. "He would never say 'tell me about your problems.' In fact, we weren't ever supposed to have any personal ones. He could not deal directly with a person's weaknesses, and he could never pat us on the back. He seemed to know when the going was rough—he always followed up his visitations with a long letter after his return to Fairbanks, and in that he often referred to situations troubling us, or gave us advice about village difficulties." Another fellow worker says, "I always thought that because he was so young when he was consecrated, he probably felt that he didn't have much wisdom to give anybody else, and consequently did not see his role as a pastor to his clergy as much as he might have, were he an older man. He was almost the same age as most of us."

This priest suggests that Bill could cope better with those under him who occasionally confronted him, or even flaunted and disobeyed his orders. He liked people to stand up to him, and it was not those whom he "fired," but rather the quiet workers who were not "roaring tigers." He wanted them to be tough, but when he "growled at them, they recoiled." These persons had their strengths, but they were often hidden behind their weaknesses, and Bill was unable, or did not want to take the time to bring them out.

On the other hand, Bill performed countless little kindnesses for his workers. Since his clergy were living on minimal salaries, he dug deep into his pockets for money to help them. Those who were ill or battling alcohol problems he sent Outside for a period of time; some who had marital problems were guided to counselors, and those who were getting married he often flew to Manley Hot Springs of McKinley Park for a few days' honeymoon. One man, who had had frequent battles with Bill, decided to leave Alaska, but could find no job opening Outside. Bill intervened and offered him an interim assistant's position in a large church in one of Alaska's cities. When Henry and Susan Chapman transferred to the church in Sitka, Bill bought them new kitchen appliances, and one summer he paid their daughter's travel to Alaska, when her parents had not seen her in two years.

Bill regularly brought his clergy together for meetings of one kind or another, often flying in renowned speakers from Outside to give them renewal and stimulation. He knew this type of activity was vital to them, and to the District as a whole. (In later years he did the same for their wives.) He also kept close tabs on who would best work where, shifting personnel around in split-second decisions, sometimes with little or no previous discussion with the person involved.

Glen Wilcox says, "I tried to bend the Bishop's ear about needing someone to share the burden of serving the three Lower [Middle] Yukon villages. I got no response. That night—we were sharing the upstairs bedroom in the Holikachuk mission house—I was about to go to sleep, and all of a sudden came his voice out of the dark saying, 'You know, you may have something there.' That was all there was to the talk that night. The next day we flew down to Shageluk and at the church service, he announced that the Reverend and Mrs. Tom Cleveland were coming; they had been scheduled to go to Eagle, but he felt it was more important for them to come to this area, and they would be based in Holikachuk. I couldn't believe my ears, and I'm sure the Clevelands were surprised, too." This incident also shows Bill's way of accepting occasional advice from workers.

The men and women of the District often joke about these unilateral decisions thrust upon them. Bill's usual approach was to say, "God wants you to go to that village, or that new position," or "The Holy Spirit is calling you to seminary." Those directives were hard to do battle with. "It was as though he was telling you what God had said," one person recalls, "but then he always added, 'You've got to think about it and make up your own mind.' " A number of people commented on the swiftness of these decisions, but Bill was never a person to spend time contemplating moves; "do it and move on" was his style from his very earliest days.

Another way Bill lent support to his workers was to fly in fresh food to them whenever he came to visit—not just a few items, but a planeload which included lettuce, tomatoes, and fruit. Bill also remembered the favorites of every family, although he often complained about the high-priced foods he was asked to bring for special occasions. However, newcomers and summer workers were never asked what they preferred to eat. Bill purchased their food on sale, using standard lists.

Grocery shopping, for Bill, was a major operation, and an important and enjoyable part of his weekly work routine. "He was recognized by every check-out person in Fairbanks," his son remembers, since the family was frequently asked for help. "He would roar into the store, grabbing five to ten carts, and some checkers quickly took their break. He always bought everything on sale, and kept track of where in town he'd find the best buys."

Gordon Charlton went on these excursions occasionally. "We would be flying to some village and we'd stop at the store en route to the plane. He could fill the back of a station wagon with groceries in thirty minutes. He'd say, 'grab a basket,' and we each went down the aisle with one. When that was full, he'd start on another, just throwing things in. Ten of this, twelve of that—light bulbs, soap, everything in sight that people might need. Then we'd load the plane until there was barely room for ourselves." The recipient of one of the loads remembers the plane coming in, the door opening, and canned goods falling out, rolling all over the air strip.

Aside from groceries, Bill carried an unusual assortment of things in his plane. "When I went to Anvik for Easter services every year, I used to take daffodils, but another time I flew two pots of Easter lilies to Shageluk. I was also carrying food supplies and three large sled dogs—about eighty pounds each—and at the last minute someone gave me two pups to deliver en route. They were only about two and one-half months old, so I put them in gunny sacks, with their heads sticking out. I didn't want them running about, or being hurt by one of the big dogs. I kept the flowers and perishable food on the front seat, to keep them from freezing. Once I got into the air, one of the pups broke loose and, terrified by the big dogs, he started running all over the plane.

That got the other dogs excited and I was afraid I'd have a riot on my hands. I decided to climb up to about 10,000 feet into thinner air, which might subdue my live cargo a bit, and keep them away from my lilies. I don't think I was ever happier to get back on the ground again."

Bill claims that his most undesirable passengers were cats. "I'm not a tremendous cat lover anyway [he hates them]. One time I flew a couple, their baby, and a dearly beloved Siamese cat. They had brought the cat to Alaska in a large cage, but there was no room for it in my plane. So, I suggested we take the cat loose. The young wife was unhappy about this, since the cat was the nervous kind. I told her, 'all I have to do is open one of the plane windows and we will see whether cats really do land on their feet when they are dropped from great heights.' I think it took her about a year to forgive me for that statement, but at least we made the trip without difficulty."

Don and Betty Hart also flew in with a Siamese cat. They remember that one of Bill's favorite comments was, "I can take your cat halfway to Fairbanks." These cat and dog stories circulated about the District for years, and people who did not know Bill well believed he hated the animals. He certainly had no love for cats, but he had been very close to his sled dogs in Point Hope, and it was only the "useless, untrained household variety" he would have no use for.

Clergy wives were among Bill's most frequent flying companions, and, with the exception of a few nervous fliers, who were unhappy in any small plane, most of the women took the sometimes hairy experience with equanimity. They felt he was a good pilot and knew what he was doing. At times when he had a solo passenger and the weather was good, Bill would reach under his seat, pull out a paperback (westerns were his favorite), and read a little. And rumor had it that he was also known to take an occasional nap. In later years, he often had planeloads of women, ferrying them to the clergy wives conferences he initiated in the mid-sixties.

Many passengers of the "Episcopal Airlines," as Bill's plane was commonly called, commented that the beginning and end of the flights were the worst parts; the beginning because one had to be at the plane on time—even a five minute delay could trigger Bill's quick temper. He always had a tight schedule to keep, and weather threats were often a concern. The end of the trip, if it was to a city, entailed driving with Bill and he became a madman behind the wheel of a car. "I can remember being very relaxed on the flight, and then I panicked during the short ride from the airport to the hostel," Dick Clarke says. "He was a very fast driver, and for the past six months in the village, I hadn't gone more than ten miles an hour by dog team."

Besides being on time for a flight, Bill's other firm rule was no drinks of any kind for three or four hours before a departure. Judy remembered his stern admonition on her first trip with him, because one of her children begged her for a drink of water. "You are dying of thirst by the time you land, because the Bishop has not let you have anything to drink all day." Rest stops were never scheduled on Bill's tight itinerary regardless of the severity of the need.

Charlotte has painful memories of a flight from Fort Yukon with Tom, and Dale Sarles. They had been attending the wedding of a fellow clergyman and while waiting for Bill to return from his first trip ferrying visitors home, they were lured into trouble. "The man who ran the local store invited us to share a bottle of champagne," Dale recounts their story. "We weren't supposed to drink in the villages, but it seemed a good way to celebrate the wedding. Our host was insidious about pouring it. I put my hand over my glass, but as soon as I took it off and looked the other way, he was filling it up again. We had gone through that bottle by the time the Bishop returned about midnight. Tom suggested we stop in the store and get some chewing gum to mask any alcoholic odor before we rushed out to the plane—no time for anything else.

"The flight from Fort Yukon to Tanana takes three and one-half hours, and the champagne started going through us like a sieve. It wasn't long before the Bishop knew that we were in discomfort. But he never said a thing. Part way to Tanana he asked if we wanted to stop at Rampart. All three of us said we thought that was really a nice idea. So the Bishop started down, going into a steep dive at first, then pulling up again. He said, 'Oh, it's too far down. We aren't going to bother to stop.' I could just feel my bladder roll right down to the bottom of my feet. You never saw three people get out of an airplane so fast when we finally reached Tanana.''

Clergy wives were often accompanied by small children, and most posed no problems. A number were infants, being returned by Bill to their village homes after their births two weeks earlier in Fairbanks. Charlotte Cleveland recalls flying back with her brand new daughter, sitting on the front seat beside Bill. The flight took longer than usual and the baby began to cry. "I said, 'Well, Bishop, I just hope you don't mind me nursing the babe.' And he replied 'Oh, no, no.' He was so shy about it. I was pretty self-conscious about it too.''

Joan Wilcox was returning with her newborn when they hit bad weather. The plane picked up ice and the engine began missing, sounding as though it was about to quit. Then his windshield frosted up, leaving him only a small hole to see through. His wings began to ice up and Bill then elected to land on the Yukon. He never allowed smoking in his plane, and Joan was a smoker at the time. While sitting on the river ice, she asked him if it would be all right for her to have a cigarette. He agreed, adding that he suspected she could really use one at that point.

Bill had more than his share of sand bar landings, and his sisters have fond memories of one, during their final departure from Alaska. Almeria and Mary Irwin had completed their work at Anvik and moved on to Huslia for a visit while waiting for a ride with Bill. Since there was no airstrip available there at that time in summer, Bill sent word via the radio program, Tundra Topics, much used by all Bush inhabitants to convey information back and forth. The message was, "To Mia and Mary Irwin—meet me at the Hog River bar Sunday at nine P.M. From Bishop Gordon.'' Neither his sisters nor many listeners allowed Bill to forget those words.

The clergy working with Bill flew with him far more frequently, and a number of stories are still repeated whenever two or more get together to reminisce. Sand bar and bad weather encounters grow monotonous after a while, and the same is true of cold weather flying. "Planes just aren't *supposed* to fly after the temperature drops to forty degrees below zero," a priest complains, but nobody ever told Bill that. One young man tells of leaving the plane when the thermometer registered sixty below. The door handle came off in his hand!

Another recalls being left at a small village at dusk, when it was fifty-five degrees below zero. "The Bishop's parting comment was a cheery 'don't freeze.' I went up to the empty mission house, found no wood had been cut, and a piece of butter that had been left on the kitchen counter was frozen so hard you could drive nails through it. I decided that house would never get warm, so I went over to the schoolteachers' home to visit, and they invited me to stay there. When the Bishop came to pick me up, his first words were, 'Did you stay with the schoolteachers?' "

Another priest will never forget his arrival at Point Hope, when the temperature was well below zero and the wind was blowing hard. In fact, he would always remember that flight itself, because it was extremely turbulent and he became airsick. He looked, in vain, for airsickness bags, and finally, in desperation, used his wool cap. Once on the ground, the Bishop asked him to get out while the engine was still running and push the plane's tail around. Forced out into the prop wash and the frigid weather, he had no recourse but to put his hat back on his head.

Bill flew his team to conferences and other gatherings; indeed he made a great effort to bring them together as often as possible, because he believed the fellowship was as important as any business discussed or teaching conducted by visitors from Outside. Not only did these gatherings help ease the isolation of village life, but it also gave everyone the feeling of a close-knit Alaskan family.

Weddings were good reason for the clergy to gather, and the fellowship on those occasions was especially good, judging from the far from dignified goings-on. Because Bill was such an avid matchmaker—his Bible school volunteer program came to a halt once all the bachelors in the District were married—a number of young men and women walked down the church aisle in Alaska.

Ordinations were also joyful times for the missionaries and villagers alike, a special occasion for a big potlatch and dance, a more elaborate ceremony in the small church, and lots of visitors flown in by the Bishop. "He was trying to help the people of the village see something of the larger family of the church in Alaska by bringing these people in," Dale Sarles recalls. "I don't remember much about my own ordination in Minto, except that I felt very much the contrast between being ordained a deacon in the Cathedral of St. John the Divine in New York City, and being ordained a priest in the community hall which held, in a squeeze, 150 people."

Taking the canonical exam required before ordination poses no problem in terms of transportation to the bishop in charge on the Outside. In Alaska, however, when someone was ready, it could mean a massive undertaking for Bill and his plane. Once, when a man on the Arctic Coast was prepared, Bill asked Gordon Charlton to accompany him, to be his examiner and his presenter. Gordon says he agreed to go, but added, "What if he doesn't pass?" Bill replied, "Look, it's a 700-mile flight up there, he's going to pass. We're not going to go all that distance and come back without ordaining him, that's for sure."

Al Reiners, also on the Arctic Coast, still had part of his Canonicals to pass when Bill and Norman Elliott dropped in on him one time. He says, "Norman was one of the examining chaplains, so the Bishop said, 'Norm, as long as you're here, let's do Al's Old Testament exam this evening.' Sitting at the kitchen table, Norman started asking me about some abstract theology. The Bishop was in the next room and finally called out, 'Come on, Norm, knock that stuff off. Just ask him a few basic content questions.' We talked on for another hour or so, and then the Bishop said, 'Okay, you pass. Let's turn in now.' "

Fellowship was as important for Bill as it was for the clergy who worked for him. But these times were few and far between, and even then Bill could never be "one of the gang" with the priests in his charge. Many comment on how lonely he must have been; to be away from home six months of the year, with no truly close friends in Alaska. The only occasion where Bill could totally relax with male companionship was on his annual moose hunts, legends now themselves. (Meat was expensive in Fairbanks and the Gordon family, like many others, depended on a good supply of moose and caribou for food.)

On his first few hunting trips, Bill prudently went with Indian friends because of his strong belief that it was their country and their game. Also, he needed their help! But after they had invited him to return whenever he wished, he asked a few of the clergy to accompany him. Don Hart went on several of these trips. "By the time the small boat was filled with the Bishop's food, there would be no room for the moose. He brought everything from apple and pecan pies to bottles of frozen milk and cases of doughnuts.

"My first trip out, I felt I was on an assault, on a par with Iwo Jima," says Don. "We steamed up the river after a pair of ears, and the Bishop was determined to shoot with the motor still going full tilt, standing from the stern of the boat. I was crouched in the middle, trying to get out of the line of fire. We hit the bank, going full speed, and while I had trouble getting out, the Bishop was in the water with one splash. Of course the moose had run off immediately, if there even was one."

Chuck Eddy, a clergyman from Anchorage, describes the hunt as "an action run fast-forward on video cassette. And the menu was Kentucky Fried Chicken with biscuits for three days, along with tea and doughnuts. Everything was done in a hurry, from almost running through the village to the boat—the people clearing a path because they knew what was up—to speeding up the river, to the hunt itself. We shot one moose and it fell into the river, so we had to haul it out, pull it up on the bank, and cut it up there. Then we shot a second, which died in a swamp, sinking straight down, legs first. We had to build about 150 yards of ramp out of alder bushes to reach it, all at 900 miles an hour. Then when we were ready to fly out, all the meat was stuffed in the plane, again in a hurry. It was a big overload, but I always felt safe flying with him."

The men all agree that they were not concerned when they flew with Bill, in spite of countless mishaps and close calls. Then the day came when it looked as though Bill's guardian angel had become tired of so much overtime, and went on strike. Bill was holding a large Eskimo-Indian conference in Kotzebue, which called for numerous trips with his plane. He had flown in most of the participants when, just before takeoff from Hughes with more delegates, he discovered his mixture control was broken. He elected to leave his passengers there and fly on to Fairbanks for repairs, but he had to wait in Nenana for almost three hours for a snow storm to clear out of the area. By the time he reached home base and the mechanic did his work, it was too dark to take off again. That meant spending the night, with people still waiting to go to Kotzebue for a meeting that was to begin the next morning.

Naturally, Bill was most anxious to make an early departure, and he reached the field about five A.M. on a cold but clear winter day. "I tried to start the engine without heating it, because the temperature was marginal, but it wouldn't turn over. So I had to warm it up with my equipment, and while I was waiting, I could see ice fog beginning to move in. When I finally got the engine started, the fog was overhead, and I had to get a special clearance for a takeoff in IFR conditions. This meant a further wait. Then I went to the end of the field, but it was too thick for any visibility there, so I thought I would taxi part of the way down the 3,200-foot runway. I figured I could get off in about 1,500 feet, since I had no passengers. I did have about twelve cans of airplane gas on board—for refueling in Hughes, since it was so expensive there.

"But the fog was pretty thick, and I couldn't see, so I pulled the plane up too fast. I noticed the red light on the panel come on, indicating an impending stall, but, not being able to see anything ahead, I was unable to do a corrective maneuver. So the plane fell off on the left wing and I dropped. I hit a Piper Super Cub on floats about thirty feet in front of the Fairbanks Aircraft hangar, plowing all the way through it, and then I hit another plane with the right wing and slid to a stop in about a one hundred foot area between two lines of parked airplanes. All this was taking place while I couldn't see anything at all in the fog. My actual landing was easier than some of those I have made intentionally. I was extremely lucky, because I very nearly plowed into the hangar, and with those cans of gas, plus the eighty gallons in the wing tanks, you can imagine what would have happened. It was a miracle that with the wing down I didn't cartwheel instead of coming down flat.

"This was one occasion when my impaired judgment put me at great risk. I did pull the plane up too soon—I was so anxious to be off and get the people to the meeting in time. Another factor that I hadn't considered was icing—while the plane sat in the fog as I preheated the engine, the wings picked up a thin layer of ice—enough to compound the problem. But I was unhurt, although my plane was demolished. The only trouble I got from the FAA was over carrying the gas illegally. I often took tins out to cache in villages—I had a supply of gas all over the Bush. It was the only way I could operate, because in many places there was no fuel available at all. I felt it was much more risky to be on dry tanks than to haul that gas once in a while. Anyway, about three hours later, I took off in our other District plane to continue my travels."

On second thought, Bill's guardian angel had not deserted him. On the contrary, he or she must have called in a whole legion of companions to help save Bill's life. Many of Bill's friends and associates became concerned following this crash, however. It was as though the many years of incidents and close calls had come to a climax, and one could not help but wonder what might happen next, since Bill was determined to continue his rigorous flying schedule and hectic way of life.

Chapter 7

"Women Are the Heroes"

Flying was not Bill's only love; he was also attracted to pretty young women. And the feeling was mutual. A secretary in the National Church office in New York remembers that "every female head turned whenever the handsome young bishop walked through their rooms, and a general sighing was almost audible." Bill attracted women of all ages and they invariably worshiped the ground he walked on. Coworkers and parishioners alike readily agreed to take on any task he requested of them, thrilled to be asked, and especially to be in his presence.

Shirley's memories of accompanying Bill on visits to churches include the inevitable social functions when she was often left alone while he was surrounded by a contingent of admirers.

One of Bill's daughters remembers going to a dinner party with him once, when Shirley was out of town, and a woman guest telling her father to let her know "if he ever became a widower, or was unattached." Bill thoroughly enjoyed these attentions, his self-esteem bolstered as it was when he was growing up among six doting sisters, his adoring grandmother, aunt, and mother. This homage also eased the loneliness from the lack of male friends and frequent absence from home.

He particularly admired and felt close to the clergy wives: "The really heroic people are not those who travel 10,000 miles by dog sled, but those who stay 10,000 days in one place," he said of them in *Time* magazine. "I believe that all of us have the capacity for one adventure inside us, but the great adventure is facing responsibility day after day." Bill recalled Shirley's lonely ordeals at Point Hope and so he went out of his way to ease the lives of isolated missionary women. Beginning in the mid-fifties, he devoted many hours of his time to flying them and parishioners to state-wide clergy wives conferences and church women organization gatherings. Once Bill brought everyone together, he remained with them throughout their sessions. Few local priests would sit through the hours of discussion, but Bill did, and he often took all the women to a movie in the evening as his guests.

When clergy wives came to Fairbanks to have their babies, and stayed in the hostel on the second floor of the office wing (added to the church parish hall in 1953), Bill frequently checked on them, taking time to chat with them around the kitchen table. He and Shirley also made them feel part of their family as they invited the women to their home for meals. They both sat with some as they went into labor, while husbands had to remain at their isolated outposts. In many cases the fathers had other children to care for at home, and besides, waiting for a baby to arrive could easily mean two months away from their village.

Joanne Reiners tells of the night her baby arrived: "I had moved into the Gordon's house to wait for the birth [the hostel was full]. I rushed into the guest room bath and took a shower, for I was determined to go to the hospital with clean hair. Shirley banged on the door, begging me to hurry so she could get me there in time. The Bishop was out of town, so it was Shirley's lot to go with me. Sarah Reiners was born quickly and she was covered with black hair, but I thought she was exquisite. When the Bishop returned to town, he came to visit me in the maternity section. I asked him if he didn't think Sarah was beautiful, and he har-rumped and said all infants were ugly. He returned on the day I was discharged and as we rode down in the elevator with a nurse holding the baby, she looked up at the Bishop, then down at Sarah and said, 'My, she certainly does look like you!' More harrumping."

Some of the women in the District, particularly those who worked for Bill, called him a male chauvinist. Even one of Bill's sisters agrees, "because he expects women to do what he wants them to do." She adds, however, that "he believes in equal opportunities for all." At the same time, Bill also expected men to do what he wanted them to do.

Anna, the third Gordon daughter, born nine years after Becky, says of her father: "I can't say I felt he limited me because I was female, nor did he push me to be a superachiever to overcome my femaleness. I think Dad did as much with his daughters as he did with his son. He encouraged me to learn to fly, and licensed me as a lay reader before I reached 'legal' age." (He did not know there was a national age limit.)

Before calling Bill a male chauvinist, one must look at the meaning of the word: unreasoning devotion to one's race, sex, country, etc., with contempt for other races, sexes, and countries. This definition does not fit him, and for those who feel it does, their perspective is clouded by three factors: his manners as a southern gentleman; his insistence on having his way, whether with a man or a woman; and the cultural mores of the 1950s.

Bill has typical southern mannerisms that show deferential respect to a woman, such as holding open doors, disliking the slacks Shirley wore on board ship (this one vanished quickly!) and leaving the cooking to Shirley. He did some of the dishwashing, however, and he always pitched in to help when he was a visitor. He also adopted frontier habits quickly, expecting women to be responsible for their own baggage, to carry their share of the work entailed, and to show the same courage and maturity of emotions he expected of men.

In the Episcopal Church during the 1950s, women could not be lay readers, much less deacons or priests. Yet Bill allowed Bessie Kay and Amelia Hill to conduct services "illegally" in Allakaket because he realized the importance of their work, and he fully supported them. He did not, however, include them in the first clergy conference he held in Fairbanks in 1950, which one male lay reader attended.

"Looking back, I am embarrassed about this oversight," Bill says today. "We simply took for granted that women like Miss Kay and Miss Hill, and countless others, would carry out the kinds of tasks committed to them faithfully and well. Bishop Rowe once commented that the most difficult missions in Alaska were often manned by women. Yet at that time we could not even license a woman to be a lay reader, according to National Church canons. Then, in 1961 at the General Convention, I pointed out this terrible inequity, asking for a change to include women lay readers. I had to fight hard, and I finally persuaded the group, but the wording stated that a woman could be licensed when there was no qualified man available. How far we've come in twenty-five years since that seeming breakthrough!''

Bill had grown up watching his mother doing "a man's job," traveling about the South on speaking and teaching engagements, with never a word said about her need to stay home to look after the seven children. And as a young man, he witnessed the strong leadership of the Eskimo women along the Arctic Coast in a culture where females had to take their place working beside the men in order to survive. When he became bishop, he saw how crucial to the Church were the pioneer women missionaries, also the wives, nurses, and teachers of later years. So, in fact he, more than most leaders of that period, expected equal work and opportunities for women in the mission field within the bounds of canon law.

Many of the first women missionaries were from the influential Deaconess School of Philadelphia. Although in earlier years they wore long gray habits with flat collars, taking solemn vows to serve God and the Church, most were not set apart from society, but committed to be teachers, nurses, and helpers. Unlike women deacons today, they could not assist in the Holy Communion Services. (Anna Files and Susan Chapman were later graduates of Deaconess School.)

Deaconess Clara Carter, headmistress of the school in the early 1900s, came north to help Bishop Rowe as he began his work in Alaska. She started the mission at Allakaket, specializing in medical help, and was a profound influence on the people of the villages as well as on the women who followed her. Bishop Bentley recalls comments by his predecessor when Bishop Rowe took her and her female companion, Clara Heintz, into the remote village. "A crew of white men went along with them to build a one-room school, a little church, and a small two-story log dwelling.

"Then Bishop Rowe called the Indians and Eskimos of the two villages together and explained that he was leaving the two women among them, one to be a nurse and at the same time to hold church services, the other to be their childrens' teacher. He added that he was counting on the people there to see that the women had the fuel, wood, and water they needed, and to protect and look after them in every way. Bishop Rowe was wise enough to know that the natives would respect those two women, and would risk their own lives if need be for them. If a man had been placed in charge there, the attitude might have been less positive."

Deaconess A.G. Sterne spent thirty years teaching in the Bush, and was in so-called retirement in Tanana when Bill first became bishop. The Misses Kay and Hill, who followed Deaconess Carter, had the same attitude toward their work; they seldom took the furloughs due them. Allakaket was their home, and they almost never left it. Bill once persuaded them to fly with him to Bettles, a larger village farther north on the Koyukuk, and it was an outing that they long remembered.

Annie Farthing, founder of St. Mark's boarding school in Nenana in the early 1900s, died there following an altercation with a drunken man. She was alone at the time, exhausted from battling an outbreak of flu among her pupils, and when the man came to the school door, the quiet gentlewoman barred his way, saying he would have to kill her first. She died shortly afterward, her coworkers thought of a stroke or heart attack from the strain of the encounter and overwork.

Deaconess Kathleen Thompson, described as "weighing eighty-five pounds soaking wet," carried on the work of St. Mark's for many years. This influential school, along with a smaller one in Anvik, and another run by the Catholic Church on the Lower Yukon, were the only centers of learning at that time available to the Indian children of the vast Interior. Promising youngsters (many of them orphans) were sent from a number of villages, and many of today's native leaders owe their early education to St. Mark's. It was finally closed by Bill in 1955 when the state government assumed responsibility for schools in all areas of the Territory. "It was difficult decision that pained us all—to cease to do the work that had been carried on for fifty years," Bill recalls.

As head of St. Mark's, Deaconess Thompson was in a position

of authority when Bill became bishop, and she did not hesitate to voice her strong disapproval of the selection of such a young, inexperienced man. It took more than just good looks and charm to win over this venerable Irish lady. She finally capitulated and became one of his staunch supporters when she saw how hard he worked, and the results of his labors. When she went to a hospital in Seattle, where she learned she was dying of cancer, she asked Bill to fly her back to Nenana to live out her remaining days.

During Bill's years as bishop, many women followed in the footsteps of these early deaconesses as nurses and teachers, most of them unsung heroes who went about their work quietly and then moved on. Others worked as volunteers in the towns and cities, and then there was the elite group that formed Bill's office staff. He never had more than two paid helpers at a time, so the responsibility on their shoulders was enormous because of his frequent and lengthy absences. Their efforts included handling the mail, the financial books of the District, the schedules of events and visitors, the monthly newsletters to clergy, and the *Alaskan Churchman* (although Bill insisted on writing and editing much of this himself because he felt it so important).

They also drove personnel to and from the airport, coordinated their housing, helped newcomers with grocery lists, kept open house in their quarters for clergy coming into town—a place where they could vent their frustrations and have some drinks. These secretaries were often the go-betweens for disgruntled clergy and Bill, soothing hurt feelings, dealing with misunderstandings, assuring the young men and women that Bill would listen and be receptive. They also did much to prepare newcomers for the shock of going out into isolated villages, and they kept clergy wives, who were waiting to give birth, occupied by putting them to work sealing letters or stamping newsletters.

"We ran the office six days a week at that time, and thought nothing else about it," one secretary remembers. "But when the Presiding Bishop was visiting, he was surprised, and told us they only worked five days in New York." Bill's quick retort was, "We're working for the Lord up here." But from that moment on, the women had the weekends off. They continued to defend

Bill, however, pointing out that his work week was seven days. They say Bill was a good boss, although the atmosphere of the office was all business. He was fair, and trusted them totally, especially during his absences, when he put them in complete charge. "He was not quick to pat you on the back," one recalls, "and we were very aware of his sharp sarcastic tongue. He could say biting things to you, but they were quickly forgotten when his temper cooled down."

On a typical day when Bill was in Fairbanks, he came to the office early, laden with paperwork, and went right to his room, to a highly cluttered, disorganized desk that no secretary dared to touch. He remained in his room, with no coffee breaks, which he seldom drank anyway. "His mail was very important to him, he took it seriously, and answered every letter he received—he might dictate to a machine all morning. If someone sent a financial gift, no matter the amount, he always explained exactly how it was to be used," Dorothy Hall recalls. "At one time," she adds, "we started the day with a brief Morning Prayer service, but that didn't last long."

Bill went home for lunch, taking only an hour unless he had to mow his lawn—he never had anybody do that for him—and then he was back at his desk until five o'clock. Late in the afternoon he occasionally came out to spend a little time chatting with the secretaries. "Sometimes he had something on his mind he wanted to talk about, something we should know, or he just wanted to share," Dorothy says. "It might be village news, or any happening that was general knowledge. He wanted us to be aware of what was going on in the District so it would help us in our work when he wasn't there.

"He had a lot of Alaskans and Outside visitors drop in on him, and he was always very warm and gracious, quick to leave his desk work. If he was about to fly somewhere, you could tell his mind was on the weather—he'd come out of his office, look out my window, then go to another, then back to his. Then he might go gas up the plane, then come back and pace some more. Sometimes he began to worry about the wind and decide to go back and tie it down, or ask me to call the mechanic about some repairs. There were days when it was one thing right after another that had nothing to do with the office, and he always did the grocery store routine himself."

When Bill was out of town, the women assumed responsibility for taking care of whatever problems came along, for checking the mail, and handling accounts. All funds were deposited or dispersed by them, with a monthly accounting sheet left on Bill's desk. "He always knew where every penny came from, and where it went," Clover Jean Ward relates. "He was often given gifts for his discretionary fund, which he dispensed freely whenever the need arose."

Bill met his most formidable female adversary in the person of short, plump missionary nurse Jean Aubrey Dementi. The clash of two strong-willed personalities caused sparks to fly for years, and yet each admired the other, and Bill mentioned her work with great pride in many of his Outside talks. Jean's rare sense of humor also enlivened the pages of the *Alaskan Churchman.*

Jean was a nurse in southern California when she decided to work for the Church in Japan. Somehow, like so many others, she wound up in Alaska instead, going first to Nenana for four years to serve under Deaconess Thompson. The older woman taught her much, but Jean would not forget two bits of wisdom she learned about her Bishop. "The first was never to get between Bill and any of his clergy, and the second was the story of the great animosity he faced when he was first consecrated, and how hard he had worked to overcome it. I worshiped the ground he walked on," Jean said, and I vowed I would never say no to my Bishop about anything. Then I had a phone call from him asking me to go to Fort Yukon because the doctor had left, and he wanted me to keep it running until he found a replacement. He said it would be only for two or three months, but it became a year and a half. It was the last place I wanted to go, and besides, I was happy where I was. Of course, I went; I would have jumped into the river if he had told me."

When the new doctor arrived, Jean looked forward to working under him, but this time Bill asked her if she would become the first full time resident church worker in Shageluk. He felt Jean had the ability and personal strength to handle a village post by herself, but somehow he failed to communicate fully his reasons to her, or she in her anger, failed to hear them. She thought she was being removed from the hospital because a priest had told the Bishop she would be jealous of the doctor. And so it went, from one misunderstanding to another throughout their many years of work together.

Bill's *Alaskan Churchman* editorial of August 1955 announced that Miss Jean E. Aubrey, P.H.N., (Public Health Nurse) accompanied by 400 pounds of baggage, flew with Bishop Gordon to Anvik en route to her new post at Shageluk. It was quite a trip, because it occurred in May during break-up. Jean began with Bill in his ski plane, was transferred to a boat, then a dog team, and finally to a float plane for the last leg of her journey.

Jean wrote of her new home: "I am occupying a tiny ten foot by twelve foot cabin which is crammed full of me and my belongings. It takes only a few minutes to clean house and I can reach almost anything by stretching out an arm. One of the initial drawbacks was the lowness of the ceiling, for I can stand straight only in the center of the room. However, after one or two weeks of bumping my head several times a day, I finally learned to duck at the right times, so my head has assumed its former shape."

Meanwhile, Jean fit well into the village, quickly becoming accepted and loved by the people. She wrote a delightful account of her first Christmas in Shageluk for the *Alaskan Churchman,* "Away in a Cow-plate." "On Christmas Eve, twenty-two of us went caroling, another first for the village. Each family had been given a candle to burn in the window if they wanted us to sing to them, and it was a beautiful sight to see the glow of the single light through the thick frost on the window panes. There was a cold wind blowing, and the temperature was about ten below zero, but we managed to sing outside each cabin. We had one difficulty that is no problem to carolers Outside. The sled dogs took a dim view of the whole idea, and howled their heads off at each stop. It was a shivering bunch of singers who finally ran back to the mission house for cocoa and crackerjack, but we all agreed that we shall do it again next year, provided the temperature does not go below minus forty."

Jean worked for Bill in Shageluk, where she married Jim Dementi, and later in Anvik, spending fifteen years on the Lower

Middle Yukon. In the 1970s, the National Church canons were changed, and Bill asked Jean to become Alaska's first woman deacon, one of only twelve in the United States at that time. But once again came the clash of two strong wills. Bill wrote to Jean that he was coming through Shageluk on a certain date and could swing through Anvik and ordain her. Jean had heard many stories of other ordinations in the District, of the fun they were, of the many friends who came to help celebrate. By the time the mail plane came three days later, she had worked herself into an angry state: "If I'm going to be ordained, it will be a big ceremony and not just me kneeling on the kitchen floor," was her written reply. She added that all this time she loved the Bishop, and wanted his admiration and the knowledge that she was doing the right thing more than anything else in the world.

One day soon after this, a villager ran to tell Jean that Bishop Gordon was coming down the trail. "I had not heard him fly over because I was teaching school at the time. Another teacher took over, and we went into the kitchen where I fixed him some coffee, and he hemmed and hawed around a little bit. Pretty soon he looked at me and he had tears in his eyes. He said, 'I'm sorry,' and put his arms out and we both wept, and he gave me a big hug. Then he told me he was wrong and we were going to have an ordination the likes of which no one had seen before because I was the first woman, and he wanted it to be special."

Jean's ordination took place in Shageluk in mid-February of 1972 with Bill flying in several planeloads of guests from all over Alaska, along with all the food that would be needed for the three-day weekend. It was a historic and impressive occasion. Three other women, all long-time friends of Jean's, took part in the ceremony, as did her husband, Jim, and five clergymen assisted Bill, all wearing vestments that were offset by winter Indian foot gear (their version of the mukluk). The small church was packed, the intricately beaded embroidery on the altar cloth a contrast to the simple table that served as an altar and the rough interior of the building.

Bill would have liked to see Jean become a priest within a year, but, while he was quick to test national rules and regulations to suit his unique Territory, this was too major a step, especially at a time when many people were not ready to accept such a change. As it was, he later became one of the first bishops to support the ordination of women, and Jean eventually became Alaska's first woman priest. Jean said, "The Bishop and I have a loving and precious relationship and we agree that we gave each other our white hair!"

Despite all the women Bill worked with, or the many pretty ones whose adulation he enjoyed, the human anchor in Bill's life, his one love, his close companion, has always been Shirley. She was also the family parent. With four children to care for, Shirley was seldom able to travel with Bill, and his absences were always hard on her.

This was especially true when Bill was traveling in isolated areas, battling weather and often out of touch for days at a time. Over the years, Shirley received more than one call from the FAA reporting him missing, and although she tried to keep track of his movements via the Fairbanks Tundra Topics radio program, there was often cause for concern. Although she denies that she worried, her fingernail biting never stopped, and one of their children observes that she appeared to need the support of the Church and private prayer far more than did Bill.

When Bill did return to Fairbanks, usually for brief periods only, Shirley found it almost as hard to have to share their precious time together with the church office, the clergy and their wives, and others who stayed at the hostel. To have him home, and alone with the family, was rare.

Yet, Shirley always radiated a beautiful tranquility; as well as love, patience, and concern for everyone. When Bill was home, she became the eye of an intense magnetic storm, the center around which whirled cyclonic force winds. One close friend's words are echoed by many of the people who knew her: "I just can't imagine the life she's lived—seldom knowing where your husband is, if he is even alive or not—shouldering all that family responsibility alone. I've always felt Shirley was a saint."

"She related so well to all people," one priest recalls, "and was always warm and enthusiastic. But inside, I think she was very lonely and carried a heavy family burden."

What did Shirley do during Bill's many absences? The role

of Bishop's wife has never appealed to her. Hat and gloves, tea parties, and presiding over church women functions were eschewed; rather, she continued to enjoy her favorite bridge games, dropping everything when invited to play (Anna claims her first words as a baby were "two spades"). She was also active in the local Sourdough Square Dance Club and the League of Women Voters. She kept up with current world affairs and did far more serious reading than Bill, but she was never interested in a career of her own. "Bill is my career," she says, laughing gently. "And I've always felt content with it, not unfulfilled, as so many women complain today."

Another young priest, who spent much time in the Gordon home at one point in his career, observes that "some women who marry clergy seem to get their identity messed up with their husband's profession, to the impoverishment of both the marriage and the ministry, but Shirley stands out as one who knows herself and is comfortable with herself, and consequently allows the rest of us to be ourselves."

They were a team, say many friends and coworkers, and everyone agrees that Shirley's incredible inner strength and warm personality helped make it possible for Bill to do many of the things he did. Bill himself acknowledges that Shirley was an indispensable bridge between him and the clergy and their wives. In spite of her youth, she was their mother confessor. They all knew that conversations with Shirley were never passed on to Bill, and conversely, she claims that Bill was so close-mouthed she was the last to know of clergy goings on, or even of her husband's plans.

A long-time clergyman says that Shirley had an extraordinary way of calming the waters, as he recalls a stern confrontation with his boss after he had inadvertently kept Bill waiting on a trip. "He finally cooled down and moved on, but Shirley had observed the scene and she came over and put her arm around me. She just said, 'John, he'll get over it.' "

Shirley and Bill's home remained available to everyone, but with Bill's frequent absences, Shirley bore the brunt of their warm hospitality. All friends, members of any Episcopal Church, fellow workers, and Outside guests had an open invitation to come and go whenever they passed through Fairbanks. One year alone saw over 465 overnight guests, and there were as many as five or six people other than family present at any mealtime. In fact, it was precisely this "hotel" situation that persuaded the Presiding Bishop in Bill's earliest years to provide Outside funding to build the hostel.

One couple recalls that after going to Fairbanks to live, they met Bill at church on their first Sunday. They told him they were staying at a local hotel until they could find a home, and within one hour he was on the phone, asking them to lunch. "They even insisted we move in and stay with them for three weeks," Mary Fran Hill recalls. "He told us we would keep Shirley company [the two became close friends] and he gave Harold some chores to do."

The Gordon home was spacious, but the children often shifted into one another's bedrooms to free beds for house guests. The key to Shirley's ability to handle constant visitors (other than her love for people) was her easygoing way of dealing with the situation. Cutty Charlton, whose husband, Gordon was the priest at the church in Fairbanks in the early 1950s, reminisces, "Shirley's basement looked like a crowded warehouse—we all ordered our food in commercial quantities then, to be brought in on the railroad. When it was time for a meal and she had a houseful of guests, she never got uptight. She would say, 'Okay, folks. I'll have to pull something together—go down to the basement and see what you can find. Then get in the kitchen and start fixing it.' She did not wait on them. She couldn't, with small children to care for. And after a meal, she wasn't compulsive the way I was. I had to clean up instantly, but in the Gordon home all the dishes might be used up before anyone would get around to washing them." (The Gordon children recall Shirley cooking simple meals, using old standbys such as sweet and sour spare ribs and curried moose, still their favorite. They also ate frequent "buburgers," made from caribou meat.)

Family and friends always congregated in the kitchen; in fact everyone, including distinguished visitors from Outside, entered the house via the back door, past a garage so cluttered that it looked like a junkyard, and Shirley moved the meal to the dining room table only when dinner guests numbered over ten. No one used the living room unless there was a conference, but even it and the den, where Shirley's crossword puzzles were always ready to be worked on, looked lived in. Piles of clothing and children's belongings lined the stairway to the upstairs bedrooms.

One of Billy's friends from kindergarten days spent many of his early years in the Gordon home, the gathering place for the neighborhood children. He can hardly remember Bill being there, and when he was, "things were much tenser for Billy and me— we would eat quickly, usually in the dining room, and then leave. And if he was upstairs, we would go down. Mrs. Gordon was always nice to all of us kids; she almost adopted me when my parents were divorced. But she let us get away with just about anything."

Billy's friend says that the two led a carefree, mischief-filled life in the small frontier town, where everyone knew everyone else. They were allowed to roam day and night, with few rules, no curfews or restrictions. "I really think Billy did some of the especially naughty things just to attract his father's attention. A lot of pressure was put on all the kids to succeed, but they didn't have constant, clear directions to follow. Billy was very smart, got good grades in school when he worked, and usually got what he wanted.

"When we left church on Sundays to go to Sunday School, we followed the other kids out the side door, but then went on down to the river bank to play. We'd help ourselves to the barrels of squaw candy [strips of dried fish] in the basement, sneak a few coins from Mrs. Gordon's purse for candy bars, and then we'd be all set for a full day on our own.

"When Billy was about eleven, we taught ourselves to drive, using a VW parked on the Gordons' front lawn. Once we took off for a whole night's drive—I was in the Bishop's brand new Jeep pickup. We refueled from his aviation gas pump at the airfield, and no one was ever the wiser."

Billy does not recall ever feeling any pressure from towns-people to behave because he was the Bishop's son, but Becky admits she occasionally felt the need to prove she was normal. However, when Billy reached fifteen years of age, Shirley felt she could no longer cope with a teenage boy, and he was sent to St. Paul's boarding school in New Hampshire. Bill says today that "Shirley had a hard time with Billy. She had to assume a new role, a take-charge role not natural to her." He adds, "If I ever failed anyone, I failed him. We were never intimate, and he was one of the casualties of my job. It cost him more than any of the others. Paneen, as the eldest, was close to her mother, and she always worked to capacity in everything she undertook. Becky was the princess type, with several boys at a time hanging about the house to gain her attention. She was very bright, got straight A's, but felt that stigma and never let it be known."

Everyone agrees that Anna came from a different mold, born so much later that it was almost as if she had a different set of parents. Self-confident and always a crusader, she and Paneen were the only two who remained churchgoers. Anna was still a baby when the Gordon children acquired their first dog, an extraordinary event in light of Bill's feelings about household pets. Billy brought the cocker spaniel pup home from a friend's house one evening, and he and his two sisters pleaded to keep it. Bill replied they could not, but little Taffy was left in the backyard that night, pending a decision on his disposition the next day. Paneen could hear him crying from her bedroom window, and when there was silence, she peeked out, only to see her dad feeding and cuddling the animal. She was smart enough to keep quiet, and they accepted their father's edict the following morning: the dog could stay *if* he was kept outdoors. Not a week went by before Taffy became a house pet, loved by all, and Bill was the first, Shirley claims, to start letting him inside.

The children agree that they have few memories of Bill's presence at home, but then they say they accepted this as part of their lives, and they never doubted that God and service must come first for him. They sensed that their father often felt guilty about missing birthdays and other holidays, but they considered it sacrilegious "for him to put us first."

Life was different when Bill did come home. "He became very upset if we didn't treat Mother well, but I never remember him losing his temper outwardly," Billy recalls. "All the warning we needed was the tone of his voice, and his exasperated exhale spoke volumes." Becky claims it was the way he slammed down the phone when he discovered she was still on it. Becky adds, "We were a hugging, touching family—Dad used to scratch my back, and rub my legs when they hurt. He's not afraid to be tender and he could tell us he loved us." Anna says, "Once two of my friends came to spend the night because their father was drunk and told them he never wanted to see them again. Later Daddy said to me that he could never hate me; he said he would always love me no matter what. To me that sounds like perfect love."

But Billy says, "It was hard for him to give us verbal pats on the back until he thought they were really deserved. That was his style, with the people he worked with, too. The ones we did get were well remembered."

The children were unanimous about Bill's frugality (and Shirley's as well). "He avoided spending money unless he had to . . . he would threaten to charge us a nickel for every light that was on in the house. . . . He was concerned about wasting car gas, would go out of his way to buy something on sale . . . and he tapped his foot all during any long distance telephone call of ours." Becky adds, "When I was in college in California, I'd be scared to call home—it would have to be a dire emergency." Anna concludes thoughtfully, "It must have been something to do with being so poor when he grew up. He really never had any money to spend until later in life."

"It hurt when he wasn't home for birthdays, and you knew Mother had signed the card for him," adds Becky, "but I'll never forget the times he took me and a couple of friends flying with him as a special birthday treat—to a place like Circle Hot Springs for the day [a resort on the Arctic Circle, which consisted of a large wooden building containing some bedrooms, a restaurant, and an indoor swimming pool filled with warm water piped right from the ground.]" Anna says, "He used to take us on an occasional Sunday visitation to villages, except then we had to sit through the same sermon two or three times." Anna quickly gained the family reputation as disrupter of her father's services, and once, when he was telling one of his Point Hope dog team stories, she asked her mother in a voice that carried to the back of the church: "Is that really true?" Another time, in Tanana, she sat among the village youngsters in the front pew. A village elder and longtime friend of Bill's, designated as head usher, carried a stick to help keep the little ones quiet, tapping a noisy child on the head. During his sermon, Bill became aware of a commotion among the youngsters, and old Fred Starr came stamping down the aisle. When he saw that it was five-year-old Anna who was the culprit, he simply raised his hands resignedly and retreated to the back of the church.

Billy was taken on several hunting trips as Bill tried to supplement their food supply each fall, but the outcome of the first trip was almost fatal to Bill. Each year he was invited to hunt caribou with the people of Arctic Village, the smallest, most isolated Indian settlement in the foothills of the Brooks Mountain Range, 150 miles north of the Arctic Circle. In fact, he hunted there for so many years that the people named a hill northeast of the village, Bishop Vatah, meaning "Bishop's Hill." They usually camped there when Bill came, spending hours talking with one another about life and the world and God.

Bill also contributed something else to the permanent landscape: his airplane. He flew eleven-year-old Billy there for his first hunt in 1957, landing on a short sand bar twenty miles northeast of the village. After several days of shooting ten caribou (enough for the Fort Yukon hospital as well as the Gordon family), Bill decided to fly them back to the village one at a time. He cut his fuel to the minimum, and left Billy behind until the last trip out. With all these precautions, even one caribou was an overload.

The hunters heard the wracking of the plane engine, then a loud "whack," and finally silence. The plane never got into the air; it staggered in a slightly nose-high position and plowed into the top of the bank across the river. The plane was demolished, but Bill was unhurt, in spite of the heavy load of meat behind his seat. They took an Air Rescue plane home.

Bill returned two weeks later and tried to salvage at least the instruments and radio, but winter had arrived, bringing ice along the edge of the river. It had rained, too, so the water was high and well over his head. Bill recalls, "I had no choice but to swim across about a hundred feet, towing an air mattress behind me. You've heard of blue babies—well I was one real blue bishop.

I tried to build a fire by the plane by using some of the gas, but I had forgotten to bring matches. I did find a single match in an old folder in the wreck. When I threw it at the pile of wood soaked in gas (I didn't dare stand too close), I missed completely. I had to swim the river four times before I was finished.

"A year later, the people brought the fuselage back to the village and a man turned the cabin (minus its wings) on end, with the tail up and used it for an outhouse. That plane was the original *Blue Box*, and had given me 150,000 miles of flying. The church women came forward again with Thank Offering money to help fund the *Blue Box Second*, a Cessna 180 which was to serve me well for another ten years."

One adventure which the whole family faced together was the devastating flood that hit Fairbanks in 1967. After many weeks of heavy rains, the Chena River overflowed its banks and inundated most of the city with almost five feet of swiftly-flowing muddy water. Bill had been preparing to ferry several planeloads of people to Point Hope for an ordination when the flood caught up with him at home, stranding some of his passengers there as well. (The hostel was full, too.)

"I remember the flood as being a fun time," Becky recalls.

"That's because four of your boyfriends made a beeline for our house and got stuck there for three days," Billy retorts. The Gordons had a total of thirteen house guests, and the children agree that the meal situation was a strain on their mother.

The water filled their basement, coming to ground floor level and Bill and Shirley lost many stored mementos, including pictures and yearbooks. Anna recalls her dad standing with a broom at the top of the steep driveway down to the basement-level garage, trying to sweep the water back. "The water was pouring into town, peoples' homes were about to float away, and Dad was out there with a broom—boats went by causing waves, making him mad."

Bill recalls that "officials predicted the water would crest at midnight. At eleven-fifty-five P.M. it appeared on our street, and began flowing into our garage. I used a broom to push it back, figuring that in five more minutes it would not get any higher. Then I looked in the other direction—a two-foot wall of water was headed right toward us and I realized that in no way would it crest by twelve o'clock. So we frantically began moving a lot of things upstairs; three of us quickly hauled up the big freezer full of moosemeat."

The water never did get onto their first floor, although it was about five feet deep on the street outside. The Gordons were fortunate because they were on high ground, and never even lost their utilities. Also, Bill had just purchased a lot of food to take to Point Hope—thirteen loaves of bread, large boxes of doughnuts, cases of soda pop, and bags of oranges. Bill was stranded, along with all the others, for three days, although he could not resist using waders and making his way the three blocks to his office to check up on everyone there. On the second day, he borrowed a boat to go look at his plane. Fortunately it was undamaged. Although water got into the tail and messed up the radio, it did not touch the engine. The people of Fairbanks, joined by many volunteers from Anchorage had a lot of cleaning up to do. For Bill it was his basement, the office, and church.

The highlight of family life for Shirley and the children was the vacation they shared once every three years to the Lower 48. The one drawback was the long, uncomfortable ride down the Alaska Highway and back, a 1,500-mile ribbon of dust-laden, rock-strewn road connecting isolated small towns in the vast Canadian wilderness. They had to drive because the cost of flying six people was prohibitive, and also it gave Bill the opportunity to pick up a new car arranged by the Diocese of Michigan for a number of years. They always told him he could have whatever options he wished, but even with a gift he could not make "wasteful expenditures." In earlier years he would never accept a radio, but later they became standard equipment, to his childrens' joy.

Anna comments, "people talk about driving the highway for fun, and I just can't imagine it. We drove to get places!"

Becky adds, "We went from Miami Beach to Fairbanks in ten days once. That was a horrible trip."

Billy feels an explanation is needed. "That's when I broke her collarbone. I pulled her over the front seat to the back—she didn't want to come. Her arm came, but she didn't."

Anna was too young to remember and asks, "I suppose Dad

kept on driving?''

Becky answers, "Oh yes, we didn't stop for that.''
The children explain they were allowed only two rest stops
a day, and stopped for the night at the first cheap motel that
happened to turn up around nine P.M. They would go right to
bed, and at four in the morning somebody would be dressing
them, getting them back into the car. They always carried their
food with them—buying anything in restaurants was out of the
question.

Once they reached their destination, the children say they
enjoyed staying with Washington State or North Carolina relatives, but there were other times when they were left with
strangers. These vacation trips were planned to coincide with
National Conventions of the Church, as well as the two Lambeth
Conferences in England (a meeting of the worldwide Anglican
Communion every ten years, which the Gordons attended twice),
and Bill and Shirley left the children with various friends of theirs.

"It was an hour introduction, then all of a sudden, good-bye,''
Anna claims. Becky adds that her mother can't believe now that
she would do such a thing.

One of the more memorable trips down the Alaska Highway
with their father was by plane, in 1969, to Billy's wedding. After
St. Paul's, he went to the University of North Carolina, where
he met his bride-to-be. Although it was early summer, Bill says
he encountered the worst weather he had ever seen and they were
forced to wait out the storms at several small villages along the
road. First Billy and then Becky were forced to "abandon ship''
and go commercially by the time Bill reached Winnipeg, and then
he, Shirley, and Anna had to leave the plane in Wilmington,
Delaware, the day before the wedding and take the train into New
York City. While waiting to be met under the clock in Grand
Central Station, a chauffeur in uniform approached the bedraggled
threesome and asked Bill, "You wouldn't by any chance be the
Bishop of Alaska?'' Bill, who was still wearing his usual flying
outfit of a red baseball cap, rumpled khaki Eisenhower jacket,
and khaki pants—half in and half out of his scuffed cowboy
boots—had to admit that he was. "We tried for years to get Dad
to dress up a little more when he went Outside,'' sighs Anna.

On an earlier flight up the Highway, Bill was alone, and looked even more scruffy as he hitched a ride from the airport to town with a longtime Canadian Bush pilot. They shared flying experiences over breakfast the following morning, and the other man asked Bill whom he flew for, Wien or Consolidated Airlines. "Neither," Bill replied, "to be perfectly honest with you, I am the Bishop of Alaska."

The old-timer stood up and said, "Excuse me, I always thought I was a good judge of character." And off he walked.

Chapter 8

Living Christianity

Judy and Curtis Edwards were both awakened instantly by a crackling noise. It was about 5:30 A.M. on 17 March 1961 the day Bill was to arrive on his annual Tanana visitation. "You know how it is when you hear something at night," Judy says. "We jumped out of bed and ran across the small hall to the three children's bedroom. Curtis must have realized right away what was the matter, although at that moment we could not see flames or even smoke. He rushed down the stairs toward the wood stove, in the basement beneath the living room.

"I ran into the children's room; we had agreed that if we ever had to get out of the house quickly at night we would use their window. It was small and above the level of my shoulders. [Judy is only 5′2″ tall.] And it would not budge. I guess it was frozen shut because it was well below zero outside. Then I remembered the window in the hallway which opened on the roof of our new addition."

The Edwardses had just added the final touches to the living room-meeting room-church classroom and village library which Curtis had been working on all fall, the start of their second year in the village. He and Judy had painted the walls; then Judy hung frilly home-sewn curtains at all the windows just in time for the Bishop's visit. Curtis had also installed a new wood stove to take the place of the oil one. Judy recalls talk later about a building up of creosote, of trouble with the "stack robber."

"I remember going past the aluminum stove pipe which went up through the children's room, and the floor around it felt hot, but there were no flames visible. As I passed the children—the girls in the double bed and little Curtis in a small one, I remember waking them. I don't know whether I grabbed Lucy and pulled her along or whether she jumped up and ran with me as I returned to the hall.

"That window was also above my shoulders, but it was lower and bigger, and I could push it up. Curtis had gotten a ladder and was climbing up onto the roof. The opened window brought the fire roaring up the stairwell. Lucy was standing between me and it and I turned to pick her up, the flames licking at my arms, but I could not push her out the high window. [Lucy was a tall, sturdy seven year old.] Curtis called to me to climb out, that he would get her. I leaned through the opening and he pulled me out. By then the flames were coming along with me, covering my back and legs.

"I landed on the roof as Curtis went back inside, and I rolled down off the steep pitch and onto the soft snow bank below. When I got up, I could see Lucy lying on the roof. An old man who lived next door—Grandpa Swenson—ran up the ladder, brought her down, and laid her in the snow. I remember looking at her and thinking, 'I hope she doesn't suffer,' because she was just blackened. I didn't want to pick her up because I was afraid it would hurt her. Grandpa Swenson then leaned over, scooped her up, and carried her back to his house.

"I turned and ran in the snow—in bare feet all this time—across the street to Pinky's house. Someone began ringing the church bell just as I burst through their door. I could look out their window and see my home enveloped in flames, and I remembered saying that Curtis and the children were all gone. I just knew Curtis had not come back out—no one ever had to tell me.

"Pinky helped me take off my nightgown, which I remember smelled and looked burned, and then she helped me crawl into their bed. Roy, her husband, told me that he saw Tanana's one ambulance go to Grandpa Swenson's house. I knew it was picking up Lucy, so we would have to wait for it to come back. I was not in pain at that point; I only felt a burning or stinging sensation over most of my body.

"When the ambulance arrived, Pinky wrapped me in an old

blanket, a scratchy, wool one. I rode in the front seat, sitting up, and I remember we drove past our house. Of course it was still burning, and I saw the lovely plated glass window in front crack and fall apart at that very moment. When we reached the hospital, I walked inside, the old blanket still over me, and Lucy was on a guerney in the hallway. I went up to talk to her, but I don't recall that she was saying anything. Maybe she was unconscious. Then Dr. Hadley came to take me into the little clinic room. He took the blanket off to look at my back, and said in a calm voice, 'Well, I see a little first degree, maybe a couple of spots of second.' He told me later that that was the hardest thing he ever had to do, because I was covered with second and third degree burns from head to toe.

"The doctors took me to my room immediately, and about that time I began to hurt. They put Lucy in the room next to me, which I was really glad of because I could hear her talking with them. They came in soon and told me that because her lungs had been burned there was no hope for her. The doctors promised me they would keep her free of pain, which they were able to do.

"I had enough Christian belief to know that it would be better where she was going, and that she would be with the rest of the family. Lucy had always been the slow one in the family; whenever we went any place with the three children, she would always be lagging behind. I have a memory of walking out of that house and starting down the road, and Lucy hollering from behind, 'Wait for me, here I come.' "

Bill's phone rang about a quarter after six that morning. Alfred Miller, one of the maintenance men at the Public Health Service Hospital in Tanana and a close friend of the Edwards, broke the terrible news. Bill said he would fly as soon as possible.

He arrived a little after eight o'clock; "I remember approaching the village and seeing the smoke still coming up from the burning mission house. Alfred Miller was waiting at the airstrip to take me to the hospital. Actually, I did not much want to go in, but steeled myself to do so."

Lucy Edwards was terribly burned over approximately ninety percent of her body, and there was no hope for survival. She was heavily sedated, but Bill spent some time beside her in prayer.

She lived about six hours and then Bill had the difficult task of telling Judy that her third child had died.

"She took this with remarkable calmness, realizing the agony that Lucy would have suffered, that her death was really a blessing. I stayed with her all that day and the doctors and staff were magnificent in their concern and caring."

The two young doctors used what they called an 'open technique,' keeping Judy's room as sterile as possible. Besides themselves, only the nurses and Bill were allowed in. Because Judy was badly burned on both her front and back, they improvised a kind of cradle, with a couple of heat lamps inside. Any covers would give her pain. She had to be turned over every thirty minutes, a painful undertaking. To compound her misery, Judy's long red hair was in plastic rollers at the time of the fire, and they melted from the heat. Someone—Judy does not recall who—spent hours gently cutting them out.

The only pain medication they could give Judy for the first three days was whiskey, and none was available in the village, so Bill agreed to fly to Fairbanks to buy some. The doctor hated to ask this favor because he knew how Bill felt about alcohol!

Except for two brief trips to Fairbanks, Bill remained at the hospital near Judy, on call day and night for seven days. "My presence in her room seemed to be a source of strength and comfort for her. We did not talk much, she seldom complained, and never once did I hear her say, 'we shouldn't have come to Tanana.' "

Bill also felt responsibility for the grief-stricken village, and he held a service in the church on Friday evening, the day of the fire. "I tried to say something that would be helpful and faith-supporting to those loving people who had lost their shepherd. Earlier that day, I had had the difficult task of searching through the few remains of the house, to find whatever we could of the bodies of Curtis and the two children. The few remains [placed in a small square box], along with Lucy's body, were prepared for burial on a lovely hill above the Tanana and Yukon rivers following the Sunday afternoon service. Judy had asked that none of her family or Curtis's come from Texas for the funeral, but Curtis's father made the trip, flying in for the day."

Judy also asked Bill to go on with his regular visitation as best he could, and so on Sunday morning Alfred Grant, the lay reader at St. James Mission, presented the class that Curtis had prepared for confirmation. "I preached again, in a most difficult and testing situation."

That afternoon, people arrived from Fairbanks and elsewhere for the funeral, including six priests who had been close to Curtis. Looking back, Bill feels it was not an inspiring occasion. "I myself was pretty well drained from the tension and tragedy of the whole occasion." Bill does not mention it, but his hair turned from a sprinkle of gray to almost pure white during this time.

Judy, of course, remained in the hospital in severe pain and she cannot recall giving any input to the service, except suggesting the hymn "I Sing a Song of the Saints of God." She also remembers that the village women made the traditional little mittens and burial boots of white moose skin for her children. Otherwise, she has no memories of that day's sad events.

But the entire town—adults and children—as well as numerous visiting clergy, remembers. The church was packed and everyone was crying. Bill delivered a sermon and afterwards all present walked the three miles to the burial site. They had a hard time digging in the frozen ground, so they used a blow torch and loosened enough dirt to cover up the little boxes.

Bill later wrote in the *Alaskan Churchman:* "From the first, Curtis and Judy and the children became a real part of the life of Tanana. They did not come to minister to the community; they came to be a part of the vital life of the village and to bring God's strength to His family there as a part of that family. In many ways the Church in Tanana is the community; Curtis preached the Gospel, but even more important, he lived it, and anything that concerned the people of Tanana concerned him too."

"Once we made it through Sunday," Bill recalls, "we had to face the fact that the Tanana hospital was not equipped to take care of a seriously burned person over a long range, and infection was a grave concern. When I flew back to Fairbanks on Tuesday, I was dismayed to find out that St. Joseph's Hospital, the only one in our town, was full and Judy would have to be in a bed in the hall.

"The Army had built a large hospital at Fort Wainwright (on the outskirts of Fairbanks), in anticipation of the possible evacuation of casualties from the Korean War to that base, and they were admirably equipped to deal with burned military personnel. So, I began negotiations with them to take Judy under special circumstances. This proved to be very difficult and I finally ended up going to the commanding general of the Alaska Command at Fort Richardson in Anchorage. I admit I did a little threatening of some bad publicity for the Army before permission was obtained.''

Judy's sister-in-law, Maryann Munroe, a registered nurse, came to Fairbanks to be with her during her lengthy stay at the Fort Wainwright hospital. Bill continued to pop in and out frequently and Maryann recalls his jaunty red baseball cap, as well as the bunches of yellow daffodils he usually brought along. She says, "He saved Judy's life, there's no doubt in my mind. She did not know how badly she was burned, and she would have died if they had let her know how close to death she was.''

Judy says, "I remember being terribly concerned after the fire about the Bishop and Shirley having to receive such a shocking phone call. It must have been hard for him to face me for the first time. I could have been very angry; I wanted to reassure him that I didn't hold him responsible. And I worried about Curtis's family as well. I think it's a blessing when you can get to the point where you're more concerned about other people than you are yourself.

"I knew from how caring the Bishop had been about our family that he would feel some responsibility for what happened. I also knew Curtis would do just what he wanted to do—he had come to Tanana because it was where he wanted to be above anywhere else, and he went back into the house for the same reason. I think that my feeling this way was part of God's healing for me. It was a big help to me as I pulled myself back together emotionally. I had to go through periods of wondering why, but I was never mad at God.''

"Judy was a tough, cocky survivor," Bill recalls. "The doctors said she pulled through because she was physically and mentally strong. They said she was lucky not to get infections. I believe her healing and fast recovery was a miracle. They said she would be in Wainwright at least two months, and then have to undergo extensive surgery. She was out of the hospital in four weeks, with no immediate operations needed. She moved into the church hostel, and then decided to return to Tanana that summer to stay with her close friends for a number of weeks."

Judy says, "No one understood why, except the Bishop. I just did nothing there but walk, pick berries, and go on picnics and boat rides on the river. I even felt good about visiting the grave site, knowing the family was all together. I was with my friends and felt so at home and at peace with everyone there. They needed ministering to, also. They needed to see me healing."

In July, Judy returned to the families in Texas. She underwent plastic surgery for burn scars in Houston, and then moved to Arkansas, where an Episcopal bishop offered her a job in his office. Two years later, she married Bob Jones, one of Curtis's closest friends at seminary, and a priest in Kotzebue at the time. So Judy returned to live in Alaska, to live in a village once again, and both of her sons were born there. (They are now in Wyoming, where Bob is the Episcopal Bishop of the Diocese.)

The Tanana fire had an enormous impact, not only on the families directly involved, but also on all of the people in the village, and on the entire Missionary District. Paneen Gordon, who was away at college at the time, wrote her parents that she was so glad to be a Christian at such a difficult time, and how terrible it must be on those who were not. Everyone was stunned by Judy's enormous loss, as well as by her courage and faith. "The true test of one's faith," she says, "is how one can handle crisis. I think the Bishop carried us all along in helping us cling to that faith—me, Curtis's family, the village, the whole District family. A weaker man would not have been able to shoulder such a burden."

Bill says, "As I look back, it gave me the opportunity to test my own faith and see God's will that we lean on him; that even in the darkest of tragedies, goodness and strength can come if we but trust Him. Judy showed us all that."

Most of the people who knew Bill say that they saw a number of subtle changes in him following the fire. The consensus is that he became gentler, a little more mellow, not so prone to criticize or make sharp retorts. Bill says that it was the first time in his life that he was truly forced to reach beyond his own strength to rely on someone else.

It was not only the tragedy that changed Bill. He was at a stage in his career where he no longer had to prove himself to the National Church and House of Bishops, to his parishioners and team, and especially to himself. In earlier days, the office of the bishop overshadowed the brash, inexperienced young man. But, as Bill grew into the office, he became increasingly free to be both a warm pastor and a good friend. And as he relaxed, his stature as "Bishop" grew. The super confidence, stubbornness, and headstrong ways of the young priest in Point Hope were still there, but they had been molded into the necessary attributes of a forceful, courageous leader.

Although Bill succeeded in attaining one of his prime goals— filling every post—the need for funds still plagued his ever more ambitious plans, and he worked as hard, and traveled as much as ever. ("Go-go," his priests had nicknamed him.) Now he had to maintain contact with his large team, more churches needed visitations, more people had to be flown to an increasing number of District-wide meetings, and he was in great demand as a speaker in the Lower 48.

The *Alaskan Churchman* (with a nationwide circulation of about 4,000) brought the District much public relations, but it was Bill's personal appearances at church groups of all kinds that brought in the largest amount of financial support. Bill did not deliberately set out to be a fund raiser—it was against National Church rules—but his charm, enthusiasm, and his stories of Alaskan adventures drew crowds of people, along with their checkbooks.

One women's auxiliary from New York State supported a young girl dying of tuberculosis at Point Lay (she recovered, thanks to their help); a wealthy woman in California sent a $500 check each year to the Point Hope mission; a southern church group "adopted" Peel Tooyak's family; and another gave clothing to the Swans in Kivalina one winter. In later years, it was a new log house for Jean Aubrey Dementi in Shageluk, clothing and toys for the children of St. Mark's boarding school, and special equipment for the Fort Yukon Hospital. Money flowed in for specific concerns, and Bill always made sure the contributors knew in a tangible way, how much they had helped, thereby insuring continued giving.

The United Thank Offering of the National Episcopal Church Women, which collected over a million dollars from all over the country, took care of a number of Alaskan needs throughout the years, including two of Bill's airplanes—Blue Box I and II. In fact, $1,000, or one-half of the first UTO gathering in 1889, built the first church in Anvik. In 1966, when Bill approached them for funds toward a new plane, the UTO Executive Board turned him down. They cited large-scale giving to world-wide needs as the reason, and Bill was surprised and upset. The "Blue Box" airplanes had by then acquired a big following among churchwomen.

A heated exchange of letters between Bill and the Board highlights his concern about the new "detached" approach. "The Church has lost a lot with the failure to recognize the need for emotional personalization," he wrote. "Big-time, high level projects—no matter how critically needed—will not provide this. Most of these women who give are not women who deal with or think in a world-wide way. Their lives are circumscribed; things are most meaningful that they can see and understand. Obviously we do not want to keep them there, but they cannot make this jump overnight, or because we *think* they should." Bill described this exchange in what he refers to as a "catty editorial" in the *Alaskan Churchman,* one that he now wishes he could take back.

It was inevitable that such widespread exposure as Alaska's "flying Bishop" should spread into the secular world, beginning as early as 1953. "It was a cold December day," Bill recalls, "and I was sitting in the kitchen while Shirley was fixing lunch. The phone rang, and it was a man representing the National Junior Chamber of Commerce, telling me that I had been chosen one of the ten outstanding young men [under thirty-five] in the United States for that year. He asked if I could attend a banquet in our honor the end of January in Seattle. I was stunned by the news, but the request that I attend the banquet put me on the spot because, ironically, I had already committed myself to a two-week speaking tour in Florida at the same time." He was able to adjust his schedule so he could fly up just in time for the dinner, changing his clothes on the plane. Bill was especially honored to be the first person in the field of religion to be chosen since the award was begun in the 1930s.

During that same time period, the Associated Press ran a prominent story about Bill's rescuing a Fairbanks Air Service pilot missing on a flight from the village of Beaver. As chaplain of the Civil Air Patrol, Bill had been called to help search. He was supposed to go to a briefing later that morning, but, in typical fashion, he decided not to wait, and took off at first light on his own. "He was a friend, and I didn't want him to have to stay out in minus twenty-five degrees too long." A half hour out of Fairbanks, Bill spotted the plane on some river ice, and landed on a very short and narrow section. He picked up the cold and hungry, but uninjured, pilot, returning him to town before the official search had even begun.

Three films were made on Bill's work in Alaska, and all three had wide distribution, even on television networks, but Bill's first personal appearance in front of TV cameras was as a contestant on "To Tell the Truth" in 1966. He, Shirley, and Anna were en route to Paneen's graduation from Mt. Holyoke College when they stopped off in New York. Anna remembers the hot studio and bright lights, and recalls it as an exciting yet disappointing experience. "They made Dad wear a ratty-looking parka, while one of the other two men wore a clerical collar, and the third was in a lumberjack shirt. Dad sat between the impostors and was shorter and younger. All three certainly didn't look like bishops!" Bill could not hide his knowledge of Alaska. He garnered 3 of 4 votes, meaning he only won $50 for his efforts.

Bill was not one to shy away from publicity, although he did not seek it, because he was always aware of the help it could bring to the District. However, he carefully avoided personal accolades such as honorary degrees. Virginia Seminary offered him a Doctor of Divinity four years after he became bishop, but he refused it, saying he had not done anything to deserve it other than be elected. A *Southern Churchman* magazine column commented on the exclusive club called the S.R.H.D. (Society for the Refusal of Honorary Degrees). "We now hear of one—and as far as we know the only one—who deserves to be enrolled as a member."

Bill remained a "member" for years, until Virginia Seminary decided to award him one anyway, and since Bill did not show up to receive it, they sent the coveted certificate north in the hands of one of Bill's young seminarian volunteers. He arrived in Fairbanks with several classmates at 6 A.M. one June morning, and they were taken home for breakfast by Bill. He was waiting for an opportune time to present the degree, and when Bill had everyone's attention in order to say grace before they sat down to eat, he spoke up: "Bishop, I have a presentation from Virginia Seminary," and he gave him the degree. Bill replied, "Thank you very much," casually tossed it on the sideboard, and went on with his prayer. The seminarian was most impressed. "If I had gotten a D.D., I think I'd be running through the streets shouting about it, but it didn't faze him in the least."

Bill's other major goal, besides full staffing of all thirty-four posts, and one that he worked toward throughout his years as bishop, was the concept of "one family" for his District. Because of its enormous size and great diversity, Bill felt it essential to strengthen the tenuous ties among his far-flung parishioners and workers. The isolation—from village to village, to town or city, from the Arctic Coast to the Southeastern Panhandle—was a deterrant to work and growth, and the farther distance to the Lower 48 and national headquarters posed additional problems. "I believe that our coming together is important," Bill told a later gathering of delegates from all over Alaska. "The Church is not just the bishop, the clergy, or buildings; it is not some vague spiritual thing that we sometimes refer to as the Body of Christ. The Church is living people and unless those who sit in the congregations have a share in the total work of the Church, then the Church is *not* the body that Christ intended."

A priest who lived for years in Southeast Alaska says, "When the Bishop was in a given place, he gave himself fully to it, but he was also a communicator for other parts of Alaska, bringing everyone a sense of unity. We heard his sermons about the northern village peoples, we read his stories in the *Alaskan Churchman,* and in later years we met and hosted in our homes delegations from everywhere."

Bill was forced to implement his dream on a small scale at first, flying himself and a few of his team to many outlying areas. Then, on a cold, snowy day in Fairbanks on 14 February 1950 Bill held the first of many annual all-Alaska clergy conferences. Traveling almost fifteen thousand miles by boat, railroad, and air, twelve clergymen gathered at St. Matthew's Church in Fairbanks. The tradition established, Bill began asking some outstanding theologian from Outside to join them. They gathered for three to five days, listening to and visiting with their guest in the mornings and evenings, then talking about some of the needs of the District in the afternoons. These topics ranged from the moral dilemma the native people faced as they were forced into lying over beaver limits, to clarification of baptism and the marriage canon. Obvious throughout each meeting was a strong feeling of fellowship and oneness of purpose, especially appreciated by the priests who then returned to isolated posts where they might not see another missionary for many months.

Volatile issues in earlier years were often theological details that later Bill was more likely to overlook or dismiss as individual preferences. In the late 1950s, the battle over the use of the title "Father" erupted. Bill did not like the use of "father." The title "mister" was used in the Bush during the early days, while the other began to appear in town parishes. Norman Elliott was secretary of the conference in 1956, and he began reading the minutes of the previous day: "Father Cleveland said this," and "Father Mendelsohn said that." Bill quickly stopped him, asking about "all this father business." Norman told him that these men had agreed on the use of the title. Bill wanted to take an immediate poll, and he went around the room asking each man what he preferred to be called. He was surprised that Norman was right, and he never brought up the issue again.

Later Bill expanded the gatherings to include an annual one for clergy wives, for Episcopal Church Women (ECW) and then District convocations, which included lay representatives. The format always remained the same, with as much time given to spiritual revitalization and fellowship as to business, although the latter became increasingly complex as the District grew in size. Bill ran the business meetings according to a schedule, using *Robert's Rules of Order,* but he was always careful that everyone had a chance to speak, and he broadly assigned responsibilities in work and in worship, making sure that newer people were involved.

These gatherings posed an inordinate amount of work for him: "I flew thirty-eight hours in three days before and afterward, getting passengers to and from the site. That's actual air hours, and doesn't count the time spent in loading baggage, refueling, and waiting for people. That on top of presiding for five days. But it was the only way to get it done."

For many Indian and Eskimo people, these trips with Bill were a rare visit outside their own village. Staying in city homes was a treat, and a free afternoon was always planned so they could do downtown shopping. One delegate, the long-time Eskimo interpreter at Allakaket, insisted on being taken to a Fairbanks store before the conference, to buy a suit for such a big occasion. An Indian priest from the Fort Yukon area will never forget his flight with Bill. "It was bad weather. Somehow he go over top of cloud, over the mountains. Around Anchorage he is looking for the hole, and there's no hole. One place he sees a little one that is closing pretty fast. He just dived down, straight down about 9,000 feet. My right eardrum burst open. Talk about pain."

Many of Bill's priests who moved away and later attended similar meetings in Outside Dioceses say they missed the informal Alaskan gatherings, where the emphasis was not on business and politics. Also, Alaska was different in that delegates always stayed in people's homes rather than hotels. Perhaps the unique aspect of Alaskan District gatherings was the manner in which Bill introduced every participant as they all gathered for the first meal. He was able to go from person to person in a room of thirty or forty people and, without the slightest hesitation, give their full names, tell where they came from, who was in their family, what they did, and what their latest news was. Nobody recalls a slip up, nor did he ever need prompting.

This extraordinary performance, which was the highlight of

the gatherings, left everyone awe-struck, and also prompted a lot of guessing as to how Bill could possibly perform this feat. Some are sure that he practiced, but most agree that he simply knew all of the people well. Bill modestly states that it is a little of both.

On a typical evening in Juneau one year, after going around several tables, Bill encountered a local woman parishioner whom he had not seen in a year, but he knew she was a member of the State Board on Alcoholism. They happened to be convening at the same time, but she elected to attend the church dinner instead. "Why Teddy Hunter," Bill exclaimed, "aren't you supposed to be at another meeting?" At the same occasion was John Phillips, the priest from Nenana, who had spent the night before at the Gordon home en route to Juneau. When Bill introduced him, he added, "John slept in my bed last night."

The members of the town and city churches also saw Bill on his twice-yearly visitations, when he came for three days of fellowship, numerous communal potlucks, and meetings with those in charge. The parishes had gained considerable autonomy, as compared to missions that were under the direct control of the bishop, and the parish priests say that Bill always asked when they wanted him to come and just what they wanted of him. He respected their leadership and never tried to tell them what to do, in spite of some serious disagreements over the years. He listened to the people, was open to their ideas, and gave them support wherever needed. Mission clergy were undoubtedly envious!

The highlight of his weekend visit was the Sunday morning Confirmation service when Bill preached. He always used his experiences in the Bush to illustrate a few major points, a technique that made city folks feel closer to their Arctic brothers and sisters.

The Point Hope lighthouse was one of Bill's favorite subjects, as was Antonio, his teacher on many aspects of life there. Bill often said that when he was in trouble with his dog team, he would force himself to stop and think, "Now what would Antonio do if he were here beside me?" Then Bill would suggest that the congregation think in similar terms, with God being at their side in times of need. Another favorite "parable" was a story of his solo dog team trip to Barrow, when he ran out of food for his dogs. The situation looked impossible when suddenly he came across a dead seal lying on the ice in front of him and there were no holes in sight. Bill always had the rapt attention of everyone, even that of the youngest children, and over the years the people requested he repeat their favorite stories.

Bill's frequent references to the Milton Swan family and Martha's delicious pan-fried trout had many urban women vying to provide him with his favorite foods; to have him as their family's house guest for his stay was considered a real honor. Although someone called him "a caged lion" in a formal setting, Bill managed to avoid most of those, preferring the homes where he could put his feet up in the living room, make caustic remarks about any household cats and dogs, and help himself to breakfast in the kitchen.

It was not only the women who doted on their handsome, charming bishop; Bill's visits were special to the men of the city churches as well, even those who seldom attended. "He's a man's man," one says, and another adds, "He can relate to Alaska's rugged individuals 'cause he is one himself." One Juneau woman, whose pilot husband never went to church, tells of the time he was in the hospital in Seattle, and Bill, who happened to be passing through, came to see him. Her husband was speechless with surprise, and told her later: "We only talked about flying, and he didn't even insist on a prayer!"

The children enjoyed Bill's visits too, drawn toward the real life adventurer who acted and dressed as they would like to when they grew up. And, of course, Bill remembered all their names, no matter how much they changed between visits. One boy recalls: "He would touch my head and say, 'Hi, David,' and he would ask me something that was related only to me. I felt like he really knew me and he cared." Norman Elliott, as rector of All Saints Church in Anchorage, remembers potlucks in Bill's honor, when he often found the bishop downstairs playing games with the children he would be confirming the next day

Visits to the larger churches were not always so flawless and cordial; some head-on clashes over the years involved both gambling and alcohol, two issues on which Bill remained unalterably opposed. At one time, when All Saints Church was without a rector, the women of the congregation decided they would raise money for a new refrigerator by selling raffle tickets. Bill dropped in on them unannounced as he flew from Valdez back to Fairbanks, and uncovered the situation. When confronted, the woman in charge admitted "that maybe they should not have done it, and they would not undertake another." Bill replied, "you're right, but you won't do this one either—you'll have to refund all those tickets and return the refrigerator."

When he first became bishop, Bill wrote in his monthly newsletter, "No organization or group representing the Episcopal Church in Alaska may sponsor any games of chance. This includes raffles, Bingo, door prizes, etc. in whatever form. We have to take a stand and to stand clearly for something, even at the risk of being called narrow. There is no painless way to raise money. If the Church means anything to our people, then there must be sacrificial giving to make it worthwhile."

One of Bill's biggest gambling headaches was the popular annual Nenana Ice Classic, first begun by Sourdoughs (old-timers) in 1917. Most Alaskans buy one or more tickets, guessing on which day, hour, and minute the ice will break up on the Tanana River. A tripod, strategically placed, will fall over as the chunk it sits on begins to move, tripping a clock and also setting off major excitement and elation for a few lucky people who win the $100,000 pot.

During one spring clergy conference, when Bill was out of the room, a new young priest stated that he hoped the ice would go on 25 May at 3:22 P.M. because he was going to give all his winnings to the District. "We all stared at Walter," Norman Elliott recalls, "and we told him he wouldn't even be in the District if he won that pool. Walter was the only person holding a ticket who was praying he wouldn't win." An old-time pilot friend of Bill's in Fairbanks purchased tickets in the names of Miss Kay and Miss Hill for many years, and then teasingly told them about it. "They took it seriously," Bill says, "and they lived in trepidation for the big date. They felt that if they won, they would go to perdition."

Bill adds, "I never issued any directives or made a big deal over the Ice Classic, although there were a lot of jokes about it and me, and I'm sure many of the clergy bought tickets. Would you believe that one Sunday when I was in the middle of my sermon at the Nenana church, the tripod fell, setting off a loud siren. I paused for a moment—this is the biggest event of the year for the people of that town, and I expected everyone to rush right out the door. But no one budged, and I just went on talking as though nothing happened."

Bill's strong opposition to alcohol never wavered, and in fact, he encouraged and supported the successful efforts of one of his clergy to introduce the first bill in the State Legislature to address the problem of alcoholism in Alaska. Of course, Bill's unbending rules on this subject were also the source of many clergy jokes. A perennial story was of a dinner in Anchorage one year, when a parishioner served an especially spicy Mexican dinner. She also served Margaritas, but told Bill she had made him a special pitcher of lemonade, and to help himself. He found the food so hot that he quickly went into the kitchen to the refrigerator, and found the container. Since she had said it was all for him, he wasted no time looking for a glass, drinking the contents in a few big gulps. Unfortunately Bill had found the extra supply of Margaritas. It was very early to bed for the Bishop that night.

As the years went by, Bill made more frequent visits to South-central Alaska because the area was experiencing a tremendous growth in population. In Anchorage itself two more Episcopal churches were begun in the late 1950s and early 60s, also one in nearby Matanuska Valley in Palmer; two outstations were started on the Kenai Peninsula, and a mission on Kodiak Island.

Bill also flew into Seward, Valdez, and Cordova, three small towns that changed little since his first visit in 1943. All three were severely affected by the 1964 earthquake, however, as were parts of Anchorage. Valdez was so devastated that the townspeople decided to relocate. The old town had been built on the unstable silt and sand of an ancient glacial moraine. During the four-minute long, 8.6 (on the Richter scale) earthquake, the largest ever recorded in North America, the ground repeatedly opened and shut, shooting up geysers of water. Buildings were destroyed, water and sewer mains broken, and roads were torn up. Fuel tanks split open, and ignited by sparks, splashed fire over the crevassed area. Then the Valdez harbor water, stirred up by the massive shockwaves and slides from the mountainsides, rushed landward and then back causing a series of giant tsunamis that drowned twenty-eight people standing on the main dock. It was Good Friday, 27 March 1964 and supplies were being unloaded from the freighter on its monthly visit. The town of 1,100 counted thirty-one dead and 225 homes destroyed or damaged.

It did not take long for the people to select a new site on firmer ground, and by 1966 most homes and businesses were being rebuilt with the aid of large amounts of Federal disaster funds. The Episcopal church building, left standing, but forlorn among the ruins of the old town, had already survived many years of struggle. An average of fifteen people attended services on Sunday, with almost half of that number coming from other denominations.

Bill was a leader in developing the Alaska Council of Churches while he was bishop (in fact, he was their first president), and at a meeting following the decision to move Valdez, he suggested that they not all build five new small churches, but rather join together and share one. The Methodists, Presbyterians, American Baptists, and Disciples of Christ—Lutherans joined later—agreed, and began a new venture for Alaska, in a new town, with a new style of building. Dale Sarles, the priest in Minto, took charge of this experimental ministry, and the church thrived. After he left, Lutheran leadership took over, and the growth continued.

The building consisted of a multipurpose room instead of a sanctuary. Bill was strongly opposed to the latter which, with fixed pews, he figured was used only about five percent of the time and was expensive to heat and operate. He had a stiff battle with long-time Episcopalians when he tried to persuade them to accept chairs instead, and suggested if the church wished to honor him when he left office, they could burn every pew in the District. In spite of the vehement opposition, the next Convocation voted to fund future churches only if they were of multipurpose construction.

Bill left his plane behind when he traveled to the Southeastern Panhandle, a distance of 850 nautical miles from Fairbanks. The commercial travel time by DC 4 from Fairbanks to Juneau was four hours plus time for stops, and the only means of reaching the four other coastal settlements (until the ferry system was developed in the mid-60s) was by the slow ten-seat amphibious Grumman Goose. Travelers always had to allow for waits because of bad weather, so these visitations took a big chunk out of Bill's tightly budgeted time. He made a valiant effort to make two trips a year, allowing three days for each of the five towns.

Most of the missions and parishes at Juneau, Sitka, Petersburg, Wrangell, and Ketchikan have long colorful histories dating back to the earliest days of Russian occupation and the gold mine era. These include serving, or even running, local hospitals and schools. The people's occupations are oriented toward fishing, lumber, tourism, and in Juneau, Alaska's capital, state government. Some people state they felt like stepchildren to the rest of the District, with little in common, and too out of touch. Bill was conscious of their needs and concerns, and over the years, he searched for a different structure that might serve these isolated, diverse areas.

In 1963, he wrote a confidential letter to Bishop Bentley at the Overseas Department in New York, asking for his superior's thoughts about dividing Alaska into two districts. One would be north of the Alaska Range, to include Fairbanks and all the Indian and Eskimo missions, the second would cover the Southcentral and Southeast regions, and have a new bishop's office somewhere closer to these churches. Bentley's reply touched on the concern that a divided District would not provide the unity now so important to everyone in Alaska, regardless of distance. He did suggest that Bill could move to Anchorage or Juneau, then ask for a suffragan, or assistant bishop, to live in Fairbanks and be responsible for the work among the native missions.

Since this approach had no appeal whatsoever to Bill, he looked for other solutions, one of which put him into another controversy with both the National Church and some parishioners. He had long maintained close contacts with the Canadian Anglican bishops. In many ways Alaska was closer to them; sharing mutual native cultural concerns and common geographic problems. Bill began to put out confidential feelers as to how they could join even more closely. "My destination wasn't absolute," Bill says. "I just felt that we had so much in common that we certainly could profit by closer ties that someday might lead to an international tie. Somehow, his attempt reached a national newspaper and headlines stated that the Episcopal Church in Alaska was considering joining the Anglican Church. The Presiding Bishop was on the telephone within hours, asking what Bill was up to now.

That particular approach was abandoned, although the leaders of Western Canadian churches have continued to meet with Alaskans over the years, and for the rest of his tenure as Bishop, Bill sought other ways to bring his office closer to all. "Missionary Bishops were pretty absolute," he reminisces, "but with the new congregations developing in other parts of Alaska, it was time to look for a different administrative structure, perhaps to develop regional entities." Bill foresaw the coming of the diocesan structure, with its state-wide committees, and regional deaneries, where churches such as those in the Southeast could come together to share mutual concerns.

Bill moved into another controversial issue when he decided to take a strong public stand against the Vietnam War. As Bishop, Bill never hesitated through sermons, talks, and the *Alaskan Churchman* editorials to take a stand on political issues. He did not try to speak on behalf of his parishioners, but he wanted them to know exactly where he stood, and why, and then asked that they prayerfully consider their own opinions. All members of Bill's team, even those who did not always agree with him, call Bill a person of great courage, willing to stand by his convictions even when they were unpopular.

In his State of the Church address to the convocation in Fairbanks in 1967, Bill stated: "As Christians we must remind ourselves anew again and again that all war is wrong and the onus is on the Christian for moral justification for support of any armed conflict that takes the lives of men. None of us wants the war in which we are presently engaged and yet in any gathering of Christian people, strong feelings persist on both sides. What do we hope to achieve by armed conflict or armed victory, and will it be necessary for us to destroy Vietnam in order to save it, or to save us? This question as Christians we must ask ourselves, and only individually can we answer it."

Heated controversy followed. Several conscientious objectors, serving their alternate duty by working for the Church in villages, introduced a resolution condemning involvement in the Vietnam conflict. Strong opposition came from the delegates of All Saints and St. Matthew's parishes in particular, because their large congregations included a number of people from the military bases near Anchorage and Fairbanks. They declared that such a resolution did not belong on the agenda of a church meeting, and when it looked as though they had the votes, a young Church Army captain tabled it. Bill was furious afterward because he felt the group should at least have had the guts to take a yes or no stand.

One way in which Bill demonstrated his Vietnam views was to recruit a number of conscientious objectors for work in the villages. He had no organized recruiting program, but word continually spread through his talks Outside that he was looking for volunteers. One young C.O. from South Dakota immortalized himself by writing a letter back to his draft board, thanking them profusely for drafting him because he had found a new part of the world that he loved.

Scott Fisher, a city person who had never been involved in formal church work, was dropped off in the tiny Indian village of Chalkyitsik, near Fort Yukon. As he stood watching Bill's plane disappear, an elder came up to him and asked, "What are you going to do for the church service tomorrow?" Two weeks later, when the Bishop's plane came in sight again, another old-timer was showing Scott how to build a fire, again a first for him. "Actually, I didn't know whose plane it was," Scott recalls, "until some kids came running up to tell me. I decided I'd better see what the Bishop was up to, and I asked him what he was doing. 'What do you mean what am I doing? Aren't you ready to go?' was his reply. Well, I'd forgotten he was going to come pick me up and take me to a Sunday School teacher meeting in Tanana. I was told I had five minutes to pack. That's how it all started."

Scott survived, to the surprise of the Chalkyitsik villagers, where he spent the winter, and he went to nearby Beaver for his

second year. "I liked what I was doing and the people seemed
to like me," Scott says. "When the Bishop came on a later visit,
he said, 'The folks want you to stay around, so why don't you?'
I decided then that I would. A year later he then asked if I'd
thought of going to seminary. I told him bluntly I did not want
to go, but then I got one of those well-known commands: 'God
wants you to go to seminary.' He also wanted me to go to one
in Texas, my least favorite place, but I had no choice because
I had no money, and through Gordon Charlton, then dean of the
Texas Seminary, I was able to get a scholarship." Scott returned
to Alaska after seminary as a priest and coordinator of activities
among the villages. He likes to use his own interpretation of Isaiah
28:21 to describe his life journey: "Strange are the ways of the
Lord. He will complete his work, strange as it is."

By the mid-1960s, Bill had gained a reputation for strong
leadership among his fellow bishops, and he had also acquired
considerable seniority, although he was still among the younger
members. Nonetheless, he preferred a low profile at meetings,
seeking no limelight and speaking only on subjects he felt strongly
about. The late Bishop Wesley Frensdorff of Nevada, who served
with Bill for many years, said he had only the highest respect for
him. "He has that marvelous combination of enthusiasm, con-
viction, and doggedness."

Bill showed his doggedness by regularly chastising his fellow
bishops for spending money on "lavish" hotel rooms and "expensive" restaurants, insisting that they be good stewards and even
stay in people's homes if possible. Bill himself usually turned
down accommodations reserved for him and instead found a
cheap motel or a friend's house. He was equally quick to scout
out the nearest diner and fast-food outlets for his meals. During
one convention held in Hawaii many bishops did stay in homes,
much to Bill's satisfaction. He was also delighted with the
opportunity to go to the beach every day, his favorite leisure-
time activity. His friend Bishop Archie Crowley claims that
everyone on Waikiki knew when the meeting was over because
Bill showed up first each afternoon. Sundays were busy working
days for Bill, however, at all the conventions. The Bishops were
asked to speak at nearby churches, and Bill was always in greatest

demand, inevitably preaching at two places or more every time. Many of the bishops, as well as other church leaders, traveled to Alaska in droves to see for themselves the work Bill was doing, and the District was unique in that all four presiding bishops came at one time or another. Although they made the journey for official occasions, such as the one hundredth anniversary celebration of the mission at Fort Yukon, or the seventy-fifth anniversary of the start of work at Point Hope, Bill treated each of them, and other visiting dignitaries, as he would any one else—informally. In fact, his custom was to deposit them in a Bush village and leave them on their own for several days. The local clergy took these visits in their stride, glad for the company and not overawed.

Bill particularly liked to leave visitors at Minto because it was close to Fairbanks, and typical of many of the smaller villages. Joyce and Dale Sarles enjoyed all their "drop in" trade, the bishop of Zambia in particular; he baptized their new daughter, and the Sarles's later visited him in Africa. Then there was a wealthy older woman from the East Coast involved in church women's work. Dale was never quite sure why she was there, and it was in his bachelor days, so he felt awkward about sharing his one-room cabin with her. To give her some privacy, he put up a makeshift screen, and each morning he would announce he was going out for firewood. The villagers later teased him, saying he must have carried a whole cord each day.

"She noticed my organ wasn't working too well, and when she returned to Fairbanks she bought us a piano and arranged for it to be sent down by boat," Dale recalls. "The trouble was, the church could be heated only for Sunday services and a piano would never survive that kind of treatment. We had a lot of correspondence after that because she just couldn't understand. The Bishop finally told me to stop writing, to sell the piano, repair the organ, and buy myself a much needed outboard motor."

Caggie and Charlie Trapp came to visit Bill from Alaska's companion diocese of Michigan, where Caggie was state president of the Episcopal Church Women. "He decided to fly us to Minto, because Joyce Sarles was from our state," Caggie recalls. "He didn't tell us for how long—he landed the plane, unloaded supplies, and he was off, without our knowing when he would return.''

''We visited every home,'' Charlie says, ''and I thought they were all cooking large pots of soup, but they were boiling laundry instead.'' Caggie adds, ''They had a meeting the next morning in my honor—the women all lined up around the wall with their little babies. My usual speech seemed stupid there, so I decided to find out what they did in their church. The reply was 'we don't do anything for the church, we don't have time. We are too busy. We have to dry fish, take care of the old people, and the children.' They didn't have bazaars and study groups—they were living real life, real Christianity.''

Chapter 9

Change in the Wind

The 1960s was a decade of great change both for Alaska and for the Episcopal Church: the development of the concept of sacramental priests and the ordination of Alaskan natives to the priesthood, and the increased role of the laity; on the National Church level, a major change in the prayerbook, the expanded use of the Eucharist service, folk music, and the evangelistic movement.

Bill was the initiator of some of these changes, others he accepted without resistance. Unlike earlier years when someone else's innovation usually brought an initial negative reply, he became more open, not ready to change for the sake of change, but willing to find new and better means of fulfilling traditional ways. He also became more daring with his own ideas, introducing concepts never tried anywhere else.

The changes within Alaska were enormous as it became a state in 1959. A boom era arrived with the oil field development in the late sixties and the building of the oil pipeline in the seventies. While many towns grew into urban centers, the village way of life for Eskimos and Indians changed drastically and permanently. The benefits and curses of Western culture penetrated even to remote Arctic Village, bringing the people a monetary economy, frame houses that were hard to heat and required oil burners, village wells and running water, village generators and electric lights, refrigeration, television, snow machines, health aids and medicine, and stores stocked with candy, cigarettes, alcohol, and sweetened cereals.

Traditional family bonds were shaken severely as village men left for jobs related to the oil industry, and although children could now stay home and attend local high schools, most left as soon as they could to become a part of the big city life they had seen so much about on television. They were no longer interested in learning about hunting or sewing, or in the traditional dances and ceremonies of their ancestors. Nor did they feel the same ties to the village church. In fact, Pentecostal groups began moving in, offering religious options.

Indian village elders could still recall the early days when they led a nomadic way of life, far more even than the Eskimos, who foraged for food from a home base. Early Athabaskans lived in camps, following the animals and fish, seeking areas of plentiful wood for fuel. When schools were brought to the people, however, they were forced to give up roaming and settle down. This had a negative impact on the amount of game and wood available in the surrounding area; more food had to come from the local store, and government welfare support became a way of life.

The inhabitants of Fort Yukon were more fortunate in that they could sell wood to the steamers plying the Yukon River and also to the hospital. The latter supplied jobs to the young girls, in the process teaching them Western hygiene, English, and cooking. They became a nucleus of strong matriarchal influence in the years ahead. Some of today's male leaders also got a head start by boarding with Dr. and Mrs. Grafton Burke (formerly Clara Heintz) while going to school in the village. This extraordinary couple virtually adopted the boys as their own, taught them English, good manners, and life in a Western home. But for many other villages, the leap from the subsistence lifestyle to the twentieth century was wrenching, leaving in its wake a people who were unhappy in either culture.

All of these changes, together with the building of the pipeline across land of unresolved ownership and the National push to set aside wilderness lands in Alaska, set into motion the Native Land Claims movement. When the United States first purchased Alaska, the federal government recognized that the Eskimo and Indian peoples had claims, which were never spelled out or resolved. By 1961, native leaders saw that the time had come to protect their heritage before they found themselves pushed onto small reservations like their brothers and sisters in the Lower 48. Many Caucasians, including those in the state and federal governments, perceived this rise of nationalism as a threat and were not sure how to deal with it.

Bill was among the first leaders to support the native movement, initiating several important conferences; first, one with Catholic Church priests and then a second with all those concerned on the federal and state government level. He felt deeply that as Americans and Christians they all had an obligation to resolve the claim; what it was he could not say, but he could at least promote talks. He also made a number of trips to Washington D.C., to meet with the Bureau of Indian Affairs and Alaska's representatives to Congress, pleading for the urgency of the situation, startled by the lack of knowledge among officials on the subject. He succeeded in obtaining an interest-free $50,000 loan from the National Church to Alaskan native leaders when the latter took the lead in their fight for rights to the land. Bill then stepped aside, always supportive, urging them to keep from becoming bitter and belligerent; to deal with the negotiations on a fair basis as Christians.

Peter John, the chief of the village of Minto, was asked to one of the many meetings in the state during the '60s. "They ask me what am I going to do with the land I get. I tell them I hunt, pick berries. They ask me if I want money for it. I don't want no money. I say what happened to the Lower 48 Indians. I don't let that happen to the people in Alaska. That's why I come to talk about land."

The native delegates to the church convocations had always been reticent, ready to listen, but not speak. The English language was a problem for most of them, as well as assertiveness in unfamiliar surroundings. In the early '60s a few of the younger leaders who spoke English pulled their people together into a joint Indian and Eskimo caucus, which gave them great clout since they voted as a block. They continued to follow Bill's leadership, so great was their respect for him, but at one meeting a startling confrontation took place. Midway through a business session on the adoption of a constitution and canons, young Lennie Lane from Point Hope stood up and said that he would like to make a motion. He proceeded to do so in Inupiat, the Eskimo language. Then Titus Peter of Fort Yukon followed him, saying he would like to interpret the motion for his people. He then spoke in Athabaskan Qwichin. The Caucasians in the room had no idea what was said, and Bill asked the two what the motion was about. The young men remained silent. One white priest recalls, "The silence screamed loud and long. And suddenly the rest of us realized that there were enough votes between the two native groups so the motion proposed could be moved and passed with none of us being any the wiser."

At that point the young men broke their silence and explained that the motion referred to the importance of the work before the meeting, of its impact on the District for years to come, and that therefore the body should slow down and take time for interpretation, putting it in simpler terms that could be understood by everyone there. Their point was never forgotten.

Regardless of the rise of nationalistic fervor among the village people, Bill remained universally admired, considered one of their own. Luke Titus, a dynamic young Indian leader, sums up their feelings: "He knew and respected our traditional cultural values. We respected him for taking part and not just sitting back and watching."

Trimble Gilbert of Arctic Village recalls: "He knew all the people. He kept track of everybody. When he comes out of the airplane, he starts shaking hands and he knew everybody's name. Even all the little children. He learned from the people, and he could do anything with them. He'd compete with anything. He likes our food, like moosehead soup. The only thing I never did see him do was drinking with the people." David Salmon, veteran Indian priest from nearby Chalkyitsik, adds, "Bishop Gordon is really most part Indian. He worked very hard, all the time. He never did say he was tired. I remember one time he packed almost one whole caribou to the river."

Bill usually slept in the local mission house, but he spent much of his time visiting in village homes, often sharing meals with them. Once, somewhere along the Koyukuk River, he sat down at a family table to eat a meal of fish. He was handed a bowl and at that point the family dog came to his side, bared his teeth, and began an ominous growling. Bill had petted the dog when he first came in and the pup was friendly, so he asked the little boy next to him what was bothering his pet. The youngster replied, "You're eating out of his bowl."

Bill showed his concern for the people in many ways. In times of trouble he was instantly there to help. When Elsie Pitka, a veteran leader in the village of Beaver, lost her son in a Fairbanks fire, Bill flew the boy's body home, comforted the family, and held the burial service. She lost a second son to drowning and Bill was there within hours. Elsie says, "He don't say very much, but his actions say a lot. And he understands us."

Bill landed at the small village of Chalkyitsik to hold a service during midwinter one year. A midwife rushed up to his plane and told him they had a woman in labor who was having difficulties. Would he fly her to the hospital at Fort Yukon, about fifty miles away? While they bundled her into the plane, Bill told the young college volunteer stationed there to collect four gas lanterns and mark the boundaries of the landing area on the snow of a lake, since it would be dark when he returned. Bill got the woman to Fort Yukon in time, and returned to land safely.

In the early fifties, Bill became concerned that the people living along the Koyukuk had only one school, run by the Church in Allakaket. With the coming of modern ways to this area, there was a critical need for education, and so he persuaded the Commissioner of Education for the Territory to come meet with the people of Huslia and Hughes. The state agreed to send a teacher there, but a school had to be established first. So Bill worked out an arrangement whereby the Church would provide materials and the people would build the building. This was Huslia's first school.

Bill was also instrumental in bringing a much-needed Community Center to Fort Yukon in 1971, although the idea came from his hard-working young Church Army captain there. Tom Tull tells how he walked into Bill's office in Fairbanks one day and said, "We need a Community Center in Fort Yukon, and I think it's going to cost $400,000 and maybe we can get the money from the federal government." Bill's instant reply was, "If you think that's important and fills a need in the village, then I'll support your spending your time and efforts in doing it." So Tom, who was only twenty-three at the time, pulled together the plans with the help of the local congregation and obtained both a federal and state grant. Unfortunately, local moneys were required, so Bill obtained an interest-free loan from the National Church. "He took the risk, trusting me completely," Tom says proudly. It enabled the local community to work together with state and federal resources. The people built themselves a place that had a gymnasium, a library, the first laundromat north of the Arctic Circle, even showers, which meant special water and sewer lines since there was no running water in the town except at the school.

Adults from the villages were going to Fairbanks and Anchorage, but having a hard time once they got there. Tom Tull came up with the plan to take six or eight youngsters on visits to the cities—the reverse of sending kids to camp—so they would know a little bit of what to expect. Tom started with Boy Scout troops, exposing them to a safe environment; he begged and borrowed cars, as well as places to stay. Then he had his hands full teaching them about the new things they encountered, like the green arrow flashing on at the airport intersection. "How did that light know we wanted to turn left?" was the first question. Next came the shower routine; the boys wanted to stay under them all night and enjoy what seemed like endless hot water. The Community Center would soon bring this miracle to their home town.

Tom's most ambitious expedition was to take forty boys to Anchorage for three weeks. He persuaded Bill to make three round trips to Fort Yukon and other villages, and then enlisted the hospitality of a number of church families to provide housing for the youngsters. "We took the railroad from Fairbanks south," Tom explains, "after raising money for their fares with bake sales. We went on a tour of a dairy in the Matanuska Valley (the boys had never seen a cow), then watched the newspaper being put together, but their most fun was a stop at McDonald's one day. I ordered 120 hamburgers, 50 fries, and the woman had to call in extra help."

Bill himself took some native elders and priests with him when he traveled Outside to conventions or on speaking tours. Chester Seveck, Bill's longtime reindeer herder friend and later leader of the church in Kotzebue, went to the national convention in Hawaii, causing quite a stir with his summer Eskimo attire. He said it was "awful hot and after we landed I was surprised—a woman put on me a lei—grab around my neck and kiss me on the cheek!"

Titus Peter, one of the first Athabaskans to be ordained as a priest, flew with Bill and Shirley to Michigan one year, where they shared in speaking tours all over the Diocese. One of their hosts took Titus on a tour of the Ford Museum, showing him the first car Henry Ford ever made. Titus compared the car with the life of Indian people in early years—it was a constant struggle with the elements, travel was tough, leaving them in much isolation, and they had no medical help or schools. Even though modern civilization had brought complications to his people, it also brought many benefits, and while life in the wilderness looked pretty good from afar, most people would rather look at it than live it.

Bill did much to help the village people, but he had also become more aware of the dangers of paternalistic thinking. No longer were church ladies encouraged to send boxes of hand-me-down clothing, or even layettes or hymnals. Money was still gratefully accepted, but only for those projects which the people wanted and were willing to work on themselves. He got into further trouble with the National Church when he railed against the welfare systems of the Bureau of Indian Affairs and the Territory.

Paternalism toward the native people was strong throughout Alaska in the 1950s. Town and city churches regularly collected second hand "gift" boxes to send to the villages, and even the most conscientious clergy were probably unaware of these paternal feelings within themselves. It was a natural reaction to the racial intolerance of the previous decades. As late as 1940, in Anchorage many business establishments carried signs saying "NO NATIVES ALLOWED," and hotels, movie theaters, and restaurants did not even have separate sections for them. A few run-down establishments were available to them and Fourth Avenue bars became their home away from home. Twenty years earlier, following the first wave of intolerant gold seekers, incoming settlers and Indians seethed with hatred for one another and the stories of Russian occupation in Alaska's earliest history are full of bloody battles with the native peoples.

In Bill's 1961 address to the District-wide convocation, he expressed his concern on paternalism: "A man must have the right to fail! No one of us wishes failure for anyone, but when a man or woman is so propped up and protected and directed that he cannot fail no matter what decision he 'thinks' he makes—then he will never really succeed either. Finally he may lose faith in himself and his ability to decide.

"The Church must make agonizing choices in her mission. She must guide and strengthen and train and direct, but finally the peoples to whom we go as missionaries must stand with only our prayers that God will save them from false choices.

"It is possible, indeed probable, that the Church in Alaska has protected, shielded, AND DIRECTED her Indian and Eskimo children too long. We have all too often given responsibility as long as those responsible ones came up with the answers that we would have produced. It is entirely possible that solutions which immediately come to our minds may be the wrong ones in a local situation."

At that same time, Bill faced another major change head on. He had succeeded in reaching his goal of filling the clergy post in every village; many selfless seminary-trained personnel provided excellent pastoral care. However, he began to notice that the day they moved out, almost nothing happened in that community until someone else came in. Bill could see that for the Church to be planted truly, ministry had to emerge from within the village or town. Also, the salaries of these highly trained people were rising, becoming a real burden to the District, and Bill now questioned the wasted talents of the seminary graduates as they spent much of their time simply struggling to survive in the harsh conditions.

Bill became a critic of seminary training itself: "We think we can send somebody to seminary and train them for three years, like put them through a tunnel, and they all come out finely honed to fit anywhere in the world, no matter what they've done, or learned."

The Reverend Emmet Gribbin, who was national administrator for the General Ordination Examination required of all seminary graduates, recalls that Bill was "a little dubious of seminary training, if it really does what it should . . . his mildly hostile position was well known and the House of Bishops elected him to be on the General Board of Examining Chaplains, which writes the exams for all who wish to be ordained. So, either the bishops felt that his perspective was needed or that Bill was not as far off base as some people thought he was. He has done good work on the Board, and I think he has learned something about the schools that he wasn't aware of before."

Bill's concern for seminary curriculum was not the heart of the problem in Alaska, however. He had become increasingly aware of the seed planted in him at Point Hope: that of the lay people holding their own services, of the lay people taking responsibility for their church when he could not be there. Also, Milton and Martha Swan, Peel Tooyak, Sam Rock, and Tommy Knox with a minimum of education had all come forward to lead their people. Bill had long believed that in the eyes of God, the Christian who cuts firewood, or, in a town, cleans windows, is as important as the person who provides the sacraments. Here lay the key to the future of the Church in Alaska.

When Bill first became bishop, he found the same lay ministry and leadership among the Indian people of the Interior. Isaac Fisher of Anvik was a lay reader during the early days of John Chapman's ministry. David Paul of Tanacross, a small village two hundred miles from Fairbanks, became a lay reader during World War I, and later a deacon, serving the Church for over sixty years. He was one of the most saintly persons Bill had ever met, the acknowledged leader of his community, no matter who might be serving as chief at the time. "I often visited his cabin, where I invariably would find him with his Bible in his hand. We would talk together about some passage and he almost always had more profound insights from his experience with our Lord and the Bible than my more educated theological understanding.

"David Paul did not fit into any category of the traditional ordained minister, with his very limited education, difficulty with the English language and Church training. It had been the same with Peel Tooyak. I had wanted to have him made a deacon, but he died before I had to face the fact that there were no established set of guidelines to fit ordained ministry for these people. Still using the previously set pattern of the white man, we did our best with David Paul. The priest who was stationed at Tanacross worked with him closely and then presented him to our examining chaplains. He passed, and was ordained deacon in 1957."

The Church at Fort Yukon had ordained several Indians as deacons, but Albert Tritt was the only survivor when Bill became bishop. He was an outstanding example of strong native leadership at isolated Arctic Village, as well as among Athabaskan communities for hundreds of miles around his home base. His people of Arctic Village have a history of active lay participation in their church and in raising up a number of men who later became priests.

David Salmon, the leader of the village of Chalkyitsik, became a lay reader under Albert Tritt, and then moved to Fort Yukon to study under Walter Hannum, the seminary-trained priest there for twelve years. Walter saw great potential in this handsome, strong young man with a good command of the English language, and so he spent a year giving David intensive training. There were no resource books to guide him, so he turned often to the Bible. They met every morning, five days a week for Bible study, using a fourth grade Sunday School manual. Then, two evenings a week, he and David passed on what they had learned to an adult village group.

In the afternoons the two paid visits to people's homes; on Saturday evenings, David worked with acolytes; and on Sundays he helped Walter with the services, which were varied every week so that he learned all forms and eventually conducted them by himself. "Talk about busy," David exclaims. "But in 1958 the Bishop ordained me as a deacon and I went back home to Chalkyitsik." Bill then ordained David the first Athabaskan priest in 1962, stationing him in Venetie. "Walter did a tremendous job in training David," Bill says. "He learned essentially all that seminarians do. We were still putting white faces on native people, but David could deal with it because he was an exceptional person."

Walter Hannum and Murray Trelease, another flying priest, then went a step farther and set up the Yukon Valley Training Center, with the goal of finding and training people in the villages of that area who could meet the pastoral needs of the village. Four times a year they held lay reader schools in Fort Yukon for an intensive two weeks, flying in the interested men from the various communities, even reaching out to the Arctic Coast and Tanana areas. Then Walter and David Salmon made follow-up visits to the men on their home ground, with Murray doing the flying.

One man, who spoke little English, was being trained to be the village pastor, visiting those people who spoke only the Indian language in their homes. Albert Tritt's son, Isaac, whose English was also marginal, became interested in following in his father's steps, and approached David Salmon. "I asked Isaac if he be willing to be a deacon after his father died," David recalls, "and every day for two months I teach him everything I learned from Walter Hannum. I had to translate it all."

Language was a serious hindrance as the villagers came forward to begin some form of training. The people of the Fort Yukon area were fortunate that the Bible and prayer book had been translated into the similiar Canadian Old Crow dialect. The same was true for the Eskimos, although they had only the prayer book translation, but in other parts of the vast Interior, Indians had to learn English first. Even with the translations, the younger people, whose English was good, did not want church services held in the native language.

Trimble Gilbert remembers the first visit by a white priest to Arctic Village when he was a small boy and could say only "hello." As a young man, he trained to be a lay reader, following in his father's footsteps. He and Isaac Tritt shared services in their church, using the Canadian translation. Then English began to be used more frequently and Trimble recalls how he hid in his darkened home the day the white priest came to ask him to read the Bible lesson in English for the next Sunday.

When Trimble first went to Fort Yukon before he began his training, he was afraid to go to church because he knew no English and had no "fancy" clothes. "I was really poor—afraid people

would laugh at me. I heard the bell for two Sundays, and wanted
to go. Finally I remembered my mother always told me don't miss
church, so I went. Almost all of Fort Yukon went, so the building
was packed. I arrived during the sermon, the swinging door made
a little noise and people turned around. I was so nervous, afraid
the people would laugh at me. I could find no seat in the back,
so I had to walk all the way up front." Today Trimble is an
ordained priest.

Titus Peter was another young man in Fort Yukon who initially
showed no interest in the Church. But Walter Hannum urged him
on and enticed him to the Training Center. Titus's struggle was
not with the language, but with alcoholism, the scourge of so
many native peoples. Years after he was ordained a priest, Titus
wrote a forthright and courageous article for the *Alaskan Churchman* telling of his battle against the disease.

Bill believes Titus has been a remarkable witness to his own
people by showing how he has had to deal with imperfection.
He also brought a new dimension to the Indian clergy, who up
until then accepted outwardly the statements and directives of
the white clergy and particularly the bishop. Titus raised questions
in a positive and aggressive way, challenging traditional concepts.
He helped Bill to deal with some of the real issues and problems
of human life in Alaska. "Without his gentle prodding and
counsel, I would have been a much poorer bishop."

Luke Titus also became an Indian church leader, but his home
was Minto, far from Fort Yukon. His English was excellent
because he attended the Mount Edgecombe School in Sitka for
native boarding students. He became involved in church work
at an early age, becoming a lay reader when he was still in grade
school. When he graduated from high school, Bill sent him to
the Cook Christian Training school in Tempe, Arizona. A non-
denominational institution, its goal is to train Indians for Christian
citizenship, particularly those who have had limited education.
It takes the person as far as he or she wants to go—academically,
culturally, and theologically—in preparing to serve his or her own
people. Bill emphasized to Luke that he was not pushing him
toward ordination, but that he wanted him to go there for
whatever education he could get.

Each fall, Bill flew a number of students (most are far beyond school age) and their families to Cook School, often all the way in his own plane. Bill usually stayed long enough to take part in conferences with the faculty and help the mothers buy bathing suits for their little ones to combat the heat. He returned from time to time throughout the year to make sure all was going well for everyone.

Luke Títus tells how the Alaskans formed a group, going places and doing things together. They did not remain completely by themselves, however; Luke met a pretty young Navajo woman during his second year there who later became his wife. He also made the decision to work toward ordination, and came home to Minto as a deacon. That was when he encountered his particular problem—the people of his village would no longer accept him as a church leader. Minto was going through a transition at that point, and Luke had been away from home a long time. Bill was supportive of his problem, but suggested he stay there and work things out. Luke did.

As pleased as Bill was with the Yukon Valley Training center work, which was also carried on in Tanana and Kotzebue, he was concerned with the time it took to train men like David Salmon and Luke Titus. The District did not have that time to wait for such talented men who could pass the seminary exams. What about the many others coming along, who were handicapped by almost no schooling and could not speak English? Men like Isaac Tritt and Milton Swan (who was the first Alaskan Eskimo ordained a deacon in 1958) were needed just as much in their own villages, but could not pass the national test. Walter Hannum and other trainers had taken a bold step, a totally new venture in the National Church, in looking at what these men needed to know in terms of their own people; also some were being examined in their own language by their peers. These were good steps forward, but the Church needed to look farther ahead, and set some specific goals.

And so Bill and Walter Hannum planned a historic five-day conference. It convened in Fort Yukon in December 1967 (where it was minus forty degrees) under the guidance of two leaders from Outside, the Reverend H. Boone Porter of the National

Church Home Department and General Seminary, and the Reverend David R. Cochran of Fort Yates, North Dakota, later to be the fourth Bishop of Alaska. All seventeen of the clergy from the native villages were present. The goal: to look at the Church's ministry to the Native peoples of the state and to determine what shape this ministry ought to take in the future. Bill took a back seat during the discussions, doing much listening and little talking.

Boone Porter drew up a brief summary, stating first that: "It was decided to concentrate on goals that could be attained in the next five years, and methods for attaining these goals . . . the great five-year goal was to have native people assume most of the responsibility for the local church in their community. Such a goal would not be totally achieved within this period in every village, but it could be largely achieved in most of them."

Specifically, these goals meant a number of changes, listed in the Porter report. White clergy must begin to withdraw from village posts wherever they could be succeeded by native clergy. (This had already happened in three places, with a fourth soon to follow.) If a native priest was to reside in every village, he must in many cases earn much of his income by his own secular work. Local people must assume more responsibility for raising and handling funds for their church, and for Christian education. Also they would be responsible for the buildings they needed in the future, choosing the kind they wanted and maintaining them.

The Porter report then addressed the required changes in methodology. The white missionary priorities would have to change. They would now be training local people to take over their jobs, and personal identification was no longer a primary objective. In many instances, missionaries should be hiring local people to assist them in providing wood, cleaning the church, etc., so that they would have the time to tutor native lay leaders. It was not proposed that Outside missionaries be eliminated from the field, but rather that they become back up resources and enablers.

Bill's response to the conference was one of gratitude and appreciation. He wrote Boone Porter: "I've been to many meetings in my time, but I do not recall any that has come forth with

as many constructive, meaningful directions for the future . . .
I only hope that we can implement this with definite forward
steps in the future." Bill concludes with the hope that the clergy
and communities in the towns of Alaska can also share in a similiar
experience. "I think much of what we discussed at Fort Yukon
is applicable and relevant to any place where we are at work in
the name of our Lord, particularly in the small towns of Alaska."
Bill commented further on the results of the conference in the
Alaskan Churchman, pointing out that "this new approach does
not in any way reflect on the work of past missionaries who,
with the tools and situations that existed, brought lovingly and
meaningfully the love of Christ into the hearts of the people. It
does say, though, that there should never be *permanent missions,*
and that we believe that God is calling us *now* here in Alaska to
rethink radically our direction based on the situation of today."
    Bill also points out that the training of ordained persons and
lay people would be an ongoing one and the Church in Alaska
would maintain trained back-up persons available in strategic
locations, who would also travel from village to village to
implement this plan. If it is carried to conclusion, the village
church clergy will largely support themselves or be supported
by the community, and then the mission will truly be *the* church
of the people. "We see now only a vision of the future—a dream
of the future—maybe an impossible dream, but a quest that we
firmly believe is God's will for us to try to achieve."
    A number of puzzle pieces were still missing from Bill's "impos-
sible dream." At a clergy meeting in the summer following Boone
Porter's conference, Bill told the group that they were talking
about every Alaskan community, not just the native villages. "We
are wrestling with how to allow God's call to ministry to spring
forth in local people: native men and women, city storekeepers,
people in business, teachers—people in secular employment who
are willing to keep their jobs and yet become part of a network
of reinforcing persons who will support the many aspects of
Christian ministry." At least a dozen small towns currently had
no ordained minister, so sacramental services took place intermit-
tently, if at all. "How do we meet this challenge," he asked,
"since by Church canon only ordained ministers can offer the
sacraments?"

Later that fall, Don Hart, who was finishing his fifth and final
year in Huslia, went along on a moose hunt with Bill. In the
relaxed environment (they got their moose the first day), Don
recalls "Bill did a lot of thinking out loud. I also remember hearing
the wolves that first night. They were especially close, making
the most incredible sounds I ever heard—different sounds like
imitations, talking to each other, singing in harmony. We listened
for hours.

"The next day was clear and warm, so we stretched out in the
sun and talked for a long time; he told me stories of the native
men he had already ordained, and the conversation led to Canon
eight, (National Church law) which was a big breakthrough in
his attempts to rethink the seminary-oriented training.

Bill studied the National Canons five, eight, ten, and eleven.
The unique Alaska situation should fit somewhere in the midst
of all those legal words! But does one interpret law in a restrictive
way, as if it is a guardian of something that may be lost, or in
an enabling way, as if it stands like trail markers helping toward
a goal? Or is it both? "We looked long and hard at Canon eight,
which speaks of just those isolated communities where sacramental services and ministry are almost impossible, and it provides the direction to raise up or call ordained ministers to meet
the needs. But it is also ambiguous and leaves many questions
unanswered."

In March 1970 Bill started his sacramental program at St. Mary's
Church in Anchorage, by then the largest parish in the state and
one that had much active lay participation. Ten men showed up
to hear more about this new form of lay ministry, one which,
after two years of intense study, would lead to ordination as a
sacramental priest. They met every Saturday morning and had
an average of ten hours of reading a week, in addition to their
regular jobs. Don Hart and Norman Elliott of Anchorage took
turns supporting Chuck Eddy as instructor, and Bill dropped in
frequently to check on their progress.

Four of the original ten stayed with it and were ordained in
1972. Their unpaid work for the Church, which was in addition
to their fulltime jobs, would free up their priest, Chuck Eddy,
to become more of an enabler and teacher for other parish lay

involvement there as well as to other churches in the area. While these men could not be in charge of a church, they were able to conduct services, which included the sacraments, particularly for outlying, unmanned churches with no clergy.

Bill did some amazing explaining to persuade the National Church that Anchorage, a large city by 1972, could be classified as "small, isolated and remote"—the words of the Canon. "He was really stretching the old Canon eight," recalled Bishop Frensdorff. "He was taking some risk for coming under criticism, but when he was not called up for censure, I was willing to follow suit—we had a similar situation in Nevada." Bill's plans and ideas have since spread to many areas of the Anglican Church around the world, not without controversy or questions, but increasingly with acceptance.

With the Anchorage project working well, Bill turned to the two on-going training centers at Fort Yukon and the Arctic Coast. Changes were needed to accommodate his plans for ordaining sacramental priests in every Bush community as quickly as possible. The villagers themselves had to begin to think in terms of raising up one of their own, after sixty or seventy years of living with the custom of a white priest provided by the Bishop literally out of the blue. Bill traveled to each village, encouraging them to pick someone within their congregation whom they could support and follow. "We wanted to avoid volunteers at all costs because they usually wished to be priests for all the wrong reasons," he says.

In a few places the process did work, at Point Hope, Kivalina, and Arctic Village in particular, which had long histories of lay involvement in church activities. In many other villages, however, Bill had to take the lead in choosing the first group of candidates. He was remarkably well suited to do it because he knew the people so well, and he had a rare sense for spotting leadership and spiritually gifted people. For the most part, he recommended respected village elders and chiefs. Inability to read or write, or knowledge of English aside, these men were the people's authority and they were deeply committed to the Church.

Bill had begun a pioneer effort, ordaining twenty-eight men under Canon eight in the following three years, with no other examples or books to help chart his course, and in typical fashion, he felt the need to forge ahead without lengthy planning and years of preparation for the congregations involved. Inevitably, some mistakes in judgment were made, and he incurred criticism from many directions. As for those persons who complained that Bill rushed into the program, it is important to note that within five years of ordaining the sacramentalists, native nationalism had developed with such a fervor that it was difficult for white priests to live in any of the villages. Yet the churches remained, staffed by native clergy.

Don Hart admits that "the whole program had a harder time because we used a system that was so completely dependent on Bill Gordon. But he had an extraordinary ability to look ahead and act positively. He'd say we could search out all the problems we wanted to, but let's talk about the good that can happen. So, often he was ahead of us, leading the way, but he did very little about the details—he left them with us."

One Outside bishop commented: "He got hold of the idea and ran with it mighty fast. While I might have been critical in that I felt it would have been better to take time to build in structures of supervision, continuing education, and a better preparation of congregations, the plain fact is it wouldn't have happened unless he did pick it up and run with it."

A priest in Alaska recalls, "the Bishop was not a follower of canon law or he would never have been so innovative with Canon eight. But better to misuse it than not to do anything at all. We are all going to make mistakes if we step ahead."

Bill replies, "In a very experimental, brand new program, you do the best you can. We obviously would have done some things differently if we had had much option, but it was critical that we get going. There are several ways of defining a mistake: one is that it is something that never should be done. Another is that it would have been better if it had been done some other way. We went with what we had, and on the whole, I think we did pretty well."

One of Bill's major regrets was that he was unable to ordain women to the priesthood. "Gosh, that canon changed in 1976, after I left, opened a whole new field, and I was envious. We would have done a whole lot better if we could have ordained some females in the beginning. In many cases, the most qualified person in the village was a woman." Bill rebuts some criticism by admitting that many of the people he ordained had a long way to go, and needed a lot more training. "We certainly visualized continuing education, but we felt they could begin by providing the sacraments, doing that as well as anybody else. They were filling a big void in the Church at that time."

"In retrospect, I believe it was good that we moved as fast as we did and ordained those twenty-eight clergy just before the nationalism fervor became so strong. Then it became very difficult for white priests to work in the villages, and it would have been impossible to implement our plan. As it was, we had an Eskimo or Indian priest in almost every village at that point, and the people couldn't say that it was a white man's church. Some day, things will level out—I think that the next generation of native leadership is going to be able to deal with some of the pressures of the modern world way better than their parents. They will be able to sort out and evaluate, and come out of it better, and the seeds that were sown in the churches during our push for local involvement will still be there to build on."

The historical implications of Bill's crusade have already reached beyond Alaskan borders. One of his fellow senior bishops says "Bill's move to ordain natives with a relatively small amount of formal theological education was a great step forward and one of the important advances in extending the mission of the church to more remote areas in many parts of the Anglican world. It has been copied and will be copied more."

Bill concludes: "We knew absolutely what the destination was, but we weren't sure about the road at times. We were out in the unknown, and as I look back, I can't believe how far off in left field we were, compared with the rest of the Church."

Another of the most exciting aspects of Bill's innovative program was the development of total ministry, of the complete involvement of all lay people. The ordination of sacramental priests was a message to them: These persons are giving a lot of their time to one church function without getting paid for it, how about the rest of us? How about pastoral care, Christian education, preaching, youth work, social involvement? The earlier concept of ministry to and for the people had shifted to the belief that every baptized Christian has a job to take on as a part of his or her faith; the team concept that Bill was later to introduce in seventy-eight dioceses throughout the United States and overseas.

In large parishes, like St. Mary's, where Chuck Eddy was a strong enabler, the theme quickly became, "you too are a minister," while the parishioners of those small-town churches who had no priest at all were forced into more lay responsibilities. Lay persons from these populated areas also looked beyond their own circle and offered to help Bill with their expertise in the Bush. One distinguished ear, nose, and throat specialist, who flew his own plane, offered to spend a month each summer visiting those remote villages without health care. Several doctors offered their time for similiar work, as did an accountant, a carpenter, a contractor, a lawyer, and pilot. The latter helped Bill with flying at those times when he had large numbers of people to ferry about.

This team ministry concept took longer to develop in villages, where the people were so used to having everything done for them by the priest. (Again, Point Hope and Kivalina were the exceptions.) Bill gave strict instructions to the traditionally trained priests: "I want you to work yourself out of a job. Every day I want there to be something you no longer have to do because you have trained some one else to take over."

Rick Draper tried an idea he had picked up from Bill. He took $100 out of his discretionary fund and sent $10 to each of ten people in the church. "Take the money," he wrote them, "and use it for someone else, the way you think Jesus would. I don't want to know who did what, but I'd like to hear what happens, so I've enclosed a post card back to me. Don't sign your name on it, but tell me what happened with this $10."

It took six months for some of the cards to be returned, but all of them came back. Every situation was truly special, like the alcoholic, whose every penny usually went to liquor. He bought $10 of groceries for an old woman who had nothing. Someone else bought song books for a group so they could sing for people. A woman who complained about their dirty church bought a broom and pail and cleaned it up. She felt so good about it that she went right on doing it once a week from then on. She could not resist sharing her experience with Rick because it had changed her whole attitude toward giving, and what a pleasure it was even when she had almost nothing to start with.

The development of lay ministry and the sacramental priest program was influenced by several factors. The first was Bill's increasing use of young volunteers and conscientious objectors, a helpful spinoff he had not counted on. These men and women with no special church training went into villages heavily dependent on local people for help. Their zeal as lay persons giving their time to the Church also made them perfect role models.

The second influence came from the Lower 48. A strong charismatic movement swept through the National Episcopal Church in the late 1960s, bringing emphasis on a deep personal commitment to God through the power of the Holy Spirit, as well as a joyous, more spontaneous kind of worship. Bill was pleased with the results of this latest change and encouraged and supported it. The village of Minto was caught up in an old-time revival, introduced by the young people. Berkman Silas, an Indian priest in the village, tells of "forty kids in Minto all excited. I so happy I start crying. They wake up the whole village, stay up all night, have prayer meeting, read the Bible, sing."

It was the folk songs that appealed particularly to Bill, although he had no musical talent. Minto young people formed a singing group, accompanied by several "hot" guitarists, and Bill flew them all over the state whenever he had the room. Bill recalls he had to put a limit on the number of guitars he could take, however, following one trip when he squeezed in four instruments and four people. Bill also commented on the Minto landing strip, saying it was one of the worst he dealt with because it went uphill, was surrounded by trees and buffeted by crosswinds—a foreshadowing of yet another close call to come.

Chapter 10

Hail and Farewell

In 1973 and 1974 three events had a strong impact on the course of Bill's life. One took place at the Minto airstrip. Bill had flown his mother, his sisters Nancy and Grace, and Shirley to Minto for the ordinations of Anna Frank and Ken Charlie. The exciting weekend finally over, he had already flown out one planeload of people and was on his way back in his Piper Cherokee to pick up his family. Bill was proud of this latest six-passenger plane, which he had purchased following the sale of Blue Box II. He had put it to a lot of hard use, and he even accepted all the good-natured teasing over its FAA serial number: 60 "Whiskey."

"I flew in real low over the village to alert them that I was there, and the engine suddenly made a loud rattling noise and lost power while I was still about three-quarters of a mile from the airstrip. I tried to land downwind, since I was closest to that end, but I didn't quite make it, and the plane landed about 200 feet short in the trees. It was the end of 60 "Whiskey." I only bruised my arm and shoulder—I had been reaching for the flaps when the plane hit and something struck me there. I really wasn't hurt much—I walked away from it." But a little girl had seen the plane go down and she ran back to the village to Bill's family and all the people waiting and told them that the plane crashed. Berkman Silas and Luke Titus, the two village church leaders, told Bill's mother and sisters and Shirley to stay there while they went to see what happened. Berkman stopped in the doorway, came back to Bill's mother, and placed the beaded cross that hung from his neck over her head.

Bill's sister Nancy recalls, "We were all ready to leave the village when an Indian came and told us there had been an accident, that we should wait in the house where we'd had lunch. Nobody knew what had happened to Bill. We'd had a service the night before with song books, and they were still at the house, so somebody began a gospel hymn, and we sang for about half an hour. Then I heard a woman, who was standing at the window, give a strange cry. It sounded like she was wailing. Later I learned she was praying in tongues. My mother and Shirley were sitting close, holding hands. There was an enormous feeling of faith and love in the room. We felt that Bill was going to be all right, and if he wasn't, this was something that God, and the whole weekend there, had prepared us for. It was the most emotionally intense experience. Then the door opened and a man said 'He okay.' We stood and had a prayer. There was no hysteria, just a great outpouring of thanksgiving."

Luke Titus recalls reaching the airstrip and seeing Bill walking toward them from the woods. "I met him. I felt helpless at that point and I asked him if he was okay. He said yeah, he think he hurt his arm or his shoulder. I told him I didn't know what to say. He said, 'Just stay by me. That's all I need.' "

Just another plane crash, yes, and the third in which the plane was destroyed. But this incident left many people, including Bill, shaken and concerned. He said it was engine trouble at the time, but as he went over and over the moments before the crash, he realized that it had really been pilot error. He had let down swiftly, throttling back to buzz the camp, then pulling up to head for the airstrip. At that moment he heard the loud noise and thought he might have broken a piston. He was reluctant to give the engine more power, and tried instead to glide toward the landing area. So he himself stalled it out into the trees.

Another event that had an enormous impact on Bill was the sudden change of Alaska's status from a missionary district to a diocese, the form of church structure used everywhere in the Lower 48. (The 1973 General Convention voted to abolish those missionary districts within the U.S.) As one veteran priest put it: "Alaska was kicked out of the Overseas Department without even being asked if we were ready to go it alone or not." There had been talk as early as the 1950s about asking for diocesan status. The clergy were unhappy with the constraints of the Overseas Department. Although Bill shared these feelings, he was cautious and did not advocate self-support. However, he did some advance preparation by appointing committees to begin work on a required constitution and canons.

It was an inevitable step and a good one for the Alaskan churches which were moving more and more toward local autonomy anyway, and the new structure of shared leadership, which the diocesan status required, was critically needed. Everyone would have to share in the new diocese's financial concerns. The Bush areas of Alaska as well as the town and cities were now called to pull together for the good of the Diocese and the common mission they shared.

How ironic that the very movement Bill was promoting—the development of lay participation—would in the end have such a profound effect on Bill as an autocratic missionary bishop! Now he would have to share decision-making and budgets with a Standing Committee made up of clergy and lay persons; no longer could he alone control the purse strings, carrying the treasury around in a bottomless hip pocket. One of his friends described the situation by telling of a time when Bill was guest chaplain at his favorite North Carolina camp. On the first evening there, he told the guests that it was a democratic organization and he wanted to involve them in all decisions during that week. He began with the question of location for Evening Prayer service; did they want it in the chapel or outside where it ought to be?

The climactic event in Bill's life that year was his return to Virginia Seminary to attend the Center of Continuing Education for six weeks of study and renewal. In his *Churchman* log, Bill calls this sojourn as being, "the most creative and deepening experience of my ministry. I did not realize how much I needed this refreshing and sharing and evaluation until I actually took part. I hope I can and will be a better bishop, a better father and husband because of this time." Bill adds that a bishop, particularly one in a remote area, seldom gets anything but petty or fawning critique, and this was a unique opportunity to receive some honest, objective feedback from a few caring, congenial friends. A number of Bill's clergy commented on a change in him on his return; he was more relaxed, affable and open. One veteran priest sensed a profound difference, and wonders if perhaps Bill had always pushed and worked himself to the limit because he believed he had to earn his way to salvation. And now, while finally taking time off for spiritual reflection, the great truth of Christianity came to the fore: only faith can save anyone.

On 11 May 1973 the second convention of the church's new Diocese met in Fairbanks at St. Matthew's Church. It began with the usual supper, with delegates from all over the state greeting long-time friends, with much talk and laughter, and with Bill's introducing each person in his inimitable way. Then everyone gathered in the sanctuary for the opening service. The church was packed, the voices of the clergy booming out the opening hymn. Bill stepped to the lectern to deliver his address on the State of the Church. He began by introducing visiting dignitaries and spent about fifteen minutes touching on the diocesan business about to come before the delegates. Then he came to his concluding paragraph:

"Next Thursday, 18 May, I will have been bishop of Alaska for twenty-five years. Some of you know that I have been wrestling for the past year with my own future and that of this diocese. I believe now that the time is approaching when this diocese needs new leadership and that change will be best for both the diocese and me. So this afternoon I have submitted to the Standing Committee of the Diocese my resignation as Bishop of Alaska, effective on the date of the consecration of my successor, but no later than 1 September 1974. I ask the concurrence of this convention and that machinery be put in motion for the election of my successor. I am not sure just what I will do with the remaining years ahead, but I am sure that God has some plan for my talents—what they are—and that He will reveal them to me. I know too with all my mind and heart that God has some definite and glorious plan for the Church in this Great Land and that this will be revealed and empowered also. May we go forward together in His Name and in the Power of His Holy Spirit.''

Audible gasps came from all over the church as Bill said the words "my resignation," then a deathly silence fell over the gathering. Everyone was stunned and saddened by Bill's announcement. It came without forewarning, because, though Bill had been wrestling with the decision since his return from Virginia Seminary, he did not decide until the day before the convention met whether he was going to do it. On the morning of his talk, he dictated his statement to secretary Dorothy Hall. The only others Bill told were his family. He called his mother, Paneen, and Billy by telephone, and then talked with Shirley, Becky, and Anna until well into the night. All were as shocked as the people in church the following day. Shirley was as calm and accepting as ever, undoubtedly experiencing feelings of deep relief, although she did not express them.

Anna, however, a fifteen-year-old, was inconsolable. She could not imagine her father as anything but the bishop of Alaska, and thought he was making a terrible mistake. Later in the evening, Bill found her on the back steps, sobbing. He went to her side and tried to explain how he had made up his mind, but no words could convince her that he was doing the right thing. She cried again, along with Shirley, when Bill made his announcement publicly.

Bill's official resignation letter to the presiding bishop says in part: "I will have been bishop of this Diocese for twenty-five years. I believe this is too long both for the Church in Alaska and for me, particularly in these changing times." The official resolution introduced to the House of Bishops at their October meeting that year stated: "It is the understanding of the House that Bishop Gordon resigned for the missionary strategy of the Church."

Bill came close to the decision while at the seminary renewal program. "I felt it was a good time for me to make a change. I had been bishop a long time, and I could see the changes in the Diocese coming. Obviously local people needed to take more of the responsibility that I had had for a long time. I had been making most of the decisions, and it was only right that many of them should be passed on to committees and councils. But it would be very hard for me to make that kind of transition. Then I decided that for all concerned it would be best to step aside instead. At that point, too, I truly felt I had accomplished all that

I set out to do twenty-five years earlier."
Bill admits that the Minto plane crash played a part in his decision.

He did not feel that, at fifty-six, he was too old to fly (airline pilots must retire at sixty), but he did wonder how much longer he could keep up such a demanding schedule without having another serious accident, perhaps one endangering other people's lives.

Bill's final year in office, while the Standing Committee of the Diocese searched for candidates to succeed him, was spent as usual, in visits to every church in the Diocese to perform confirmations and a number of ordinations, but this time it was also to say good-bye, and Shirley was at his side. There were many tearful partings, although most of the village people never quite accepted the fact that Bill was actually leaving for good. In fact, people working in the office in following years recall Eskimo and Indian parishioners arriving to ask for Bishop Gordon. Bill's successor, the Reverend David Cochran from North Dakota (who was two years older than Bill, but not a pilot), became used to going to isolated areas and being asked, "Where's Bishop Gordon?"

During his final days in office, Bill and Shirley were given a large farewell party in Anchorage, and contingents of native peoples came from the Arctic and Interior regions. They sang and danced for him, and gave him magnificent gifts, such as a walrus tusk carved into a dog team and sled. The evening brought many nostalgic feelings, and tears flowed freely when the Point Hope people sang "Til We Meet Again."

For Bill, the moment that tore him apart occurred at David Cochran's consecration in Fairbanks. Almost 400 people crowding about the new bishop, while Bill stood alone. He was suddenly innundated by feelings of sadness and nostalgia, but he was also thinking, what have I gotten myself into? His future was indefinite, with no plans other than to move on to Washington State for a while. Many ideas and suggestions had been considered, including an offer to become a bishop in Florida, and strong urgings to enter Alaskan politics, but none seemed appropriate.

For Shirley and Bill, the actual packing to move on was easy. Shirley told a friend, "We don't own a home or even furniture—

they all belong to the Church. We moved to Alaska with the clothes on our backs, and we will move out the same way." Shirley and Anna left first, driving down the Alaska Highway with some suitcases and a few boxes of memorabilia. Bill decided to fly the old diocesan plane Outside for an overhaul in the Seattle area, and Shirley and Becky would go along. On the day before Bill left, he attended the usual Wednesday morning service at St. Matthew's church. Somehow, word went out that he would be there to celebrate Holy Communion, and the place was packed. The organist came, too, although they did not ordinarily have music at that time. It was an emotion-packed hour, and everyone was reluctant to leave. They lingered and sang all the songs that Bill loved, bringing tears to everyone's eyes.

Bill decided that it would be easiest if the family simply slipped out to the airfield alone the following morning. Betty Hart and Dorothy Hall drove them there, and watched while Shirley and Becky climbed in quietly. Bill threw some suitcases into the back, then walked around the plane making his final preflight checks. He kicked a tire, climbed in, shut the door, started the engine and took off, just as he had done so often in his twenty-six years as bishop.

EPILOGUE

On the morning of August 30, 1974, a blue and silver Cessna 180 lifted off Phillips Field in Fairbanks and made a right turn, heading southeast into the sun. Bishop Gordon, at the controls with his wife Shirley in the right seat and daughter Becky in the back, was headed for Seattle—this his last 13 of nearly 9,000 flying hours as captain of "Alaska Episcopal Airlines."

They refueled in Whitehorse, Yukon Territory; thence across 550 miles of lonely wilderness to an overnight stop in Prince George, British Columbia, and finally to the shores of Puget Sound. The Cessna was headed for an overhaul in Portland, and Bill Gordon was headed to two years' service for the national Episcopal Church with Project TEAM (Teach Each A Ministry).

During those two years, Bishop Gordon was the staff of Project TEAM, his own creation, supported by the Episcopal Church Foundation and the United Thank Offering. He shared his vision—nurtured in his service in Alaska—of the total ministry of all the people of the Church, visiting 78 dioceses in the U.S., Canada, England, Central and South America, Africa and Australia, speaking 720 times on the "Total Ministry of the People of God."

Then from 1976 to 1986 Bishop Gordon served as Assistant Bishop of the Diocese of Michigan, with responsibility for 50 congregations in the northwestern part of that large diocese. He more or less retired on January 1, 1986, and he and Shirley resided in Midland, Michigan.

When asked how he would like to be remembered, Bill Gordon replied, "I'd like written on my tombstone, 'He dared to Dream.'"

[From notes that Bishop Gordon sent to Tay Thomas in 1989. Bill Gordon died in Midland, Michigan, on January 4, 1994, and Shirley Gordon then returned to Alaska.]

Bill on a return visit to Alaska in 1981, now as assistant bishop of the Diocese of Michigan. Note his sermon notes in his pocket.

A number of Athabaskan and Caucasian priests gather at Fort Yukon in 1971 as Bill ordains Philip Peter to the priesthood.

Shirley and Bill about 1967. The portrait behind them is of Peter Trimble Rowe, Alaska's first bishop (1895-1942).

Presiding Bishop John Hines stands with Bill, one of two hundred guests to fly to remote Point Hope on July 4, 1965, for its 76th anniversary of the founding of the mission.

An Eskimo woman in her traditional dress is thrown high in a blanket toss (Nalukatuk) *during the celebration.*

Bill takes his turn. The round walrus skin is held tight by many villagers, and they can toss a person 20 feet high. It takes skill and courage as legs can be broken.

A rare formal Gordon family portrait, taken about 1965. Paneen, Billy and Becky are standing. Shirley and Bill sit, with Anna at Bill's side.

Curtis and Judy Edwards with their three small children at the Tanana mission house just three months before it burned down, taking the lives of all but Judy.

Bill's Cessna 170 upside down on the tundra inland from Kotzebue following his forced landing when the weather closed in.

Bill at the controls of his Cessna 170 (Blue Box 1) in 1959. He wears his traditional baseball cap, parka and boots.

The Alaska delegation to the 1955 General Convention in Hawaii, planting a monkey pod tree in Honolulu. (L to R) Mrs. J.C. Fontaine and Mrs. Howard Day, Margaret Hall, the Reverend Hugh Hall, Shirley, Bill, and Chester Seveck.

Point Hope Whaling crews cut up the much-prized meat, to be shared with every family in the village.

Villagers with a dog team meet Bill in 7360 "Kilo" on a lake near Tetlin in 1950. Snow drifts rendered their air strip unusable.

Blue Box I, Bill's Cessna 170, on its back at the edge of the Kotzebue Friends' graveyard in June of 1953. The engine failed because water had collected in his gas.

Milton Swan, the first Eskimo to be ordained a priest, and his home in Kivalina, 1959.

A precocious two year old, the only son and much-loved by parents, sisters, grandmother and aunt, Bill was already eager to take off behind a wheel.

A member of the cross country and track teams at the University of North Carolina, Bill began with a pre-med major before he accepted his calling to the priesthood.

Bill, on the front row, far right, a member of the Virginia Episcopal School's basketball team. He excelled in sports after first trying to overcome the "preacher's kid" image through rebellion.

On the occasion of his ordination to the diaconate on 24 January, 1943, Bill stands with his close friend, Dr. Syd Alexander.

Pretty twenty year old Shirley Lewis and Bill met on the ship headed for Alaska. It was a whirlwind romance and they were married in Seward four months later.

Bill's 1930 Chevrolet, dubbed "Anesthesia," took him all over the South on college weekends when he became president of the Young Peoples' Service League, showing organizational skills at an early age.

Shirley sits on the Point Hope mission steps, wearing the typical women's decorative cotton parka worn over fur.

Bill was ordained a priest on 25 July, nine days after his marriage in Seward. Bishop John Bentley stands beside him, accompanied by priests Warren Fenn, Elsom Eldridge and Arnold Krone.

In front of the Point Hope school house, Bill wears the colorful parka given him by Antonio Weber during his first Christmas at Point Hope.

The misses Kay (on the left) and Hill, dressed in native winter clothing to ward off minus 50 degree temperatures at Allekaket.

Bill sheds his robes and does his laundry during a summer visit to Allekaket.

The villagers of Allekaket come to one of the first services held by Bill. The misses Hill and Kay are in the left foreground.

St. John's in the Wilderness, the log church at Allekaket. The inscription on the bell in the tower reads "O YE ICE AND SNOW BLESS YE THE LORD; PRAISE HIM AND MAGNIFY HIM FOREVER."

Peel and Beatrice Tooyak about 1938. Peel interpreted Bill's sermons, read the Bible Lessons in Eskimo and played the small organ. He also helped teach school and ran the mission during Bill's frequent absences.

Point Hope Eskimos celebrating at the annual whaling feast, singing to the beat of large drums fashioned from seal intestines, sheltered from a cold wind by an upturned umiak.

St. Thomas's Mission Church at Point Hope in 1943. A colorful painting of St. Thomas hung above the altar, which held an ornate brass cross and many candlesticks. The imported pews were made of oak.

A wedding at Point Hope in 1951. Bill marries Nicholas and Mable Hank. People had no rings for weddings, and the words of the service in the prayer book were beyond their understanding.

An Athabaskan at a summer fish camp is confirmed by Bill during his first trip on the Godspeed in 1948.

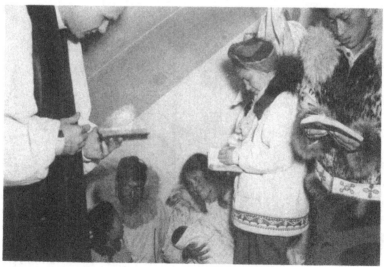

Bill baptizes young Billy Stone in a tent on the Arctic coast in 1951. Dora Tooyak and Calvin Oktollik look on.